ESPAÑA Y PORTUGAL

Copyright by C. S. HAMMOND & CO., N.Y.

ESCALA

KILÓMETROS

0 50 100 150 200

MILLAS

0   50   100   150   200

Capitales ⊛

Límites Internacionales

FRANCIA

ANDORRA

CATALUÑA

Pirineos

Barcelona

Tarragona

ISLAS BALEARES

Menorca

Mallorca

Palma

Ibiza

Mar Mediterráneo

ARAGÓN

NAVARRA

VIZCAYA

San Sebastián

Bilbao

Río Ebro

Zaragoza

Golfo de Gascuña

Covadonga

Oviedo

ASTURIAS

León

Burgos

Valladolid

CASTILLA LA VIEJA

Río Duero

Segovia

Escorial

Madrid

NUEVA

Cuenca

Valencia

Alicante

Murcia

Cartagena

ESPAÑA

Ávila

Zamora

Salamanca

CASTILLA LA

Toledo

Río Tajo

Almería

Granada

Río Genil

Málaga

ANDALUCÍA

Río Guadalquivir

Córdoba

Sevilla

Itálica

Gibraltar (Brit.)

Tarifa

Estr. de Gibraltar

Cádiz

EXTREMADURA

Badajoz

Río Guadiana

Sierra Morena

GALICIA

La Coruña

Cabo Finisterre

Santiago

Vigo

Río Miño

Río Miño

Oporto

Río Duero

PORTUGAL

Lisboa

Océano Atlántico

Longitud Oeste de Greenwich

40°

8°

4°

0°

36°

Intermediate
Conversational Spanish

INTERMEDIATE
Conversational SPANISH

GREGORY G. LAGRONE
The University of Texas

MIGUEL ROMERA - NAVARRO
Late of The University of Texas

VICTORIA DE ROMERA - NAVARRO

New York
HENRY HOLT AND COMPANY

PREFACE

This book, which presupposes an introduction to the basic forms of Spanish, is designed to enable the second-level student to increase his vocabulary, to develop fluency, and to gain a clearer insight into the nature of the language.

Part I contains fifteen model passages in Spanish—usually in dialogue form—together with appropriate exercises: (1) questions in Spanish, (2) suggestions for a summary in Spanish, (3) drill exercises, (4) translation from English to Spanish, and (5) topics for related conversation and composition.

Part II contains eight units giving an analysis of the important aspects of syntax from a new perspective, using for the examples and the exercises the same vocabulary that is used in Part I, and with emphasis on oral expression in the three types of exercises: (1) drill, (2) comprehension, and (3) completion.

The two parts of the book are presented in this order in the belief that at the intermediate level informal practice may profitably precede formal analysis. Actually, however, the two parts, though carefully integrated, form complete units in themselves, and can easily be used (1) independently, (2) simultaneously, or (3) in either order. This flexible arrangement has seemed best because the needs and interests of intermediate students vary considerably.

The collaboration which has produced this book began several years ago. The late Professor Romera-Navarro prepared the model passages and some materials for the exercises. His widow, Victoria de Romera-Navarro, has made the minor alterations needed in the model texts, and has collaborated in producing the Spanish parts of the exercises. With the help of my wife, Margaret Allyn LaGrone, I have supplied the other materials of the book. It is my hope that this collaboration has produced a second-level text with really authentic Spanish, presented in a usable form.

Austin, Texas   G. G. L.
February 15, 1958

CONTENTS

Part I

Preface   v

Informal Practice

   1   Empieza el día.   1

   2   Diálogos y bullicio en la Universidad.   7

   3   Charlando en el restaurán.   13

   4   Velada tranquila y quehaceres menudos. . .   19

   5   Del tren a la oficina.   25

   6   Pequeños asuntos que atender.   31

   7   Conversaciones en una tienda.   37

   8   Charla sobre el cine, el teatro y Hollywood.   43

   9   Coloquios galantes en el baile.   49

  10   Plática de los deportes.   55

  11   Diálogo del tiempo y solo de teléfono.   61

  12   Cartas de amigos.   67

  13   Diálogo del campo y la ciudad.   73

  14   Volando sobre las nubes.   79

  15   El libro que más me ha impresionado.   85

Part II

Formal Practice

1	Articles	92
2	Nouns and Adjectives	98
3	Personal Pronouns	104
4	Possessives and Demonstratives...........	110
5	Negatives, Adverbs, and Prepositions......	115
6	Idiomatic Verb Usage	121
7	Tenses of the Indicative...............	127
8	Uses of the Subjunctive.................	133

Appendix (Verb Forms) 141

Vocabularies i

Index lvii

Intermediate Conversational Spanish

PART I

Empieza el día

Empieza el día en el hogar,[1] y empieza con mucha calma. No ha sonado el despertador;[2] el chico no se ha levantado. Pero grita[3] la madre desde su alcoba:[4]

— ¡Levántate, hijo, que ya es tarde!

5 — ¿Pues qué hora es?

— Son ya las ocho: ¡arriba, arriba![5]

— Ya voy, madre.

De prisa y corriendo,[6] el muchacho se echa la bata[7] encima. Va al cuarto de baño[8] y empieza su aseo.[9] La
10 maquinilla de afeitar,[10] la brocha[11] y el jabón[12] están en su lugar. Ahora, a lavarse. Se seca[13] con la toalla. ¿Y el cepillo de dientes[14] y la pasta dentífrica? ¡Ah, sí, aquí están! Ahora, el peine[15] y el cepillo de cabeza. De vuelta en[16] la alcoba, acaba de vestirse. Ya listo,[17] entra en el
15 comedor.[18]

— Buenos días, madre; dame un beso.[19]

— Buenos días, hijo.

---

1 hogar *home*
2 despertador *alarm clock*
3 grita *calls out*
4 alcoba *bedroom*
5 ¡arriba! *get up!*
6 de prisa y corriendo *very quickly, on the run*
7 bata *bathrobe*
8 cuarto de baño *bathroom*
9 aseo *grooming*

10 maquinilla de afeitar *safety razor*
11 brocha *brush*
12 jabón *soap*
13 seca *he dries*
14 cepillo de dientes *toothbrush*
15 peine *comb*
16 de vuelta en *back in*
17 listo *ready*
18 comedor *dining room*
19 beso *kiss*

—¡Hay que ver![20] Primer día de clase, y el despertador descompuesto.[21]

—No importa, ahora desayuna con tranquilidad. Aquí tienes el jugo de naranja[22] y el cereal.

—Venga,[23] venga el huevo[24] y la tostada.   5

—A ver si te atragantas[25] con tanta prisa.

* * *

—Oye, madre, mi amigo Fernando vendrá a buscarme.[26]

—Será él quien llama ahora; voy a abrir.

—Buenos días, señora.   10

—Bien venido,[27] Fernando. Pasa,[28] que Alfonso está terminando.

—¡Adelante,[29] hombre, adelante!

—¿Qué, dormilón,[30] se te pegaron las sábanas?[31]

—El pícaro[32] despertador que no ha sonado. Pero ya 15 termino.

—Pues, andando.[33] Que usted lo pase bien,[34] señora.

—Adiós, Fernando. Y tú, hijo, abrígate,[35] que la mañana está fresca.

—Con Dios, madre, y otro beso.   20

20 ¡hay que ver! *isn't that something!*
21 descompuesto *broken*
22 jugo de naranja *orange juice*
23 venga *let's have*
24 huevo *egg*
25 a ver si te atragantas *you're going to choke*
26 vendrá a buscarme *will come by for me*
27 bien venido *welcome*
28 pasa *come in*
29 ¡adelante! *come in!*
30 dormilón *sleepyhead*
31 ¿se te pegaron las sábanas? *did you get up late?, couldn't you get out of bed?*
32 pícaro *rascally, darned*
33 pues, andando *well, let's get going*
34 que usted lo pase bien *good-by*
35 abrígate *wrap up*

Poco después, ya en la calle, plantados[36] los dos muchachos en la esquina:[37]

— Y ese tranvía[38] sin venir.

— No tardará mucho.[39] Pero mira, mira quién viene
5 por allí.

— ¡Linda muchacha!

— Buena compañía, no empieza mal la mañana.

EXERCISES

A. QUESTIONS.

1. ¿Cómo empezó el día en el hogar de Alfonso?
2. ¿Por qué no se había levantado el muchacho?
3. ¿Quién le llamó desde su alcoba?
4. ¿Qué preguntó Alfonso a su madre?
5. ¿A qué hora se levantó el muchacho?
6. ¿Cómo se echó la bata encima?
7. ¿Dónde hizo su aseo?
8. ¿Dónde acabó de vestirse?
9. Ya listo, ¿adónde fué?
10. ¿Qué le dijo a su madre al entrar en el comedor?
11. ¿Qué tomó de desayuno?
12. ¿Qué le podía pasar si comía de prisa?
13. ¿Quién vino a buscarlo?
14. ¿Qué hizo la madre cuando llamó el amigo?
15. ¿Cómo la saludó Fernando?
16. ¿Qué dijo Alfonso al despedirse de su madre?
17. ¿Por qué debía abrigarse el muchacho?

36 plantados *standing*
37 esquina *corner*
38 tranvía *streetcar*

39 no tardará mucho *it won't be long
(in coming), it'll be here soon*

18. ¿A qué aguardaban los amigos en la esquina?
19. ¿Quién vino a tomar el mismo tranvía?
20. ¿Qué pensaron del encuentro los dos muchachos?

B. Report.

Tell in Spanish how Alfonso fared on his first day of classes: getting up, grooming, breakfast, arrival of his friend, waiting for the streetcar.

C. Drill.

1. *Read the following lists of related expressions.*   1. dormilón, alcoba, despertador; dormir, pegársele a uno las sábanas, despertar, levantarse, vestirse; sonar, estar descompuesto.   2. aseo, cuarto de baño; maquinilla de afeitar, brocha, jabón, toalla, peine, cepillo de cabeza, pasta dentífrica, cepillo de dientes; asearse, afeitarse, lavarse, secarse, peinarse, limpiarse (cepillarse) los dientes.   3. desayuno, comedor; jugo de naranja, cereal, huevo, tostada, café; desayunar(se), tomar, comer, atragantarse.   4. buenos días, bien venido, pasa (pase usted), ¡adelante!; adiós, con Dios, que usted lo pase bien.

2. *Complete by supplying appropriate ideas.*

1. Al que quiere dormir mucho se le llama ＿＿＿.
2. El cuarto donde se duerme se llama ＿＿＿.
3. «Pegársele a uno las sábanas» quiere decir ＿＿＿.
4. El reloj que nos despierta se llama ＿＿＿.
5. El despertador no suena cuando está ＿＿＿.
6. Se hace el aseo en ＿＿＿.
7. Muchos se afeitan con ＿＿＿.
8. La toalla sirve para ＿＿＿.
9. Para peinarse se necesita ＿＿＿.
10. Los dientes se limpian con ＿＿＿.
11. El cuarto donde se come se llama ＿＿＿.

12. De desayuno muchos toman _____.
13. Se saluda a un amigo diciéndole _____.
14. Al amigo que llama a la puerte se le dice _____.
15. Al despedirnos decimos _____.

3. *Make sentences using the following ideas.* 1. levantarse tarde. 2. sonar el despertador. 3. ir al cuarto de baño. 4. usar la maquinilla de afeitar. 5. limpiarse los dientes. 6. acabar de vestirse. 7. entrar en el comedor. 8. tomar jugo de naranja. 9. comer de prisa. 10. tardar mucho.

D. TRANSLATION.
1. I get up a little before seven.
2. For breakfast I have orange juice, cereal, egg, toast, and coffee.
3. The first class that I have is at nine.
4. Sometimes a friend comes by for me.
5. We always take the streetcar.
6. We wrap up well when the mornings are cool.
7. This morning I got up late.
8. The alarm clock didn't go off because it was broken.
9. It was already seven when my mother called me.
10. I threw on my bathrobe and went to the bathroom.
11. I shaved quickly with the safety razor.
12. I washed myself and brushed my teeth.
13. I finished dressing and went into the dining room.
14. I ate breakfast quickly.
15. I had not finished when Fernando arrived.
16. My friend called me a sleepyhead because I got up late.
17. We went to the corner to wait for the streetcar.
18. It was not long in arriving.
19. A pretty girl took the same streetcar.
20. The morning wasn't beginning badly.

E. CONVERSATION AND COMPOSITION.

Topics: 1. Your morning routine.   2. A good breakfast.
3. Some people that you see each morning.

Diálogos y bullicio[1] en la Universidad

Estamos en el vestíbulo de la Universidad. Unos entran, otros salen, muchos conversan en grupos. Hay abrazos,[2] saludos y empujones.[3]

—Aquí todos hablan, y nadie escucha—observa un
5 estudiante grave.

—Sí, la agitación y el bullicio de siempre.

—¡Hola, Fernando! ¿Cómo estás?

—Bien, gracias, ¿y tú?

—Y a ti, Alfonso, ¿cómo te va?

10 — Muy bien, contento de verte. ¿Qué tal pasaste el verano?

—Fueron unas vacaciones deliciosas allá en el campo. ¡Qué pronto se acabaron!

—Bien lo puedes decir. Y ahora a trabajar.

15 —¡A sudar tinta![4] Para mí comenzaron los trabajos al matricularme ayer: dos horas estuve haciendo fila[5] para abonar[6] los derechos[7] de matrícula.

—También yo perdí la mañana arreglando el programa de asignaturas.[8] Y menos mal que[9] tengo un con-
20 sejero[10] hábil[11] y diligente: lo llaman Carambitas.

---

1 bullicio *hubbub, noise*
2 abrazos *embraces*
3 empujones *shoves*
4 sudar tinta *"sweat blood"*
5 haciendo fila *standing in line*
6 abonar *pay*

7 derechos *fees*
8 programa de asignaturas *program of studies, list of courses*
9 menos mal que *fortunately*
10 consejero *adviser*
11 hábil *able*

—Ya lo conozco, y me hace gracia[12] también su eterno
¡Caramba,[13] chico, caramba!

—Quería que tomase la Química, pero no me gusta ni
es curso obligatorio; lo reemplazamos con la Física.

—También voy a tomarla yo este semestre. Seguiré,[14] 5
además, tres cursos electivos: sintaxis francesa, lengua
alemana, literatura española, pues ya sabes que estoy especializando en lenguas modernas.

—¡Para mentir[15] no te basta[16] una sola lengua!

—Tienes gracia,[17] aunque me llames embustero.[18] Pero 10
más gracia deben tener esos del grupo. Mira cómo se ríen.

—Buenas carcajadas sueltan.[19]

—Sí, y cada uno con su voz:[20] ¡ja, ja! ¡je, je! ¡ji, ji!

—Parece un concierto. ¡Toma,[21] pues ahora callan!

—Porque allí viene el Rector[22]... y el Vicerrector. 15
¡Pues no falta ya más que el Decano![23]

—¡Y la Facultad entera! ¿Sabes una cosa? Tengo al
Decano de profesor de Historia.

—Te felicito.[24] Es hombre de sabiduría y bondad.[25]
Lo que no me agrada[26] es que dicen que pasa lista[27] todos 20
los días.

—Así habrá menos alumnos que hagan rabona.[28] Oye

12 me hace gracia *amuses me*
13 ¡caramba! *gracious!, confound it!*
14 seguiré *I'll take*
15 para mentir *for lying*
16 no te basta *is not enough for you*
17 tienes gracia *you're funny (clever)*
18 embustero *liar*
19 buenas carcajadas sueltan *they're really roaring (with laughter)*
20 voz *(tone of) voice*
21 ¡toma! *why!, well!*
22 rector *president*
23 decano *dean*
24 te felicito *I congratulate you*
25 de sabiduría y bondad *learned and kindly*
26 no me agrada *I don't like*
27 pasa lista *he calls roll*
28 que hagan rabona *who will cut class (play hooky)*

¿me quieres acompañar a la librería?[29] Tengo que comprar unos libros.

—También yo necesito un lápiz[30] y un cuaderno.[31]

—Pues, andando, y luego iremos a la casa de huéspe-
5 des.[32]

—No, mejor será almorzar hoy en el restaurán.

EXERCISES

A. QUESTIONS.

1. ¿Qué pasaba en el vestíbulo de la Universidad?
2. ¿Qué hacían todos, según un estudiante grave?
3. ¿Qué hay siempre allí?
4. ¿Dónde pasó el verano el amigo de Fernando y Alfonso?
5. ¿Qué tienen que hacer ahora?
6. ¿Cuántas horas estuvo haciendo fila uno de los muchachos?
7. ¿Cómo perdió la mañana otro de ellos?
8. ¿Cómo es el consejero a quien llaman *Carambitas?*
9. ¿Por qué lo llaman así?
10. ¿Qué quería *Carambitas* que tomase el muchacho?
11. ¿Por qué no tomó ese curso?
12. ¿Con qué curso lo reemplazaron?
13. ¿Qué cursos va a tomar el muchacho que se especializa en lenguas modernas?
14. Según su amigo ¿por qué se especializa en lenguas?
15. ¿Cómo se reían algunos de los muchachos?
16. ¿Por qué callaron?
17. ¿Cómo es el Decano?

29 librería *bookstore*
30 lápiz *pencil*
31 cuaderno *notebook*
32 casa de huéspedes *boarding house*

18. ¿Por qué habrá pocos alumnos que hagan rabona?
19. ¿Qué tenían que comprar los muchachos?
20. ¿Qué pensaban hacer después?

  B. REPORT.

Tell in Spanish about the hubbub in the vestibule of the
University: who was there and what they talked about.

  C. DRILL.

  1. *Read the following lists of related expressions.* 1. agitación, bullicio; abrazos, saludos, empujones; entrar, salir,
conversar, hablar, escuchar. 2. matricularse, hacer fila,
abonar los derechos de matrícula, arreglar el programa de
asignaturas. 3. semestre, consejero, curso obligatorio, curso
electivo; química, física, historia, lenguas (modernas); estudiar, tomar, seguir, especializar(se). 4. rector, vicerrector,
decano, facultad; profesores, alumnos, estudiantes; pasar
lista, hacer rabona. 5. librería, libro, lápiz, cuaderno.

  2. *Complete by supplying appropriate ideas.*
1. En el vestíbulo hay siempre agitación y ＿＿.
2. Los buenos amigos se saludan dándose ＿＿.
3. Lo contrario de entrar es ＿＿.
4. Muchos se reúnen en grupos para ＿＿.
5. Todos hablan y nadie ＿＿.
6. Antes de empezar los cursos, los estudiantes tienen
   que ＿＿.
7. Hay que hacer fila para abonar ＿＿.
8. El año académico se divide en dos ＿＿.
9. El consejero ayuda a arreglar ＿＿.
10. Los cursos pueden ser obligatorios o ＿＿.
11. Hay muchos que se especializan en ＿＿.
12. Los que gobiernan la universidad son ＿＿.
13. Los otros miembros de la facultad son ＿＿.

14. Si el profesor no pasa lista, habrá muchos alumnos que ____.
15. En la librería compramos ____.

3. *Make sentences using the following ideas.* 1. haber bullicio. 2. hacer fila. 3. arreglar el programa de asignaturas. 4. tener un consejero diligente. 5. tomar cinco cursos. 6. ser curso obligatorio. 7. seguir cursos electivos. 8. especializarse en lenguas modernas. 9. pasar lista. 10. comprar libros.

D. TRANSLATION.

1. In the vestibule of the University there always is excitement and hubbub.
2. There are many embraces, greetings, and shoves.
3. Today we were talking about the courses and the professors.
4. We were all roaring with laughter.
5. Everybody quieted down when the Dean arrived.
6. How soon the vacation ended!
7. It was a delightful vacation there in the country.
8. Now to work! To sweat blood!
9. I enrolled yesterday.
10. I spent two hours standing in line to pay my matriculation fees.
11. I had already wasted the morning arranging my program of studies.
12. My adviser isn't able nor diligent.
13. He wanted me to take French syntax.
14. I already have enough with the Spanish language!
15. I am majoring in chemistry.
16. I also like physics.
17. They say that the history professor calls the roll every day.

18. He doesn't like the students to cut class.
19. Now I have to go to the bookstore.
20. Afterwards we can have lunch at the boarding house or in the restaurant.

E. CONVERSATION AND COMPOSITION.

Topics: 1. Getting enrolled. 2. The best courses.
3. A scene at the University.

Charlando[1] en el restaurán

—Éste es el restaurán que te decía, el de los buenos alimentos.

—Pues adentro,[2] que vengo con apetito.

—Por fortuna llegamos temprano, y no hay que hacer
5 cola.[3]

— ¡Pasen, pasen, señores! Allí al fondo[4] tienen ustedes una mesa vacía.

—Vas a ver que aquí se practica el gran arte de comer, que es comer bien y barato[5]... Mira, ahí tienes una per-
10 cha[6] para el sombrero.

—Me gusta esto. Todo está limpio y bien cuidado.[7]

—Venga el menú: sopas, asados,[8] pescados,[9] ensaladas, legumbres[10]... ¡Buena lista de platos para un gastró-nomo![11]

15 —Y envidia[12] del que esté a régimen.[13] Oiga, cama-rero,[14] tráigame esta sopa de hierbas[15] y unas chuletas de cerdo[16]... No, mejor será el asado de cordero[17] con puré de patatas.[18]

1 charlando *chatting*
2 adentro *let's go in*
3 hacer cola *wait in line*
4 al fondo *at the back*
5 barato *cheaply*
6 percha *clothes tree, hat rack*
7 limpio y bien cuidado *clean and well kept*
8 asados *roast meats*
9 pescados *fish*
10 legumbres *vegetables*
11 gastrónomo *gourmet*
12 envidia *envy*
13 a régimen *on a diet*
14 camarero *waiter*
15 sopa de hierbas *(Spanish) vegetable soup*
16 chuletas de cerdo *pork chops*
17 cordero *lamb*
18 puré de patatas *mashed potatoes*

—Y a mí un bisté[19] con patatas fritas y una ensalada
de lechuga.[20] Es lástima que no me atreva con[21] el arroz
con pollo,[22] porque aquí lo hacen muy rico: un plato
suculento, una magistral obra culinaria.

—Hombre, parece que lo estás saboreando;[23] con tanto   5
gusto lo dices.

—Y tanto me llené de[24] ese arroz el otro día que cogí
una indigestión.

—¡Glotón! Tú no eres de los que necesitan píldoras
de vitamina.   10

—Aquí tienen, señores, el servicio.[25]

—Gracias, todo parece sabroso.[26]

—Pruébelo[27] y verá, señorito.

—Hazme el favor de la pimienta,[28] Fernando.

—Ahí va. Pásame tú la sal.   15

—Para sal,[29] la de aquella que entra ahora. Mira qué
linda es.

—Sí, graciosa muchacha. Me parece que la he visto
antes. Pero a comer y no quebrantar la costumbre,[30]
porque tengo notado que en el restaurán pasa al revés   20
que en la sala de clase; aquí las chicas se dan más cuenta
de[31] los muchachos que ellos de las chicas: ellas a mirar
de reojo,[32] y ellos a tragar.[33]

19 bisté *beefsteak*	27 pruébelo *try it*
20 lechuga *lettuce*	28 pimienta *pepper*
21 que no me atreva con *that I don't dare have*	29 sal *salt = charm*
22 arroz con pollo *chicken and rice*	30 quebrantar la costumbre *break the custom*
23 saboreando *savoring*	31 se dan más cuenta de *notice... more*
24 tanto me llené de *I stuffed myself so much with*	32 de reojo *out of the corner of their eyes*
25 servicio *meal, order*	33 tragar *swallow, eat a lot*
26 sabroso *tasty*	

— ¡Se me hace la boca agua!

— ¿Mirando qué? ¿la cara[34] bonita o esa fruta que lleva el mozo[35] en la bandeja?[36]

— Las dos cosas.

5   — Pues híncale el diente[37] al bisté y cómetela a ella con los ojos[38] si quieres.

* * *

— Y ahora ¿qué postre[39] desean los señores?—pregunta el camarero.

— Yo cualquier fruta que tengan, pero fresca, no en
10 conserva.

— Y yo un pastel de manzana[40] y café con leche.

— Muy bien, señores. Ahora mismo se lo traigo.

— Y a éste ¿qué le damos de propina?[41]

— Ninguna, aquí no hay propinas. Cuando nos deje
15 la cuenta[42] y acabemos de almorzar le damos un *¡Adiós, gracias!* y a pagar a la cajera.

EXERCISES

A. QUESTIONS.

1. ¿Dónde almorzaron los muchachos?
2. ¿Por qué no tuvieron que hacer cola?
3. ¿Dónde había una mesa vacía?
4. ¿En qué consiste el gran arte de comer?
5. ¿Cómo estaba todo en el restaurán?

34 cara *face*
35 mozo *waiter*
36 bandeja *tray*
37 híncale el diente *sink your teeth*
38 cómetela a ella con los ojos *feast your eyes on her, stare at her*
39 postre *dessert*
40 pastel de manzana *apple pie*
41 propina *tip*
42 cuenta *bill*

6. ¿Era buena la lista de platos?
7. ¿Qué platos había en el menú?
8. ¿Qué clase de carne pidieron los muchachos?
9. ¿Tomaron los dos puré de patatas?
10. ¿Qué ensalada tomó uno de ellos?
11. ¿Cómo es el arroz con pollo de ese restaurán?
12. ¿Qué le pasó al muchacho que se llenó tanto?
13. ¿Por qué no necesita éste píldoras de vitamina?
14. ¿Cómo parecía el servicio al traérselo el camarero?
15. ¿A quién vieron entrar los muchachos?
16. ¿Conocían ellos a la muchacha?
17. ¿Cómo miran a veces las chicas?
18. ¿Qué postres tomaron los muchachos?
19. ¿Qué le dieron de propina al camarero?
20. ¿A quién pagaron la cuenta?

B. REPORT.

Tell in Spanish about the boys' lunch in the restaurant: their arrival, the meals ordered, their conversation.

C. DRILL.

1. *Read the following lists of related expressions.* 1. restaurán, mesa vacía, percha; mozo (-a), camarero (-a), cajero (-a); menú, lista de platos, alimentos, servicio, cuenta, propina. 2. traer, pasar, hacer el favor de, hacer cola, pagar. 3. sopas, carnes, asados, pescados, ensaladas, legumbres, postres; sopa de hierbas, asado de cordero, bisté, chuletas de cerdo, arroz con pollo, patatas fritas, puré de patatas, ensalada de lechuga, fruta (fresca, en conserva), pastel de manzana, café con leche. 4. apetito, gastrónomo, glotón; comer (bien, barato), estar a régimen, tomar píldoras de vitamina; rico, suculento, sabroso; probar, saborear, hacérsele a uno la boca agua, hincar el diente, tragar, llenarse, coger una indigestión.

2. *Complete by supplying appropriate ideas.*

1. No hay que hacer cola en el restaurán cuando hay ____.
2. Los sombreros se ponen en ____.
3. Al salir se paga la cuenta ____.
4. En la mesa se deja una propina para ____.
5. Los platos de un menú son ____.
6. Una de las carnes que me gustan más es ____.
7. Tráigame chuletas de cerdo con ____.
8. Quiero fruta fresca, no en ____.
9. De postre voy a tomar ____.
10. Al que conoce el arte de comer bien se le llama ____.
11. El que come demasiado es ____.
12. No pueden comer mucho los que están ____.
13. El arroz con pollo lo hacen aquí muy ____.
14. Se me hace la boca agua al mirar ____.
15. El que se llena mucho de un plato suculento puede coger ____.

3. *Make sentences using the following ideas.* 1. hacer cola. 2. tener una mesa vacía. 3. traer arroz con pollo. 4. pasar la sal. 5. hacer el favor de la pimienta. 6. estar a régimen. 7. tomar píldoras de vitamina. 8. coger una indigestión. 9. dar de propina al camarero. 10. pagar a la cajera.

D. TRANSLATION.

1. In this restaurant one eats well and cheaply.
2. They say that this is the great art of eating.
3. Everything is clean and well kept.
4. Those that arrive early don't have to wait in line.
5. But never are there many empty tables.
6. There is no tipping here. (Here there are no tips.)
7. One pays the cashier.

8. Here we have the menu: soups, roast meats, fish, salads, and vegetables.
9. There is always a good bill of fare.
10. Yesterday I had lunch here with María.
11. I took roast lamb with mashed potatoes and vegetables.
12. For dessert I had apple pie.
13. María took soup, lettuce salad, and fruit.
14. It's too bad that she is on a diet.
15. All these dishes were very tasty.
16. María said that her mouth was watering.
17. The most delicious dish that they make here is the chicken and rice.
18. It is a masterly culinary production.
19. Today I am going to take that rice.
20. I'm not one of those that need vitamin pills.

E. CONVERSATION AND COMPOSITION.

Topics: 1. Dining out.   2. Good food.   3. Your favorite restaurants.

Velada tranquila y quehaceres menudos[1]

PART ONE

4

INFORMAL
PRACTICE

—Esta mañana dejó aquí la cuenta el lavandero.[2] Sube a dos dólares y veinticinco centavos.

—Pues yo no mandé más que unas pocas piezas de ropa interior,[3] tres pares de calcetines[4] y hasta media docena
5 de pañuelos.[5]

—Ya ajustaremos cuentas.[6] Pero mira esta camisa,[7] no está que digamos[8] muy bien planchada.[9]

—Tampoco me han limpiado a mí bien el traje[10] en la tintorería.[11] Todavía se conoce la mancha[12] en la
10 manga[13] de la americana.[14] El pantalón puede pasar.

—Si te parece, haremos un ratito de limpieza,[15] que por la mañana nunca hay tiempo para nada. Yo voy a dar betún a los zapatos[16] y a quitar el barro[17] a los chanclos de goma.[18]

15 —Y yo a cepillar el abrigo[19]... Oye, no me pongas más tu impermeable[20] encima del abrigo. ¡Toma, y debajo[21] aparece tu piyama!

---

1 velada tranquila y quehaceres menudos *a quiet evening and some small chores*
2 lavandero *laundryman*
3 ropa interior *underclothing*
4 calcetines *socks*
5 pañuelos *handkerchiefs*
6 ya ajustaremos cuentas *we'll settle accounts later*
7 camisa *shirt*
8 que digamos *we might say*
9 planchada *ironed*
10 traje *suit*
11 tintorería *dry cleaner's*
12 mancha *spot*
13 manga *sleeve*
14 americana *coat*
15 un ratito de limpieza *a little cleaning*
16 dar betún a los zapatos *polish my shoes*
17 barro *mud*
18 chanclos de goma *overshoes*
19 abrigo *overcoat*
20 impermeable *raincoat*
21 debajo *underneath*

—Dispensa,[22] hombre, tendré más cuidado.[23]

—¿Quieres poner la radio?

—¿En onda larga[24] para escuchar música española?

—No, en onda corta, que a esta hora tiene un programa interesante la estación ABC.   5

—También me gusta a mí esa emisora:[25] el noticiario[26] es muy completo, el comentarista un hombre bien informado, y la música con buena orquesta y cantantes[27] célebres.

—Sólo el anunciador se pone un poco pesado.[28] Ojalá 10 no haya estática y la recepción sea clara.

*   *   *

—Basta de limpieza y de música, y ahora a estudiar, que tengo un par de lecciones difíciles para mañana.

—Y yo a escribir mi tema de francés, que el catedrático[29] es bien exigente.[30]   15

*   *   *

—Son ya las once y media. ¿No te parece que es hora de meterse en la cama?[31]

—A la cama, pues. Mañana sacaré en limpio[32] mi tema.

*   *   *

—Durillo es este colchón.[33]

---

22 dispensa *pardon me*
23 tendré más cuidado *I'll be more careful*
24 onda larga *long wave*
25 emisora *station (broadcasting station)*
26 noticiario *newscast*
27 cantantes *singers*

28 pesado *boring*
29 catedrático *professor*
30 bien exigente *very strict*
31 cama *bed*
32 sacaré en limpio *I'll make a clean copy of*
33 durillo es este colchón *this mattress is a little hard*

—Tampoco es muy blando[34] el mío. Apaga[35] cuando
quieras. Y cuando te duermas me avisas[36]...

—En broma lo dirás,[37] pero yo tengo un tío que vaya
si[38] nos avisa cuando se duerme: ¡da unos ronquidos que
5 ya, ya![39]

EXERCISES

A. QUESTIONS.

1. ¿A cuánto subía la cuenta del lavandero?
2. ¿Qué ropa había mandado uno de los muchachos?
3. ¿Por qué parecía mal una de las camisas?
4. ¿Qué se conocía todavía en la manga de la americana?
5. ¿Por qué hicieron su rato de limpieza por la noche?
6. ¿Con qué se limpian los zapatos?
7. ¿Qué había que quitar a los chanclos?
8. ¿Qué iba a cepillar uno de los muchachos?
9. ¿Dónde estaba el impermeable del amigo?
10. ¿Y dónde estaba su piyama?
11. ¿Qué programa de radio había en onda larga?
12. ¿Por qué pusieron la radio en onda corta?
13. ¿Cómo es el noticiario de la estación ABC?
14. ¿Por qué les gusta el comentarista?
15. ¿Qué les parece la música de esa estación?
16. ¿Quién se pone un poco pesado?
17. ¿Cuándo es clara la recepción?
18. ¿Por qué se pusieron a estudiar los muchachos?
19. ¿A qué hora se acostaron?
20. ¿Cómo les parecieron los colchones?

34 blando *soft*
35 apaga *turn out the lights*
36 me avisas *let me know*
37 en broma lo dirás *you may be*
joking, you're probably joking
38 vaya si *certainly*
39 ¡da unos ronquidos que ya, ya!
he really snores!

B. REPORT.

Tell in Spanish how the boys spent the evening: cleaning clothes, listening to the radio, studying lessons for the next day.

C. DRILL.

1. *Read the following lists of related expressions.* 1. lavandero (-a), tintorería; limpieza, mancha, barro; lavar, planchar, limpiar, cepillar, dar betún a, quitar el barro a. 2. camisa, pieza de ropa interior, par de calcetines, pañuelos, piyama; traje, americana, pantalón, abrigo, impermeable; zapatos, chanclos (de goma).   3. radio, onda larga, onda corta, recepción, estática; estación, emisora, anunciador, comentarista; programa, noticiario, música, orquesta, cantante; poner, escuchar, oír.

2. *Complete by supplying appropriate ideas.*

1. A la mujer que lava ropa se la llama _____.
2. Se limpian los trajes en _____.
3. No está limpio un traje si se le notan _____.
4. Algunas piezas de ropa que se lavan son _____.
5. Hay que planchar las camisas y _____.
6. Se limpian los zapatos dándoles _____.
7. A los chanclos hay que quitarles _____.
8. Dos prendas de vestir que se ponen los hombres son _____.
9. Sobre un traje se puede llevar un abrigo o _____.
10. Se puede poner la radio en onda larga o en _____.
11. La recepción no es clara cuando hay _____.
12. La estación de radio puede llamarse también _____.
13. Dos de las personas que hablan por la radio son _____.
14. El programa en que se dan las noticias se llama _____.
15. Los programas de música son buenos cuando tienen _____.

3. *Make sentences using the following ideas.* 1. limpiar el traje. 2. conocerse una mancha. 3. estar bien planchado. 4. hacer un rato de limpieza. 5. dar betún a los zapatos. 6. cepillar el abrigo. 7. poner la radio en onda larga. 8. escuchar un programa de música. 9. ser completo el noticiario. 10. ser clara la recepción.

D. TRANSLATION.

1. The laundryman left my clothes here this morning.
2. The bill comes to two dollars and twenty-five cents.
3. I sent some shirts, underclothes, handkerchiefs, socks, and pajamas.
4. Everything is very clean, and the shirts are well ironed.
5. They also cleaned my suit well at the dry cleaner's.
6. You don't see the spot on the coat.
7. Now I'm going to brush my overcoat (the overcoat).
8. I am also going to polish my shoes.
9. On doing a little cleaning, I like to listen to the radio.
10. There are good programs on long wave and on short wave.
11. Station ABC always has an interesting program.
12. The newscast is very complete, and the commentator is a well informed man.
13. They have Spanish music with good orchestras and famous singers.
14. But I don't like the announcer because he gets a little boring.
15. I see that there isn't any static and the reception is clear.
16. That's enough cleaning, and now to study.
17. I have a couple of difficult lessons for tomorrow.
18. The professors are quite strict.
19. I will have to make a clean copy of my Spanish theme.
20. It is already time to get to bed.

E. CONVERSATION AND COMPOSITION.

Topics: 1. Some daily chores.   2. Evenings at home.
3. Your favorite programs.

Del tren a la oficina

— ¡Ay, cielos, qué mañanita! ¡qué carreras,[1] amiga mía!
Éste es el primer momento de descanso[2] que tengo.

— Cuente usted, Rosario, cuente.

— Fuí a tomar el tren, y habían cambiado el horario.[3]
5 Quise tomar el autobús, y el que salía entonces iba llenito hasta los topes.[4] De taxis, no hay que hablar; con la
lluvia,[5] ninguno libre. Tuve que aguardar en la estación
más de tres cuartos de hora. Viene el tren... mucha gente
en el andén[6]... una mujer delante de mí que trata de subir
10 al coche[7] con dos chiquillos[8] y un sin fin de bultos.[9] ¡Ya
podía haber facturado el equipaje![10] Pero no, allí quería
meterse con dos maletas[11] y tres o cuatro bultos de mano.
Y como era muy gorda[12] y estaba muy azorada[13]... con los
chiquillos, con los bultos... parecía que nunca iba a aca-
15 bar de subir. Y el revisor[14] que mete prisa, y el tren que
está para partir, y yo aguarda que te aguarda,[15] pensando
¡Dios mío, si perderé también este tren!... ¡Oh! ¡le digo
a usted que pasé un ratito!

— Me lo figuro.[16]

20 — En mi asiento, al fin. Respiré... ¡Sí, sí, otra buena

---

1 carreras *rushing around*
2 descanso *rest, peace*
3 horario *schedule*
4 llenito hasta los topes *jam-packed*
5 lluvia *rain*
6 andén *platform*
7 trata de subir al coche *tries to get
   in the coach*
8 chiquillos *children, kids*
9 bultos *bundles*

10 ¡ya podía haber facturado el equipaje! *she could at least have
   checked the luggage!*
11 maletas *suitcases*
12 gorda *fat*
13 azorada *excited, upset*
14 revisor *conductor*
15 aguarda que te aguarda *waiting
   and waiting*
16 me lo figuro *I can imagine*

me esperaba![17] Llegó el revisor, abrí mi bolso,[18] y el billete de abono[19] por ninguna parte. Quise comprar un billete de ida y vuelta, para aprovecharlo[20] al volver esta tarde. Y el revisor diciendo que no podía ser, que no podía darme sino uno sencillo.   5

— ¡Ah, pues sí que han sido calamidades! ¡Ni que[21] las estuviera usted inventando!

— ¡Sí, sí, para invenciones estoy yo![22] ¿Y qué, cree usted que terminaron ahí las calamidades? ¡Ca!...

— ¡Vamos, vamos, no me asuste![23]   10

— Llego aquí y pregunto al botones del ascensor[24] si ha llegado el jefe,[25] y me responde: «¡Toma, un rato ya largo!» Entro por esa puerta, y la mecanógrafa[26] me dice con una sonrisita:[27] «El amo[28] preguntando por usted toda la mañana.» ¡Ya ve usted, así, *toda la mañana...!* ¡La 15 muy fresca! Y luego la cajera: «El amo está que trina.»[29] Y a coro[30] los otros oficinistas, hasta ese bobo del mensajero:[31] «¡Ya, ya, Rosarito!» «¡Bien, bien, chica!» ¡Tendrán mala sombra![32] ¡Pero, Señor! ¡ni que hubiera yo robado la caja![33] ¡ni que hubiera pegado fuego[34] a la ofi- 20 cina!

— ¡Hay que ver!

—Entro, al cabo,[35] en el despacho[36] del jefe, y allí él

17 otra buena me esperaba *there was more to come*
18 bolso *purse*
19 billete de abono *commutation ticket*
20 para aprovecharlo *to use it*
21 ¡ni que...! *one might think that...!*
22 ¡para invenciones estoy yo! *I'm in a fine mood for making things up!*
23 no me asuste *don't frighten me*
24 botones del ascensor *elevator boy*
25 jefe *boss*

26 mecanógrafa *typist*
27 sonrisita *little smile, smirk*
28 amo *boss*
29 está que trina *is in a huff*
30 a coro *in chorus*
31 hasta ese bobo del mensajero *even that silly messenger boy*
32 ¡tendrán mala sombra! *are they an unpleasant bunch!*
33 caja *safe*
34 pegado fuego *set fire*
35 al cabo *finally*
36 despacho *office*

muy repantigado[37] en su butaca, como si nada pudiera hacer sin mí: «¡Vaya, vaya, taquígrafa![38] Tardecito llegamos ¿no?» Y yo sofocada:[39] «Lo siento, señor.»

— ¡Bah, no se apure usted![40] Hoy anda el jefe de mal
5 humor, pero ya se le pasará.

—¿Cómo no he de apurarme? Si precisamente hoy pensaba pedirle aumento de sueldo.[41]

— ¡Pues sí que está usted divertida![42]

EXERCISES

A. QUESTIONS.

1. ¿Por qué no tomó Rosario el mismo tren de siempre?
2. ¿Cómo iba el autobús que salía entonces?
3. ¿Por qué no había ningún taxi libre?
4. ¿Cuánto tiempo tuvo ella que aguardar en la estación?
5. ¿Qué quería hacer la mujer gorda?
6. ¿Qué debía haber hecho con el equipaje?
7. ¿Qué pensaba Rosario mientras la mujer acababa de subir?
8. ¿Dónde creía haber puesto su billete de abono?
9. ¿Por qué no pudo comprar un billete de ida y vuelta?
10. ¿Qué le preguntó al botones?
11. ¿Qué noticia le dió la mecanógrafa?
12. ¿Qué le dijo la cajera?
13. ¿Qué dijeron los otros oficinistas?
14. ¿Qué opinión tiene Rosario del mensajero?
15. ¿Qué hacía el jefe al entrar ella en el despacho?
16. ¿Qué le dijo él?

37 muy repantigado *sprawled out, lolling*
38 taquígrafa *stenographer*
39 sofocada *embarrassed*
40 no se apure usted *don't worry*
41 aumento de sueldo *a raise in salary*
42 divertida *in a predicament*

17. ¿Cómo contestó ella?
18. ¿Cómo andaba el jefe ese día?
19. ¿Por qué no debía apurarse la chica?
20. ¿Qué es lo que pensaba pedir Rosarito?

B. REPORT.

Tell in Spanish about the secretary's misfortunes: waiting at the station, getting on the train, buying a ticket, remarks by the office workers, the boss's bad mood, her real disappointment.

C. DRILL.

1. *Read the following lists of related expressions.* 1. taxi, autobús, tren; libre, lleno (hasta los topes); estación, andén, coche, asiento; revisor, horario, equipaje, bulto (de mano), billete (sencillo, de ida y vuelta, de abono). 2. comprar, dar, facturar; tomar, perder; aguardar, subir, meterse, salir, partir, llegar, volver. 3. oficina, despacho, caja, butaca, puerta; oficinista, jefe, amo, taquígrafo (-a), mecanógrafo (-a), cajero (-a), mensajero, botones del ascensor; sueldo, aumento de sueldo. 4. calamidad, mal humor; apurarse, trinar; ¡ay, cielos!, ¡Dios mío!, ¡oh!, ¡ah!, ¡ca!, ¡bah!, ¡vamos!, ¡toma!, ¡ya, ya!, ¡ya ve usted!, ¡pero, Señor!, ¡hay que ver!

2. *Complete by supplying appropriate ideas.*

1. Si queremos tomar un taxi, buscamos uno que esté

_____.

2. No podemos subir al autobús cuando va _____.
3. El lugar de la estación donde se sube al tren se llama

_____.

4. En el tren se sienta uno en _____.
5. El que revisa los billetes se llama _____.
6. Para saber la hora de los trenes hay que mirar _____.
7. Tres clases de billetes para el tren son _____.

8. Cuando el equipaje es mucho hay que ____.
9. Se pueden llevar a mano ____.
10. Cuando se pierde un tren, hay que ____.
11. El revisor mete prisa cuando el tren está para __
12. Para ver al jefe de la oficina, entramos en su ____.
13. Los nombres de empleados de una oficina son ____.
14. Las calamidades nos ponen de mal ____.
15. Algunas exclamaciones corrientes son   .

3. *Make sentences using the following ideas.* 1. tomar
el tren.   2. comprar un billete.   3. aguardar en la estación.
4. facturar el equipaje.   5. llevar bultos.   6. perder el tren.
7. llegar tarde.   8. entrar en el despacho del jefe.   9. andar
de mal humor.   10. pedir aumento de sueldo.

D. TRANSLATION.

1. I work in an office.
2. To go to the office, I take the train.
3. Sometimes I take the bus or a taxi.
4. This morning my friend Rosario arrived late at the office.
5. It amused me to hear her tell about her calamities.
6. She went to take the train, and they had changed the schedule.
7. She tried to take the bus, but it was jam-packed.
8. She looked for a taxi, and there wasn't any free.
9. She had to wait at the station three quarters of an hour.
10. When the train came, there were a lot of people on the platform.
11. In front of her was a fat woman with two kids and no end of packages.
12. It seemed that they would never finish getting on the train.

13. The conductor was hurrying things up because the train was about to leave.
14. Rosarito was thinking: "Good Lord! Will I miss this train, too!"
15. In her seat at last, she breathed a sigh of relief.
16. But the calamities didn't end there.
17. She couldn't find her ticket, and had to buy another.
18. When she arrived at the office, they told her that the boss had asked about her.
19. The boss was in a bad mood.
20. And precisely today Rosarito was intending to ask him for a raise in salary.

E. CONVERSATION AND COMPOSITION.

Topics: 1. Means of transportation.   2. A day that you were late.   3. Some office workers that you know.

Pequeños asuntos que atender[1]

—¡Qué hermosos edificios!

—Sí, ya llegamos al Centro.[2] Aquí están los grandes establecimientos comerciales y las tiendas más lujosas[3] de la ciudad. Verá usted cómo le gusta esto.

5 —¡Y qué movimiento![4]

—Demasiado, con tanta circulación de coches y tanto transeúnte.[5]

—Valiente es usted, Felisa, para conducir:[6] ¡coches a la izquierda, coches a la derecha, y por delante y por 10 detrás! Le digo que a mí me va a dar miedo[7] guiar el automóvil por estas calles.

—Ya se acostumbrará,[8] Elena, cuando lleve aquí algún tiempo.

—Trabajillo me va a costar[9]... ¡Cuidado,[10] cuidado, 15 que cambian las luces![11]

—No se apure, que ya las veo. Después de esta parada,[12] en la bocacalle[13] que viene torceremos a la derecha y estacionaremos[14] el auto en un garaje o en cualquier

1 pequeños asuntos que atender *little errands (little matters to attend to)*	7 dar miedo *frighten*
	8 ya se acostumbrará *you'll get used to it*
2 centro *business district*	9 trabajillo me va a costar *it won't be easy*
3 tiendas más lujosas *most luxurious stores*	
4 movimiento *movement, traffic*	10 ¡cuidado! *careful!*
5 tanto transeúnte *so many pedestrians*	11 luces *lights*
	12 parada *stop*
6 conducir *drive*	13 bocacalle *intersection*
	14 estacionaremos *we'll park*

espacio vacante junto a la acera,[15] ¡que, de seguro, no lo
habrá! Y luego, a pie, a corretear.[16]

* * *

— Ahora, libres ya del coche, vamos a la Central de
Correos,[17] que está ahí mismo, para certificar[18] esa carta
y remitir el paquete postal. También yo tengo que com- 5
prar sellos[19] y tarjetas postales.[20]

— Como usted guste.

— Luego al Banco Nacional, que está al lado, para que
cobre usted el cheque. Bastará con que yo lo garantice
con mi firma.[21] Y después a las tiendas.   10

— Muy bien.

— Tengamos cuidado al cruzar la calle, que el pavimento está mojado[22] y algo resbaladizo.[23]

* * *

— Quiero certificar esta carta.

— Muy bien... Son cincuenta y tres centavos, incluso 15
el franqueo.[24] Tome usted el recibo.

* * *

— ¿Cuál es el importe[25] de este paquete?

— Setenta y nueve centavos.

* * *

— Déme veinte sellos de a tres, y diez tarjetas postales.

— Aquí los tiene.   20

15 acera *sidewalk*	20 tarjetas postales *post cards*
16 corretear *go from place to place*	21 firma *signature*
17 central de correos (*main*) *post*	22 mojado *wet*
office	23 resbaladizo *slippery*
18 certificar *register*	24 franqueo *postage*
19 sellos *stamps*	25 importe *amount*

* * *

— Buenas tardes, señoras.

— Yo quisiera cobrar este cheque. Va endosado[26] con la firma de mi amiga, que tiene cuenta en este banco.

— Está bien, señora. ¿Cómo quiere usted el dinero?

5 — En billetes de diez dólares.

— Tome usted: diez, veinte, treinta, cuarenta, cincuenta.

— Gracias.

— De nada. Que ustedes lo pasen bien.

EXERCISES

A. QUESTIONS.

1. ¿Cómo son los edificios del Centro?
2. ¿Qué establecimientos están allí?
3. ¿Cómo son las tiendas del Centro?
4. ¿Cuándo se dice que hay mucho movimiento en la calle?
5. ¿Por qué le va a dar miedo a Elena conducir por las calles del Centro?
6. ¿Cuándo se acostumbrará?
7. ¿Le será fácil?
8. ¿Dónde hacen parada los coches?
9. ¿Cuándo lo hacen?
10. ¿En qué lugares se puede estacionar un automóvil?
11. ¿Por dónde va uno a pie en la calle?
12. ¿Adónde pensaban ir las dos señoras?
13. ¿Adónde fueron primero?

26 endosado *endorsed*

14. ¿Qué hicieron en Correos?
15. ¿A qué banco fueron?
16. ¿Dónde está ese banco?
17. ¿Qué hizo Elena en el banco?
18. ¿Cómo garantizó su amiga el cheque?
19. ¿Por qué había que tener cuidado al cruzar la calle?
20. ¿Adónde irán las señoras al salir del banco?

B. REPORT.

Tell in Spanish about the ladíes' errands downtown: driving and parking, going to the post office and the bank, plans for shopping.

C. DRILL.

1. *Read the following lists of related expressions.* 1. ciudad, centro; edificio, tienda, establecimiento comercial, banco, central de correos; grande, hermoso, lujoso. 2. movimiento, circulación, parada; coche, auto, automóvil, transeúnte; calle, bocacalle, acera, pavimento, luces, garaje, espacio vacante. 3. guiar, conducir, estacionar, torcer, cruzar, corretear, ir a pie, tener cuidado; a la derecha, a la izquierda, (por) delante, (por) detrás, al lado (de), junto (a), ahí mismo. 4. carta, sello, tarjeta postal, paquete postal; franqueo, importe, recibo; certificar, comprar, remitir. 5. cheque, firma; cuenta, dinero, billete; cobrar, garantizar, endosar.

2. *Complete by supplying appropriate ideas.*
1. Los edificios de la ciudad son muy _____.
2. En el Centro están las tiendas más _____.
3. Por las calles hay mucha circulación de _____.
4. Hay que parar cuando cambian _____.
5. Los coches hacen parada en _____.
6. Se puede estacionar un automóvil en _____.

7. Los que van a pie por las calles son _____.
8. Debemos tener cuidado al cruzar _____.
9. No sé si hay que torcer a la derecha o _____.
10. Hay coches por delante y por _____.
11. Vamos a la Central de Correos para certificar _____.
12. En Correos se pueden comprar _____.
13. También se remiten allí _____.
14. Vamos al banco para cobrar _____.
15. Un amigo puede garantizar el cheque con _____.

3. *Make sentences using the following ideas.* 1. llegar al Centro. 2. guiar el automóvil. 3. torcer a la derecha. 4. estacionar el auto. 5. ir a la Central de Correos. 6. certificar una carta. 7. remitir un paquete postal. 8. comprar sellos y tarjetas postales. 9. cobrar un cheque. 10. tener cuidado.

D. TRANSLATION.
1. What beautiful stores!
2. These are the most luxurious stores in the city.
3. I'm going to like this city a lot.
4. It still frightens me to drive on the downtown streets.
5. There is so much traffic.
6. My friends tell me that I will get used to it soon.
7. We will park the car in a garage.
8. There is never a vacant space on the streets.
9. Now let's go to the Post Office to buy stamps and post cards.
10. I also have to register a letter and mail a package.
11. To go to the Post Office, do we turn right or left?
12. It is right over there.
13. Then we can go to the bank.
14. I have to cash a check.
15. The National Bank is beside the Post Office.

16. The lights have changed; now we can cross the street.
17. Careful! The pavement is rather slippery.
18. Yesterday I came downtown with my friend Rosario.
19. We had to attend to several matters.
20. We didn't have time to go to the stores.

E. CONVERSATION AND COMPOSITION.

Topics: 1. Some recent business in town. 2. Getting around downtown. 3. Size and appearance of the city.

Conversaciones en una tienda

—¡Qué animada está la tienda! ¡qué concurrencia![1]
¡Y qué bien iluminada! Esto da gusto.

—En este piso[2] podemos comprar los pañuelos, el kimono, las chinelas[3]... ¡Adiós, muy buenas![4]... Son unos
5 vecinos,[5] un matrimonio del barrio.[6]

—Parece que ella lleva el marido a remolque.[7]

—Sí, no parece que va de muy buena gana.[8]

—Lo mismito que el mío cuando lo traigo de tiendas.
¡Se pone más impaciente! No es que le duela soltar los
10 cuartos,[9] no; sino que le cansa y pone de mal humor este
ajetreo de ir[10] de acá para allá. No sabe el pobre el gustito que nos da a las mujeres ir parándonos[11] cada cuatro
pasos ante un mostrador[12] y otro, mirar los artículos, buscar los saldos,[13] palpar los géneros,[14] notar su calidad,
15 probarnos[15] alguna cosa, discutir un poquito con el dependiente.[16] ¡Vaya, yo le digo que aquí estoy en mis glorias!... Pero, mire, mire estos precios;[17] no es aquí muy
cara[18] la ropa blanca,[19] ¿verdad?

1 concurrencia *crowd*
2 piso *floor*
3 chinelas *house slippers*
4 ¡adiós, muy buenas! *hello! good afternoon!*
5 vecinos *neighbors*
6 un matrimonio del barrio *a couple from my neighborhood*
7 lleva...a remolque *has...in tow*
8 de muy buena gana *very willingly*
9 no es que le duela soltar los cuartos *it's not that he minds spending the money*
10 este ajetreo de ir *this bustling around*
11 ir parándonos *to go along stopping*
12 mostrador *counter*
13 saldos *(clearance) sales*
14 palpar los géneros *feel the materials*
15 probarnos *try on*
16 dependiente *clerk*
17 precios *prices*
18 cara *expensive*
19 ropa blanca *linen*

—Ni barata, tampoco. Fina sí es, y el surtido[20] muy completo. Pero si usted quiere, subiremos primero al segundo piso, que es donde tienen la ropa de vestir.[21]

—Pues, vamos arriba.

* * *

—Buenas tardes, señoras. Tomen ustedes asiento.   5

—Gracias.

—Muchas gracias.

—No hay de qué. ¿Y en qué puedo servirlas?

—¡Ay, ay! Se me ha corrido un punto en la media.[22]

—Estas medias tan finas son una lata.[23]   10

—Bueno, pues desearía un traje estilo sastre,[24] y mi amiga un vestido de noche.[25]

—De los dos tenemos unos modelos primorosos,[26] y a precio razonable.

—En el escaparate[27] he visto uno de noche, azul pá- 15
lido,[28] que creo me irá bien.[29] ¿Cuánto es?

—Con la rebaja[30] de precios que hoy tenemos en los vestidos, cuarenta y nueve dólares, con noventa y cinco centavos. Una verdadera ganga.[31] Créame que vale muchísimo más. Y le sentará a usted divinamente.   20

—Pues me lo probaré. Mi talla[32] es del treinta y cuatro.

---

20 surtido *stock, supply*
21 ropa de vestir *wearing apparel*
22 se me ha corrido un punto en la media *I've got a run in my stocking*
23 lata *nuisance*
24 estilo sastre *tailored*
25 vestido de noche *evening dress*

26 primorosos *lovely*
27 escaparate *show window*
28 azul pálido *pale blue*
29 me irá bien *will look well on me, will be becoming to me*
30 rebaja *reduction*
31 ganga *bargain*
32 talla *size*

—En seguida,[33] señora. Hagan ustedes el favor de pasar al cuartito de pruebas, que yo vengo en un instante con el vestido y con la modista.[34]

EXERCISES

A. QUESTIONS.

1. ¿Cómo estaba la tienda al entrar las señoras?
2. ¿Qué pensaban comprar en el primer piso?
3. ¿A quiénes vieron en la tienda?
4. ¿Cómo parecía llevar la mujer al marido?
5. ¿Por qué a los hombres no les gusta ir de tiendas?
6. A las mujeres ¿qué les da gusto hacer en una tienda?
7. ¿Qué les pareció la ropa blanca que vieron?
8. ¿Dónde se vendía la ropa de vestir?
9. ¿Cómo las saludó el dependiente?
10. ¿Qué exclamó una de las señoras?
11. ¿Qué ropa de vestir deseaban comprar?
12. ¿Eran caros los modelos?
13. ¿Qué habían visto en el escaparate?
14. ¿Cuánto costaba el vestido de noche?
15. ¿Por qué dijo el empleado que era una ganga?
16. ¿Cómo le sentará el vestido a la señora?
17. ¿De qué número es su talla?
18. ¿Adónde pasaron las señoras para probarse el vestido?
19. ¿Tuvieron que aguardar algún tiempo?
20. ¿A quién iba a traer el dependiente?

B. REPORT.

Tell in Spanish about the ladies' shopping trip: browsing, commenting, and making their purchases.

---

33 en seguida *right away*   34 modista *dressmaker, fitter*

C. DRILL.

1. *Read the following lists of related expressions.*
1. tienda, piso, mostrador, escaparate, cuartito de pruebas; dependiente (dependienta), modista.   2. artículo, géneros, modelo, surtido, talla; ropa blanca, ropa de vestir; pañuelos, kimono, chinelas, medias, traje (estilo sastre), vestido (de noche).   3. calidad, precio, rebaja (de precios), saldo, ganga; caro, barato, razonable, fino, primoroso; valer, ir (bien), sentar (divinamente).   4. ir de compras, ir de tiendas; entrar, subir, pararse, tomar asiento, mirar, buscar, palpar, notar, probarse, discutir; comprar, vender, costar, valer.

2. *Complete by supplying appropriate ideas.*
1. En esta tienda la ropa de vestir está en el segundo ____.
2. Los artículos de una tienda se exponen en ____.
3. Para probarse un vestido hay que entrar en ____.
4. El empleado de una tienda se llama ____.
5. Para traer un traje el dependiente necesita saber ____.
6. Algunas prendas de vestir que se llevan sólo en casa son ____.
7. Otras prendas de vestir son ____.
8. La señora desearía un traje estilo ____.
9. Se palpan los géneros para notar ____.
10. Cuando un artículo cuesta mucho, decimos que es ____.
11. Los artículos son más baratos cuando hay ____.
12. A un artículo baratísimo se le da el nombre de ____.
13. Cuando un artículo no es caro ni barato, decimos que el precio es ____.
14. Nos gustan los trajes que nos sientan ____.
15. Vamos de tiendas para hacer ____.

3. *Make sentences using the following ideas.* 1. ir de compras. 2. comprar unos pañuelos. 3. subir al segundo piso. 4. pararse ante el mostrador. 5. buscar los saldos. 6. tomar asiento. 7. pasar al cuartito de pruebas. 8. probarse un vestido. 9. tener un surtido completo. 10. sentar bien el vestido.

D. TRANSLATION.

1. I like the suit that I bought yesterday.
2. It is becoming to me and is a real bargain.
3. With the price reduction, it cost only $59.95.
4. The prices in this store seem very reasonable.
5. Also they have a complete stock of all the articles.
6. The linen isn't very cheap, but it certainly is of good quality.
7. It is a joy (It gives pleasure) to see the store so animated.
8. That woman seems to have her husband in tow.
9. Men never go shopping very willingly.
10. They get most impatient.
11. We women like to stop in front of all the counters.
12. We always look for the sales.
13. If you wish, we'll now look at the dresses.
14. The wearing apparel is on the second floor.
15. They have some lovely models.
16. Good afternoon, ladies. Have a seat.
17. What can I do for you? (In what can I serve you?)
18. I would like to see an evening dress, pale blue, like the one that is in the show window.
19. My size is 36.
20. I'll be back in a moment with the dress and with the fitter.

E. CONVERSATION AND COMPOSITION.

Topics: 1. A shopping trip.   2. Your favorite stores.
3. Likes and dislikes in shopping.

Charla sobre el cine, el teatro y Hollywood

—¡Me gusta el cartel!¹ Buena escena romántica, lindo el título.

—Y famosos los peliculeros,² aunque me agrada más la actriz que el actor.

5 · —¿Qué localidad³ compramos? ¿billetes de galería o de butacas?⁴

—Me es igual, pero apresúrese, que no le tomen el puesto.⁵

* * *

—Haga el favor, taquillera,⁶ de dos butacas.

10 —Aquí las tiene, señor.

—Gracias.

* * *

—¿Le parece que aguardemos en el saloncillo de fumar⁷ a que termine esta sección?

—Sí, es preferible. Cogeremos así mejor asiento, y 15 veremos la película⁸ desde el principio.

—Pues, adelante.

—Tome un cigarrillo.

---

1 cartel *show bill*
2 peliculeros *movie actors*
3 localidad *seat*
4 butacas *orchestra seats, main floor seats*
5 apresúrese, que no le tomen el
puesto *hurry, so they won't get your place*
6 taquillera *ticket seller*
7 saloncillo de fumar *smoking lounge*
8 película *film, picture*

[43]

—Se agradece[9]... Este encendedor[10] no funciona.

—Para seguros,[11] los fósforos. Encienda.[12]

—Gracias. Conque ¿apasionado del cine, eh?

—Lo soy. La cinematografía es una de las maravillas
modernas. Aquí podemos ver, en la pantalla,[13] un drama,   5
una comedia, una revista musical. Hay para todos los
gustos, desde los dibujos de muñecos[14] en tecnicolor, que
a mí me aburren, pero encantan a los niños, o la película
policiaca,[15] tan del gusto de los adolescentes, hasta la gran
ópera. ¿Y a quién, hombre o mujer, niño o anciano,[16]   10
no le interesarán los noticiarios, esa actualidad viva[17] de
lo que acontece[18] en el mundo?

— ¡Sí que es usted un entusiasta! Y tiene razón. Una
película con argumento interesante, con buenos artistas y
con esa perfección técnica que a veces logran[19] en Holly-   15
wood...

— ¡Hollywood, Hollywood! ¡cómo fascina ese nombre
en el mundo!

—Sí, sí, amor, arte, modas[20]...y escándalos.

— ¡Quién visitara[21] aquellos estudios...!   20

—Pues, no sé. Porque allí estuve yo una vez viendo
impresionar[22] una película, y créame no fué cosa muy
divertida.

— ¡No me diga!

—Como usted lo oye.   25

9 se agradece *thank you*
10 encendedor *lighter*
11 seguros *dependable*
12 encienda *have a light*
13 pantalla *screen*
14 dibujos de muñecos *cartoons*
15 película policiaca *detective film*
16 anciano *elderly person*

17 actualidad viva *live account*
18 acontece *happens*
19 logran *attain*
20 modas *fashions*
21 ¡quién visitara...! *I wish I could
visit...!*
22 viendo impresionar *watching...
being shot*

—A ver, a ver.

—Era una escena entre un galán y su dama. A ella se le caía[23] el pañuelo, y él se bajaba a recogerlo[24] y se lo devolvía. Esto era todo. «¡No, no es así!», gritaba el
5 director. Y repetían la misma acción. Tampoco ahora estaba bien: el fotógrafo pedía que cambiasen ligeramente de posición para enfocarlos mejor. Tornaron a ensayar.[25] «¡Que no, que no!», y el director le mostraba a ella cómo había de dejar caer el pañuelo. Vuelta a
10 ensayar, y vuelta a protestar él, porque el galán, aunque lo recogía con naturalidad, no se lo devolvía a ella con bastante gracia. Otra vez...y otra...y otra más. Duró aquello del pañolito media hora. Yo no pude resistir más,[26] y me marché.

15   —Con todo, a mí me gustaría ver uno de esos estudios y sus estrellas[27]... Pero parece que ha terminado la sección. ¿Vamos dentro?

—Vamos.

EXERCISES

A. QUESTIONS.

1. ¿Por qué parecía bueno el cartel?
2. ¿Por qué debía apresurarse el que iba a comprar los billetes?
3. ¿Qué billetes compró?
4. ¿Por qué era preferible aguardar un rato?
5. ¿Dónde podían aguardar?

---

23 a ella se le caía *she would drop*
24 se bajaba a recogerlo *would stoop down to pick it up*
25 tornaron a ensayar *they rehearsed again, they tried again*
26 yo no pude resistir más *I couldn't stand it any more*
27 estrellas *stars*

6. ¿Con qué encendieron los cigarrillos?
7. ¿Qué clases de películas vemos en el cine?
8. ¿A quiénes encantan los dibujos de muñecos?
9. ¿A quiénes les gustan las películas policiacas?
10. ¿Qué se necesita para hacer una buena película?
11. ¿Qué se piensa en general de Hollywood?
12. ¿Qué le pareció al señor cuando vió impresionar una película?
13. En la escena del pañuelo ¿qué hacían el galán y su dama?
14. ¿Qué gritaba el director?
15. ¿Qué hacían los actores después?
16. ¿Qué pedía el fotógrafo?
17. ¿Quién le mostró a la actriz cómo dejar caer el pañuelo?
18. ¿Cómo lo recogía el galán?
19. ¿Qué no le pareció bien al director?
20. ¿Cuánto tiempo duró la escena del pañuelo?

B. REPORT.

Tell in Spanish about the men's observations at the movie: looking at the show bill, buying the tickets, waiting in the lounge, commenting on types of movies, movie production, and Hollywood.

C. DRILL.

1. *Read the following lists of related expressions.* 1. cine, teatro; cartel, taquillero (-a), película, pantalla, sección; asiento, localidad, billete, galería, butaca, saloncillo (de fumar); comprar, aguardar, apresurarse, ir dentro. 2. título, argumento, escena; drama, comedia, revista musical, gran ópera, película policiaca, noticiario, dibujos de muñecos (en tecnicolor). 3. estudio, director, fotógrafo; peli-

culero (-a), actor, actriz, artista, estrella, galán, dama; ensayar, enfocar, impresionar, protestar, gritar, mostrar, cambiar, repetir. 4. apasionado, entusiasta; bueno, lindo, famoso, divertido, interesante, romántico; perfección técnica, maravilla moderna; interesar, aburrir, gustar, agradar, encantar, fascinar.

2. *Complete by supplying appropriate ideas.*

1. Se anuncian las películas en ____.
2. La mujer que vende los billetes se llama ____.
3. Se proyectan las películas en ____.
4. Antes de entrar en el teatro hay que comprar ____.
5. Los asientos más caros son ____.
6. Las localidades más baratas son de ____.
7. Se puede aguardar en ____.
8. Los géneros de películas que más me gustan son ____.
9. Se impresionan las películas en ____.
10. En la impresión de una película toman parte ____.
11. A los artistas famosos del cine se les llama ____.
12. Muchas veces el director se pone a ____.
13. Al que le gusta mucho una cosa se le llama ____.
14. Nos agradan las escenas que son ____.
15. Lo contrario de interesar es ____.

3. *Make sentences using the following ideas.* 1. gustar el cartel. 2. comprar los billetes. 3. aguardar en el saloncillo de fumar. 4. terminar la sección. 5. coger buen asiento. 6. tener un argumento interesante. 7. encantar a los niños. 8. visitar los estudios. 9. ver impresionar una película. 10. ensayar la escena.

D. Translation.

1. Two main floor tickets, please.
2. The first show has not ended yet.

3. Let's wait in the smoking lounge.
4. I prefer to see the picture from the beginning.
5. Besides, that way we'll get a better seat.
6. Have a cigarette. . . Have a light.
7. We liked the picture that we saw last week.
8. The plot was very interesting and the actors were good.
9. There were some very romantic scenes.
10. I like the actress better than the actor.
11. There are films for every taste: dramas, comedies, and musical revues.
12. Sometimes the musical revues bore me.
13. Neither do the detective films interest me very much.
14. I always like the cartoons and newsreels.
15. I once visited a Hollywood studio.
16. I always wanted to see a picture being shot.
17. They made them repeat the same action so many times.
18. The director was shouting: "No, it's not that way!"
19. The photographer was asking the actors to change position to focus better.
20. Believe me it was not very entertaining.

E. CONVERSATION AND COMPOSITION.

Topics: 1. A recent movie.   2. Your preferences in films.   3. Some ideas about Hollywood.

Coloquios[1] galantes en el baile

— ¡Dichosos los ojos que la ven,[2] Maruja!

— Buenas noches, Enrique.

— Para mí superiores, teniéndola a usted aquí. ¿Y Emilio, qué hizo usted de él?

5 —Se quedó en la taquilla del guardarropa,[3] pero ya viene.

— A ver cuándo riñen[4] ustedes y lo suplanto yo.

— ¡Qué bromista![5]

— Es que tengo yo aquí en el pensamiento escrito el
10 nombre de usted.

— Pues táchelo usted.[6]

— Parece mentira[7] que sea conmigo tan dura de corazón[8]. . .

— Aquí viene Emilio.

15 — ¡Y él a divertirse[9] y yo a sufrir! Hasta luego, hermosa.

—Adiós.

⁂

1 coloquios *conversations*
2 dichosos los ojos que la ven *it's surely good to see you again*
3 guardarropa *checkroom*
4 riñen *have a quarrel*
5 bromista *joker*

6 táchelo usted *erase it*
7 parece mentira *it seems unbelievable*
8 dura de corazón *hard-hearted*
9 divertirse *have fun, have a good time*

— Pero, Emilio, cuánto has tardado.

— Es que me he encontrado en el vestíbulo con una pareja[10] que te voy a presentar. Ya llegan... ¡Eh, Antonio, aquí estamos!

—Parecen simpáticos. ¿Son novios,[11] no?   5

—Lo son... Maruja, tengo el placer de presentarte a Adelita Vance.

—Tanto gusto.

—El gusto es mío.

—Y éste es mi amigo Antonio Martín.   10

—Me alegro, Antonio, de conocerle.

—Encantado, Maruja.

—Está el salón muy animado ¿verdad? Y la orquesta parece buena.

—Sí, esos músicos tocan bien, sobretodo el pianista, 15 a quien yo conozco, y los dos violinistas. Y lo mismo[12] nos tocan un vals que una rumba.

— Prefiero el tango.

—Pues ahora empiezan una conga. ¡Ea!, a bailar, que esta música se baila sola.[13] Después nos veremos.[14]   20

—Y tomaremos algo en el ambigú.[15]

—Hasta más tarde, Maruja.

—Que usted lo pase bien.

—Adiós, Adela, hasta la vista.

—Adiós.   25

✿ ✿ ✿

10 pareja *couple*
11 novios *sweethearts*
12 lo mismo...que ...*as well as*
13 se baila sola *is made for dancing*
14 nos veremos *we'll meet*
15 ambigú *refreshment counter*

—Pero, Emilio, qué de prisita has cortado la conversación; ¡ni que fueras un tren expreso!

—Quiero hablar contigo sola. Y quiero sólo tu palabra y tu sonrisa.

5 —¡Lisonjero![16] ¡siempre con palabritas dulces!

—Tú decías ayer que tu corazón era una hojilla en blanco[17] ¿no? Pues yo quiero escribir en él cuatro letricas:[18] *amor*.

—Bueno, hombre, escribirás, escribirás... Pero no
10 corras tanto,[19] que parece que vuelas,[20] y ahora a bailar ese *fox-trot* que están tocando. ¡Anda, vamos!

—Contigo, Marujilla, al cielo.

EXERCISES

A. QUESTIONS.

1. ¿Qué exclamó Enrique al ver a Maruja?
2. ¿Dónde se había quedado Emilio?
3. ¿Por qué quería Enrique que riñesen Maruja y Emilio?
4. ¿Qué le pareció esto a ella?
5. ¿Dónde dijo Enrique que tenía escrito el nombre de Maruja?
6. ¿Por qué le pareció que era dura de corazón?
7. ¿Por qué tardó tanto Emilio?
8. ¿Quiénes son los amigos que presentó a Maruja?
9. ¿Qué dijo para presentar a Adela?
10. ¿Qué dijeron Maruja y Adela?
11. ¿Cómo estaba el salón esa noche?

16 lisonjero *flatterer*
17 hojilla en blanco *blank piece of paper*
18 letricas *little letters*

19 no corras tanto *don't go so fast*
20 parece que vuelas *you seem to be flying, you're fairly flying*

12. ¿Qué les pareció la orquesta?
13. ¿Cuáles de los músicos tocaban mejor?
14. ¿Qué clase de música tocaban?
15. ¿Dónde pensaban los amigos tomar algo después?
16. ¿Por qué cortó Emilio tan de prisa la conversación?
17. ¿Por qué le llamó lisonjero Maruja?
18. ¿Qué había dicho Maruja acerca de su corazón?
19. ¿Qué palabra quería escribir en él Emilio?
20. ¿Qué le contestó ella?

B. Report.

Tell in Spanish about the events at the dance: meeting of
Enrique and Maruja, arrival of Emilio, introductions, flat-
tering remarks.

C. Drill.

1. *Read the following lists of related expressions.* 1. vestíbulo, taquilla del guardarropa, salón, ambigú; quedarse,
tardar, llegar, encontrarse con, verse, tomar algo. 2. música, orquesta; vals, rumba, tango, conga, fox-trot; músico,
pianista, violinista; tocar, bailar. 3. amigo (-a), novio (-a),
pareja; amor, palabras dulces, sonrisa, pensamiento, corazón; hermoso (-a), duro (-a) de corazón, simpático (-a),
lisonjero (-a), bromista; hablar, reñir, suplantar, divertirse,
sufrir. 4. tengo el placer de presentarte (presentarle) a;
encantado (-a), tanto gusto, el gusto es mío, me alegro de
conocerle (conocerla).

2. *Complete by supplying appropriate ideas.*
1. Al entrar en el baile se deja el sombrero en ____.
2. Después de bailar un rato se toma algo en ____.
3. El lugar donde se baila se llama ____.
4. Para bailar se necesita ____.
5. Algunos de los bailes que me gustan son ____.

6. La orquesta ha empezado a ____.
7. El mejor músico de esa orquesta es ____.
8. En los bailes nos agrada encontrarnos con ____.
9. En el corazón los novios sienten ____.
10. Al que dice palabritas dulces se le puede llamar ____.
11. Al que dice bromas se le llama ____.
12. Si una persona no nos corresponde, pensamos que es ____.
13. Para presentar a un amigo se puede decir ____.
14. La persona a quien es presentado puede decir ____.
15. El amigo presentado puede contestar ____.

3. *Make sentences using the following ideas.* 1. tardar mucho. 2. encontrarse con. 3. tomar algo en el ambigú. 4. estar animado el salón. 5. tocar bien. 6. parecer simpático. 7. ser novios. 8. decir palabras dulces. 9. tener el placer de presentar. 10. alegrarse de conocer.

D. TRANSLATION.
1. We had to wait in line at the checkroom window.
2. In the vestibule I met a friend that I want to present to you.
3. Here he comes. . . Hey, Antonio!
4. Maruja, I have the pleasure of presenting to you my friend Antonio Martín.
5. It's a pleasure.—The pleasure is mine.
6. The ballroom is very gay this evening.
7. There are already many couples dancing.
8. The orchestra is very good.
9. They play waltzes, tangos, and rumbas.
10. I know the pianist and one of the violinists.
11. This music is just made for dancing.
12. Later we'll meet to have something at the refreshment counter.

13. Good-by. See you later.
14. Antonio seems very nice.
15. He is Adela's sweetheart.
16. What did she do with Henry?
17. They had a quarrel last month.
18. And who is Henry's sweetheart now?
19. Now he doesn't have a sweetheart.
20. He likes to say sweet words to all the girls.

E. Conversation and Composition.

Topics: 1. A recent dance.   2. Your favorite music.
3. Courtesy and gallantry.

Plática de los deportes[1]

—Dígame, José, ¿cuáles son los deportes que cultivan allá en su país?

—Pues en España, Rosalinda, se cultivan todos los deportes conocidos. Los más comunes entre nosotros, en
5 la Universidad española, son el baloncesto,[2] el balompié,[3] que también llamamos futbol, y el rugby.

—Pero ¿habla usted en español o en inglés...?

—En los dos, a medias, porque son juegos que ustedes los norteamericanos, y sus primos[4] los ingleses, nos han
10 llevado allá.

—Y los jugarán con viveza[5] española, pero con mala pronunciación, porque ¿quién entenderá aquí en mi tierra eso de *rugby* dicho a la española?[6]

—También españolizamos algunos: ahí tiene usted
15 *balompié*.

—¡Tiene gracia, *ball-foot* por *foot-ball!* ¡capricho[7] español!

—Mi capricho...mi capricho va a ser...una personita muy graciosa...

20 —¡Al deporte, José, al deporte! ¿Cuáles otros cultivan?

---

1 plática de los deportes *a chat about sports*
2 baloncesto *basketball*
3 balompié *football, soccer*
4 primos *cousins*
5 viveza *liveliness, vivacity*
6 a la española *in the Spanish way*
7 capricho *caprice*

[55]

—El boxeo, la lucha[8] y la pelota vasca.[9] También el tenis y la natación.[10]

—¿Cuáles son los equipos[11] que más se distinguen?

—Suelen ser[12] los de las Universidades de Madrid y Barcelona, que son las dos mayores.   5

—Ustedes los de Andalucía…, porque usted es andaluz ¿no?

—Para servir a usted.

—Pues preguntaba yo ¿ustedes los andaluces se diferencian en su gusto de los de Castilla o Asturias?   10

—Pero, Rosalinda, me está usted haciendo un examen, y tan seria, tan doctoral, que ni una maestra.[13] ¡Y qué lástima que no lo sea usted de verdad! ¡Con qué gusto iría yo a su clase!

—Gracias, José, usted siempre tan galante, pero vamos   15
al asunto.[14]

—Pues dicen que los andaluces damos[15] los mejores jugadores de tenis. Los castellanos suelen ser los campeones del atletismo.[16] En los partidos de pelota ganan[17] con frecuencia los vascongados. El campeonato de ba- 20
lompié pertenece por lo común a los gallegos y asturianos.

—Y dígame ¿se puede señalar[18] en cuáles juegos sobresalen[19] los chicos y chicas de cada Facultad?[20]

8 lucha *wrestling*	14 asunto *subject*
9 pelota vasca *pelota (Basque ball game)*	15 damos *produce*
10 natación *swimming*	16 atletismo *athletics, track*
11 equipos *teams*	17 ganan *win*
12 suelen ser *they usually are*	18 señalar *indicate, point out*
13 que ni una maestra *one might think you were a teacher*	19 sobresalen *excel*
	20 facultad *school (university division)*

—En general, las chicas se destacan[21] en el tenis, que es su deporte favorito. Entre los muchachos yo creo que la aptitud y vocación deportivas dependen principalmente del factor regional. Dicen los aficionados[22] que los
5 alumnos de Filosofía y Letras[23] suelen dar buenos equipos de baloncesto, y los de Medicina los mejores equipos de rugby.

—¡Será porque si se fracturan, la cura[24] les sale barata...!
10 —Eso dicen ellos también, en broma.

EXERCISES

A. QUESTIONS.

1. ¿Qué deportes se cultivan en España?
2. ¿Cuáles son los más comunes?
3. ¿Quiénes han llevado algunos deportes a España?
4. ¿Cómo juegan los españoles?
5. ¿Cuál es la forma españolizada de *futbol?*
6. ¿A qué llama Rosalinda capricho español?
7. ¿Quién va a ser el capricho de José?
8. ¿Qué otros deportes se cultivan en España?
9. ¿Cuáles son los equipos que más se distinguen?
10. ¿De qué región es José?
11. ¿Por qué le parece a José que la muchacha le está haciendo un examen?
12. ¿Por qué le parece lástima que ella no sea maestra?
13. ¿En qué deporte se destacan los andaluces?
14. ¿Quiénes suelen ser los campeones del atletismo?

21 se destacan *stand out*   23 filosofía y letras *liberal arts*
22 aficionados *fans*   24 cura *treatment*

15. ¿Quiénes ganan con frecuencia en los partidos de
pelota?
16. ¿A quiénes pertenece por lo común el campeonato de
balompié?
17. ¿Cuál es el deporte favorito de las chicas españolas?
18. ¿Quiénes suelen dar buenos equipos de baloncesto?
19. ¿Quiénes dan los mejores equipos de rugby?
20. ¿Por qué será que los estudiantes de Medicina sobresalen en el rugby?

B. REPORT.

Tell in Spanish about sports in Spain: the best-known
sports, the best teams, regional differences, school preferences.

C. DRILL.

1. *Read the following lists of related expressions.* 1. deporte, juego, partido, equipo, jugador, aficionado; baloncesto, futbol, balompié, rugby, boxeo, lucha (libre),
atletismo, pelota vasca, tenis, natación. 2. campeón, campeonato, aptitud, vocación deportiva; mejor, favorito, cono-
cido, común; cultivar, jugar, ganar, sobresalir, destacarse,
distinguirse. 3. país, tierra, región; español, inglés, norteamericano; andaluz, asturiano, castellano, gallego, vascongado. 4. Universidad de Madrid, Universidad de Barcelona; Facultad de Filosofía y Letras, Facultad de Medicina.

2. *Complete by supplying appropriate ideas.*

1. Los jugadores de un deporte forman _____.
2. Mañana van a jugar un partido de _____.
3. La forma españolizada de *futbol* es _____.
4. Mi deporte favorito es _____.
5. Las chicas suelen destacarse en _____.
6. Otros deportes comunes son _____.

7. El campeonato pertenece al equipo que gana más ____.
8. Andalucía, Castilla y Asturias son ____.
9. El rugby fué llevado a España por ____.
10. Uno de los deportes que cultivan mejor los españoles es ____.
11. Los deportes en que sobresalen los norteamericanos son ____.
12. Los que son de Andalucía se llaman ____.
13. Otros nombres regionales de España son ____.
14. Las dos universidades más grandes de España son ____.
15. Entre las varias Facultades figuran ____.

3. *Make sentences using the following ideas.* 1. ser el deporte favorito. 2. dar buenos equipos de baloncesto. 3. pertenecer el campeonato de balompié. 4. dar los mejores jugadores de futbol. 5. destacarse en el rugby. 6. ser los campeones del atletismo. 7. ganar en los partidos de pelota. 8. jugar un partido de tenis. 9. distinguirse los castellanos. 10. diferenciarse en su gusto.

D. TRANSLATION.

1. My favorite sports are basketball and football.
2. I also like tennis and swimming.
3. Our university usually has good teams.
4. Last year we won the basketball championship.
5. We saw a good game last Saturday.
6. My friend José says that the same sports are cultivated in Spain.
7. The most common are basketball, football, and rugby.
8. They play them with Spanish vivacity.
9. The best teams are usually those of the Universities of Madrid and Barcelona.
10. They also cultivate boxing, wrestling, pelota, tennis, and swimming.

11. The girls' favorite sport is tennis.
12. Among the boys the aptitude for sports depends on the regional factor.
13. The Andalusians produce (give) good tennis players.
14. The best pelota players are usually the Basques.
15. The Castilians are outstanding in track.
16. The football championship often belongs to the Galicians and Asturians.
17. The boys of the various schools (Faculties) also differ in their preference.
18. The liberal arts students (The students of Philosophy and Letters) prefer basketball.
19. The Medical students have the best rugby teams.
20. They say that if they get fractured, the treatment proves inexpensive for them.

E. CONVERSATION AND COMPOSITION.

Topics: 1. Your favorite sports.   2. The best teams.
3. Regional or school preferences.

Diálogo del tiempo y solo de teléfono[1]

—Mala noche hace para salir.

—Sí, prima, el tiempo no puede ser peor. La lluvia es fuerte,[2] y ahora veo que empieza a granizar.[3]

—¡Cuándo vendrá el buen tiempo y se acabarán las
5 nevadas![4]

—Ojalá sea pronto, que ya hemos visto bastante nieve este invierno.

—¡Cómo ha de ser![5] Lo que dice el tío: ahora nos quejamos[6] del frío, llegará el verano, y entonces a pro-
10 testar del calor.

—Es verdad, que tampoco me gusta el verano; se suda,[7] se corren los polvos[8] y queda la nariz[9] como un espejo.[10] Para mí, en cuanto a estación,[11] la deliciosa primavera con sus días apacibles,[12] su sol y sus flores.

15 —Y si no, el otoño, que en este clima, ya verás, es lo mejor del año: ni frío, ni calor, noches largas, mucha luna... ¿Qué? ¿ponemos el gramófono? Tengo algunos discos nuevos.

—Como quieras, pero acaso molestemos a tu padre,
20 que veo ahí en el despacho leyendo un periódico. ¿Por qué no echamos una partida de naipes?[13]

1 solo de teléfono *telephone solo*	7 se suda *one sweats, you sweat*
2 fuerte *strong, heavy*	8 polvos *powder*
3 granizar *hail*	9 nariz *nose*
4 nevadas *snowfalls*	10 espejo *mirror*
5 ¡cómo ha de ser! *what can you expect!*	11 en cuanto a estación *as to seasons*
	12 apacibles *mild*
6 nos quejamos *we complain*	13 partida de naipes *game of cards*

— Pues traeré la baraja,[14] si es que la encuentro, porque mi hermano anduvo anoche con ella.[15] Jugaba con Jacinto... ¿no sabes?...el sobrino[16] de Doña Soledad. ¡Y daban unos gritos![17] «¡La sota de bastos!»[18] Y ¡pum!, daba un golpetazo.[19] «¡El caballo de copas!» «¡El rey de 5 oros!» ¡Pum! ¡pum! «¡El as, el as de espadas!» Y duro con los palos[20] de la baraja, vengan golpes y vengan trampas[21]...

*   *   *

— ¡Enriqueta! ¡Enriqueta!, el teléfono; es para ti.

— ¡Ya voy, papá! Dispensa, Juana, un momento.   10

—Anda, anda. No te apresures en volver; yo me entretendré haciendo solitarios.[22]

*   *   *

— ¡Hola! ¿Con quién hablo?... Sí, sí, aquí Enriqueta... ¡Vaya si he reconocido[23] tu voz!... No, chico, estuve esperando tu llamada toda la tarde... ¡Ah! ¿sí? 15 Pues el telegrama no ha llegado... Sí, lloviendo también aquí todo el día... ¿Qué dices ahora?... ¿Qué? No oigo bien... Será la Central, que estará escuchando... ¿Una bomba,[24] dices? ¡Ja! ¡ja!... Pues has asustado a la telefonista; ya nos deja tranquilos... Tienes 20 razón... Bien, hombre, bien; se agradece... ¡No me digas!... ¡Anda, pícaro, no te creo!... Bueno, hasta mañana... ¿Qué?... No, ¡por Dios!, no me mandes eso

14 baraja *deck*
15 anduvo con ella *used it*
16 sobrino *nephew*
17 ¡y daban unos gritos! *and they were really shouting!*
18 sota, caballo, rey *(face cards corresponding to jack, queen, king); oros, copas, espadas, bastos (suits: diamonds, hearts, spades, clubs)*
19 daba un golpetazo *he would give a bang*
20 palos *suits*
21 trampas *tricks (cheating)*
22 haciendo solitarios *playing solitaire*
23 vaya si he reconocido *of course I recognized*
24 bomba *bomb*

por teléfono: va a resonar demasiado... ¡Chist, chist![25]
¡qué escandaloso!... Adiós, adiós.

* * *

— Hablaba, prima, con Pepe. No pudo tomar el tren
de las dos, y acaba de llegar ahora. Telefoneaba desde
5 la estación.

— Tengo ganas de conocerlo. Un novio tuyo no puede
dejar de ser[26] simpático.

— Pues mañana lo verás. Vendrá para acompañarnos
a la iglesia,[27] a misa de diez.[28]

10 — Así me gustan los hombres, con amor y con religión: dos valores espirituales ¿verdad?

— Bien puedes decirlo.

EXERCISES

A. QUESTIONS.

1. ¿Cómo era la noche?
2. ¿De qué nos quejamos en el invierno?
3. ¿De qué protestamos en el verano?
4. ¿Por qué es deliciosa la primavera?
5. ¿Por qué, en algunos climas, es el otoño lo mejor del
   año?
6. ¿Qué hacía el padre de Enriqueta?
7. ¿Por qué no pusieron el gramófono las muchachas?
8. ¿Quién había andado con la baraja?
9. ¿Con quién había jugado el hermano de Enriqueta?
10. ¿Cómo jugaban los dos?
11. ¿Para quién era la llamada del teléfono?

25 ¡chist, chist! *sh! sh!*   27 iglesia *church*
26 dejar de ser *fail to be*   28 misa de diez *ten o'clock mass*

12. ¿Cómo pensaba entretenerse Juana?
13. ¿Qué dijo Enriqueta al ponerse a hablar en el teléfono?
14. ¿Cuánto tiempo había estado esperando la llamada?
15. ¿Quién podría estar escuchando la conversación?
16. ¿Qué dijo Enriqueta de lo que le iba a mandar por teléfono?
17. ¿Por qué había llegado Pepe tan tarde a la ciudad?
18. ¿Desde dónde telefoneaba?
19. ¿Adónde las iba a acompañar Pepe?
20. ¿Cómo le gustan a Juana los hombres?

B. REPORT.

Tell in Spanish what the girls talked about: the weather, entertainments, a phone call, plans for the next day.

C. DRILL.

1. *Read the following lists of related expressions.*
1. clima, tiempo; calor, frío, sol, luna, lluvia, nieve, nevada; llover, nevar, granizar, hacer (buen tiempo, calor, frío, mucho sol, mala noche), haber (sol, mucha luna), estar (frío hermoso, delicioso), ser (fuerte la lluvia, apacible el día, larga la noche). 2. año, estación; primavera, verano, otoño, invierno; empezar, acabarse, venir, llegar; sudar, quejarse, protestar. 3. baraja, palo; oros, copas, espadas, bastos; sota, caballo, rey; andar con, echar una partida (de naipes), hacer solitarios. 4. teléfono, central, telefonista; telefonear, hablar, escuchar, esperar (una llamada), reconocer (la voz de uno). 5. ¡hola!, ¿con quién hablo?, aquí...; ¿qué?, no oigo bien, ¿qué dices (dice usted) ahora?

2. *Complete by supplying appropriate ideas.*
1. En el verano hace _____.
2. En el invierno nos quejamos del _____.

3. Me gusta el tiempo cuando hay ____.
4. No sé cuándo se acabarán ____.
5. Ahora veo que empieza a ____.
6. Me parece que también va a ____.
7. No me gusta salir cuando hace ____.
8. En la primavera los días son ____.
9. Las cuatro estaciones del año son ____.
10. Para echar una partida de naipes se necesita ____.
11. Los palos de una baraja son ____.
12. Entre los naipes de más valor figuran ____.
13. Con una baraja puede uno entretenerse ____.
14. Al ponerse uno a hablar en el teléfono, dice ____.
15. Si no entiendo bien, digo ____.

3. *Make sentences using the following ideas.* 1. hacer mala noche. 2. llover todo el día. 3. empezar a granizar. 4. venir el buen tiempo. 5. quejarse del frío. 6. protestar del calor. 7. ser lo mejor del año. 8. echar una partida de naipes. 9. hacer solitarios. 10. telefonear desde la estación.

D. TRANSLATION.

1. The climate of our city is not bad.
2. At times in the winter we complain of the cold.
3. And also, in the summer we protest about the heat.
4. Spring and fall are delightful.
5. I like the mild days, the sunshine, and the flowers.
6. Today the weather is too bad (very bad) to go out.
7. It's cold, it's raining, and it's beginning to hail.
8. I'm going to turn on the phonograph and listen to some new records.
9. We can also play a game of cards if I can find the deck.
10. My brother used it last night.
11. He likes to play with his friend Jacinto.

12. They always shout a lot.
13. They also do some cheating (tricks).
14. Excuse me; they're calling me on the phone (by telephone).
15. I'll entertain myself playing solitaire.
16. Pepe telephoned from the station.
17. He called me to tell me that he had just arrived.
18. He couldn't take the two o'clock train.
19. The telegram that he sent me did not arrive.
20. He'll come by (He'll come) tomorrow to go to church with us.

E. CONVERSATION AND COMPOSITION.

Topics: 1. The climate in your city.   2. A game of cards.   3. An interesting phone call.

Cartas de amigos

30 de enero

Querida Julia:

Siento no haber podido escribirte antes, pero acá andamos de[1] exámenes de medio curso,[2] ¡y qué exámenes,
5 Dios mío! Ayer tuve dos: uno de Álgebra con el soso de
X[3] (tú ya lo padeciste[4] el año pasado), y otro de Educación
que fué sencillamente horrible. Veremos qué notas[5] saco.

La otra noche, María y yo estuvimos en un baile de
nuestra Hermandad.[6] Hacía un mes que no íbamos a
10 ninguno. Nos presentaron a un Alberto no sé qué[7] (no
puedo recordar el apellido[8]), un muchacho simpático,
aunque demasiado jovencito.[9] Bailó mucho con María.
Conocí a algunos más, y entre ellos un pajarraco chiquito
y feo[10] que me amargó[11] la velada. Su percha debía yo
15 de parecer, con esta estatura que Dios me ha dado. Y el
hombrecito empeñado en[12] bailar conmigo cuantos bailes
podía. ¡Uf, qué pelmazo![13]

Basta por hoy, porque los libros me esperan y hay más
exámenes. Cuídate,[14] simpática, y escríbeme prontito.
20 Con mucho cariño,[15]

Teresa

1 andamos de *we're having*	9 jovencito *youngish*
2 de medio curso *midyear*	10 un pajarraco chiquito y feo *an*
3 el soso de X *that insipid X*	*ugly little bird*
4 padeciste *suffered, endured*	11 amargó *spoiled*
5 notas *grades, marks*	12 empeñado en *insisting on*
6 hermandad *sorority*	13 pelmazo *bore*
7 no sé qué *something or other*	14 cuídate *take care of yourself*
8 apellido *surname, last name*	15 cariño *love*

* * *

15 de abril

Ramoncete amigo:

Cuatro letras nada más, pero que te van a levantar en vilo.[16] Rosita, tu antigua adorada,[17] ¿qué crees que hizo el sábado? Pues casi nada: casarse con[18] David. Así, de repente,[19] como quien se bebe un vaso de agua. Tenían concertada su boda[20] para septiembre; luego la adelantaron a junio; y ahora, no pudiendo aguardar más, ha sido en abril. Cuando David me dijo que se iba a casar tan pronto como encontrara un piso,[21] me quedé de una pieza.[22] Pronto lo halló, y entonces derechitos a la vicaría. Figúrate la sorpresa que fué para todos.

No he visto a la velocísima[23] pareja desde el día de la boda. Te repito que fué el sábado, y los dos tenían que volver a clases el lunes. La verdad es que a mí me gustaría una luna de miel[24] más larga. ¿Y a ti?, mala persona.

Te abraza,
Ricardo

* * *

25 de mayo

Mi amable amiga:

¿Cómo no ponerle a usted unos renglones[25] de sincero agradecimiento[26] por su hospitalidad y sus bondades con nosotros? Fué una verdadera fiesta ese fin de semana con ustedes. La sencillez y finura de su trato,[27] sus delicadas

16 levantar en vilo *bowl over*	22 me quedé de una pieza *I was dumbfounded*
17 tu antigua adorada *your old flame, your former sweetheart*	23 velocísima *very speedy*
18 casarse con *marry*	24 luna de miel *honeymoon*
19 de repente *suddenly*	25 renglones *lines*
20 boda *wedding*	26 agradecimiento *gratitude, thanks*
21 piso *apartment*	27 trato *treatment, manner*

atenciones, no podrán ser olvidadas. Y ojalá tengamos
pronto el gusto de que se vengan ustedes a pasar con
nosotros unos días. Ya lo concertará Manuel con don
Luis cuando se vean el mes próximo.

5   Con todo reconocimiento y amistad,[28] su afectísima[29]

Emilia Gay de Brentano

EXERCISES

A. QUESTIONS.

1. ¿A quién escribió Teresa?
2. ¿Por qué no había escrito antes?
3. ¿Qué opinión tiene ella del profesor de Álgebra?
4. ¿Cómo fué su examen de Educación?
5. ¿Dónde estuvieron María y Teresa la otra noche?
6. ¿Cómo es Alberto?
7. ¿Con quién bailó mucho Alberto?
8. ¿Quién le amargó a Teresa la velada?
9. ¿En qué estaba empeñado el hombrecito?
10. ¿Conoce Ramoncete a Rosita?
11. ¿Qué hizo ella el sábado pasado?
12. ¿Para cuándo tenían concertada la boda?
13. ¿A qué fecha la adelantaron?
14. ¿Qué tenían que buscar antes de casarse?
15. ¿Por qué no pudo ser larga la luna de miel?
16. ¿Por qué escribe Emilia a su amiga?
17. ¿Qué tal les pareció el fin de semana?
18. ¿Qué no podrán olvidar?
19. ¿Qué gusto esperan tener pronto?
20. ¿Cuándo lo concertará Manuel con don Luis?

---

28 reconocimiento y amistad *grati-*
tude and friendship

29 su afectísima *sincerely yours, cor-*
dially yours

B. REPORT.

Tell in Spanish the news contained in the letters: Teresa's report on her exams and the sorority dance, Ricardo's account of the wedding, Emilia's thank-you note and invitation.

C. DRILL.

1. *Read the following lists of related expressions.* 1. carta, cuatro letras, unos renglones; Querida Julia, Ramoncete amigo, Mi amable amiga; Con mucho cariño, Te abraza, Su afectísimo (-a); escribir, poner. 2. velada, baile; muchacho, hombrecito, pajarraco, pelmazo; simpático, jovencito, chiquito, feo; ir, estar, presentar, conocer, bailar, empeñarse en, amargar la velada. 3. boda, luna de miel; pareja, novios; concertar, adelantar, aguardar, buscar (encontrar) un piso; casarse (con), ir derechitos a la vicaría. 4. fin de semana, fiesta; hospitalidad, bondades, delicadas atenciones, sencillez y finura (del trato); sincero agradecimiento, reconocimiento y amistad.

2. *Complete by supplying appropriate ideas.*

1. La expresión «cuatro letras» indica que la carta no será ____.
2. Otras palabras que significan lo mismo son ____.
3. Se puede comenzar una carta diciendo ____.
4. Antes de firmar se puede poner ____.
5. Teresa conoció a varios muchachos en ____.
6. Alberto es un muchacho simpático, aunque demasiado ____.
7. A las muchachas no les gusta bailar con ____.
8. Al que nos amarga la velada le llamamos ____.
9. La luna de miel sigue a ____.
10. La fecha de la boda de Rosita se ha ____.

11. La pareja piensa casarse tan pronto como encuentren ＿＿.
12. Los que quieren casarse en seguida van derechitos a ＿＿.
13. Después de pasar unos días con unos amigos, les agradecemos ＿＿.
14. En el trato de los amigos nos agradan ＿＿.
15. El agradecimiento que expresamos debe ser ＿＿.

3. *Make sentences using the following ideas.*   1. no haber podido escribir.   2. estar en un baile.   3. bailar con.   4. amargar la velada.   5. estar empeñado en.   6. escribir pronto.   7. casarse con.   8. concertar la boda.   9. encontrar un piso.   10. poner unos renglones.

D. TRANSLATION.

1. Yesterday I had two exams.
2. Both were simply horrible.
3. I don't yet know the grades that I got.
4. Teresa and I met several boys at the dance.
5. Alberto is nice, though too youngish.
6. Teresa says that an ugly little bird spoiled her evening.
7. The little man insisted on dancing with her all evening.
8. She says that she must have looked like his hat rack.
9. Rosita married David on Saturday.
10. It was a surprise for everybody.
11. First they intended to get married in September.
12. Then they moved the wedding up to April.
13. They have found an apartment that they like.
14. On Monday they have to return to classes.
15. The honeymoon will not be very long.
16. I must write Emilia a few lines of thanks for her hospitality.

17. The weekend that we spent with them was a real party.
18. Their thoughtful attentions cannot be forgotten.
19. I hope that they will soon come to spend a few days
     with us.
20. Luis will arrange it with Manuel when they see each
     other next week.

E. CONVERSATION AND COMPOSITION.

Topics: 1. News from your friends.   2. Letters that
you must write.   3. A recent weekend.

Diálogo del campo y la ciudad

—Hemos llegado, al fin. Allí, entre aquellos pinares,[1] tenemos el hotel.

—Y bien se ha portado[2] el coche. Yo creí que nos quedábamos en mitad de la cuesta:[3] ¡cómo trepidaba[4] el
5 motor, con qué ansia,[5] con qué fatiga!

—Sí. Pero paremos aquí un momento. Esta explanada la llaman El Mirador. El panorama es hermoso ¿verdad?

—¡Lo es, lo es!... ¡Hermoso, hermosísimo! Cielo, tierra y mar[6] se juntan[7] en tanta hermosura... Estas altu-
10 ras[8] de la cordillera,[9] esos robledales frondosos[10] en sus estribaciones,[11] allá abajo en la llanura[12] los olivares[13] y los campos de trigo[14] festoneados de amapolas,[15] y al fondo el mar de plata[16] y esmeralda[17]... Y todo bajo un cielo límpido y luminoso... Razón tenía usted: ¡esto es la
15 gloria del mundo!

—Ya verá, ya, qué deliciosas vacaciones pasamos aquí. Un día, a cazar;[18] otro, de excursión al Picacho[19]... Vuélvase,[20] mírelo allá, lejos...

1 pinares *pine groves*	*groves*
2 se ha portado *has behaved*	11 estribaciones *spurs*
3 en mitad de la cuesta *halfway up*	12 llanura *plain*
the slope	13 olivares *olive groves*
4 trepidaba *vibrated*	14 campos de trigo *wheat fields*
5 ansia *anguish*	15 amapolas *poppies*
6 mar *sea*	16 plata *silver*
7 se juntan *join*	17 esmeralda *emerald*
8 alturas *heights, summits*	18 a cazar *we'll go hunting*
9 cordillera *mountain range*	19 picacho *peak*
10 robledales frondosos *luxuriant oak*	20 vuélvase *turn around*

[73]

—¡Qué alto, Señor! Piernas de acero[21] voy a necesitar.

—Las tendrá, las tendrá. Ya nos prepararemos con algunos ejercicios y excursiones menores. Y desde allí la vista es aún más hermosa. Otros días, a pasear en canoa[22] por el lago.[23] No se ve el lago desde aquí; queda al otro 5 lado del hotel. Y por las mañanas y al atardecer,[24] nuestro buen baño.[25] El año pasado vinieron más veraneantes[26] que nunca, y la playa[27] del lago estaba muy animada. Muchos bañistas, muchas señoras, lindos trajes de baño. Estaba esto delicioso.   10

—¡Magnífico!

—Subiremos otro día al Monumento. Está en aquella loma,[28] a la izquierda. Es una estatua ecuestre de cierto famoso general, bella obra[29] de escultura. Pues sabrá usted que aquí, en estos mismos parajes,[30] se dió una 15 batalla en la guerra[31] civil.

—Sí, algo he oído de eso. La victoria de la Sierra, me parece que la llaman.

—La misma. Y con ella quedó salvada la ciudad. Allá tiene usted la ciudad, a la derecha, al cabo de la bahía.[32] 20 Aunque bien distante, por las noches se ven desde aquí sus luces. También la visitaremos algún día. Tiene un Museo de Artes precioso. El edificio es de bella arquitectura, y dentro encierra algunas colecciones de pintura dignas de verse. De pintores modernos, ingleses, espa- 25 ñoles, italianos. Hay también algunos cuadros holan-

---

21 piernas de acero *legs of steel*
22 a pasear en canoa *we'll go canoeing*
23 lago *lake*
24 al atardecer *in the late afternoon*
25 baño *swim*
26 veraneantes *(summer) vacationists*
27 playa *beach*
28 loma *hill (long, low hill)*
29 bella obra *a beautiful work*
30 parajes *places, spots*
31 guerra *war*
32 al cabo de la bahía *at the end of the bay*

deses al óleo,[33] unos pocos dibujos al lápiz[34] de no sé qué
francés, y varias tablas[35] alemanas.   Así es que, poco más
o menos, están representadas todas las nacionalidades.

—Con tal que no sean de esos pintamonas[36] que ahora
5 están de moda; digo, esos modernistas o futuristas, o como
se llamen.

—¡Oh, no! Es un museo de arte, y no de perversas
excentricidades. . . . Pero si a usted le parece, nos llegaremos[37] al hotel, que tiempo tendremos de contemplar todo
10 esto.

—Bueno, como usted guste.

EXERCISES

A. QUESTIONS.

1. Durante el viaje ¿cómo se ha portado el coche?
2. ¿Cuándo trepidó el motor?
3. ¿Qué es El Mirador?
4. ¿Cómo es el panorama desde El Mirador?
5. ¿Qué se ve desde la explanada?
6. ¿Cómo parece el mar?
7. ¿Cuáles son las diversiones en la montaña?
8. ¿Por qué será difícil subir al Picacho?
9. ¿Cómo es la vista desde el Picacho?
10. ¿Qué se puede hacer en el lago?
11. ¿En qué parte del año está más animada la playa?
12. ¿Dónde está el Monumento?
13. ¿Qué representa la estatua?
14. ¿Qué batalla se dió en estos parajes?

---

33 cuadros holandeses al óleo *Dutch*   35 tablas *panels*
    oil paintings   36 pintamonas *daubers*
34 dibujos al lápiz *pencil sketches*   37 nos llegaremos *we'll move along*

15. ¿Cómo llaman la victoria que salvó a la ciudad?
16. ¿Qué museo tiene la ciudad?
17. ¿Cómo es el edificio del Museo?
18. ¿Qué colecciones de pintura encierra?
19. ¿Qué nacionalidades están representadas?
20. ¿Qué pintores están de moda ahora?

B. Report.

Tell in Spanish about the vacationists' impressions: scenic views, local history, vacation plans and recollections.

C. Drill.

1. *Read the following lists of related expressions.* 1. vista, panorama; cielo, tierra, mar; sierra, cordillera, montaña, altura, picacho, explanada, mirador, estribación, loma, cuesta, llanura, campo; arboleda, pinar, olivar, robledal; bahía, lago, playa. 2. alto, frondoso, límpido, luminoso; bello, hermoso, delicioso, precioso, magnífico, famoso, digno de verse. 3. aquí, allí, allá abajo, al fondo, lejos, a la derecha, a la izquierda, dentro, al otro lado; llegar, parar, quedarse, subir, volverse; ver, mirar, contemplar. 4. vacaciones, excursión, ejercicio, baño; veraneante, bañista; cazar, pasear (en canoa); por las mañanas, al atardecer, por las noches. 5. monumento, museo, edificio, colección; bellas artes, escultura, arquitectura, pintura; obra (de arte), estatua, cuadro (al óleo), tabla, dibujo (al lápiz); pintor, pintamonas, modernista, futurista; inglés, español, italiano, holandés, francés, alemán.

2. *Complete by supplying appropriate ideas.*
1. La vista extensa desde una altura se llama ____.
2. En un panorama se juntan cielo y ____.
3. Unas montañas enlazadas forman ____.
4. Las puntas agudas de algunas montañas se llaman ____.

5. El campo que no tiene altos ni bajos se llama _____.
6. Entre las arboledas que más me gustan figuran _____.
7. De una vista que nos agrada podemos decir que es _____.
8. Algunas frases para indicar dirección son _____.
9. Los que pasan el verano en un lugar de recreo se llaman _____.
10. La playa del lago está muy animada cuando hay muchos _____.
11. Por las mañanas, en la montaña, me gusta _____.
12. De las bellas artes, la que me interesa más es _____.
13. Entre las diferentes clases de cuadros figuran _____.
14. A los pintores malos se les llama _____.
15. Las nacionalidades que están representadas en esta colección son _____.

3. *Make sentences using the following ideas.* 1. llegar al fin. 2. parar un momento. 3. ser hermoso el panorama. 4. verse desde aquí. 5. quedar al otro lado de. 6. pasar unas vacaciones deliciosas. 7. venir muchos veraneantes. 8. pasear en canoa. 9. visitar el museo. 10. encerrar colecciones de pinturas.

D. TRANSLATION.

1. From here the view is beautiful.
2. The hotel is there among those pine groves.
3. The mountain range is very tall.
4. Down there on the plain there are some wheat fields.
5. We spent a delightful vacation here last year.
6. We made two excursions to the Peak.
7. I like to go canoe riding on the lake.
8. Many vacationists come here every year.
9. The beach of the lake is always very animated.
10. The bathing suits are prettier each year.

11. The famous Monument is an equestrian statue.
12. It is a lovely work of sculpture.
13. A certain battle was fought here in the civil war.
14. With the victory of the Sierra the city was saved.
15. The city can be seen from here.
16. Its Art Museum has some collections of painting worth seeing.
17. The architecture of the building is beautiful.
18. Many modern painters are represented in these collections.
19. There are works by Englishmen, Spaniards, Italians, and Frenchmen.
20. The Museum has a few paintings by the daubers who are now in fashion.

E. CONVERSATION AND COMPOSITION.

Topics: 1. Some scenic views that you like.   2. Your favorite vacation spots.   3. Some museums that you have visited.

Volando sobre las nubes[1]

— ¡Señores viajeros[2] del 35, al avión![3]—oímos en el altavoz.[4]

— Feliz viaje,[5] amigo mío.

— Que se conserve usted bueno.

5 Estábamos, claro es, en el aeródromo. El avión brillaba a los rayos del sol. Vimos subir al aparato el capitán aviador, el piloto y el radiógrafo, muy jóvenes y galanes en su uniforme. Subimos luego los viajeros. Los motores comenzaron a funcionar y vibró el aeroplano, nervioso
10 e impaciente por levantar el vuelo.[6] La revisora,[7] de pie ante nosotros, exclamó en voz alta:

— ¡Sírvanse,[8] señores, ajustarse las correas![9]

Y lo dijo con tan linda voz, y tan graciosa y atractiva era la joven, que yo no dejé de[10] contemplarla mientras
15 me ajustaba las correas del asiento.

Pronto arrancó[11] el avión con gran ruido[12] de motores, se deslizó por la pista,[13] veloz y sereno. Cuando despegó de tierra[14] nunca lo notamos, porque apenas[15] había pasado un minuto y ya veíamos la ciudad allá abajo como

---

1 nubes *clouds*
2 viajeros *travelers, passengers*
3 avión *plane*
4 altavoz *loudspeaker*
5 feliz viaje *bon voyage*
6 levantar el vuelo *take flight*
7 revisora *(or* camarera, azafata*)* *stewardess, hostess*
8 sírvanse *please*

9 correas *safety belts*
10 no dejé de *I didn't stop*
11 arrancó *started moving*
12 ruido *noise, roar*
13 se deslizó por la pista *it glided along the runway*
14 despegó de tierra *it left the ground*
15 apenas *hardly, scarcely*

casitas de muñecas.[16] Poco después estábamos sobre las
nubes, y por entre ellas, como si fuesen islas del cielo,
divisábamos[17] en un mismo instante pueblecillos,[18] valles,
ríos y montañas: era un panorama inmenso. Tan firme
y sereno era el vuelo, tal la sensación de seguridad, que   5
nos sentíamos tan tranquilos como si no hubiese peligro[19]
alguno.

Unas horas más tarde aterrizamos[20] en un aeropuerto.

—¡Es un encanto la navegación aérea!—dijo muy con-
tenta, al salir, una señora que yo había visto antes entrar   10
en el aeroplano algo nerviosa, con un poquito de miedo.

—¡Vaya, vaya si lo es!

—¿Decía usted que su viaje es más largo?

—En efecto, señora. Tengo que cambiar de avión.
Es de otra línea aérea, y no saldrá hasta la madrugada.[21]   15

—Pues adiós, joven, que le vaya felizmente.

—Que usted siga bien, señora.

Bien de madrugada, al avión de nuevo. Empezaba a
clarear[22] el día. De pronto,[23] en el lejano oriente,[24] una
masa de luz dorada,[25] más bien rojiza,[26] que surgía del   20
abismo como un abanico[27] de fuego. ¡Qué hermosura es
la salida del sol[28] visto desde las alturas! Y luego, mar,
mucho mar, el vasto océano, y el gran pájaro[29] de acero
cortando[30] cielo, sereno, infatigable, poderoso. Volábamos
por un espacio transparente y luminoso; abajo las nubes,   25

16 casitas de muñecas *little doll*
   houses
17 divisábamos *we could make out*
18 pueblecillos *little towns*
19 peligro *danger*
20 aterrizamos *we landed*
21 madrugada *dawn*
22 clarear *dawn*

23 de pronto *suddenly*
24 lejano oriente *far east*
25 dorada *golden*
26 rojiza *reddish*
27 abanico *fan*
28 salida del sol *sunrise*
29 pájaro *bird*
30 cortando *flying through*

como de algodón³¹ fino y aéreo; y mucho más abajo, de
vez en cuando,³² entre las nubes, se veían lagos al parecer:
era el océano. En varias horas de vuelo sólo vimos en uno
de aquellos lagos un barquito de juguete,³³ frágil, minús-
5 culo, ¡y tenía dos chimeneas, era un transatlántico!

    Tierra, al fin. Casi lo lamenté, porque ya me sentía en
el avión como en mi casa, y hasta había hecho conocimiento con varios pasajeros. En el avión, con la misma
rapidez del vuelo se contraen las amistades.

EXERCISES

A. QUESTIONS.

1. ¿Qué se oyó en el altavoz?
2. ¿Qué dijeron los amigos al despedirse?
3. ¿Quiénes subieron primero al avión?
4. ¿Cuándo vibró el aeroplano?
5. ¿Qué exclamó en voz alta la revisora?
6. ¿Por qué se quedó el viajero contemplando a la joven?
7. ¿Cuándo se oyó gran ruido de motores?
8. ¿Por dónde se deslizó el avión?
9. ¿Cómo se veía la ciudad desde el avión?
10. ¿Qué se divisaba por entre las nubes?
11. ¿Cómo era el vuelo del avión?
12. ¿Cuándo aterrizaron en un aeropuerto?
13. ¿Qué dijo una señora al salir del aeroplano?
14. ¿Cómo había estado antes, al entrar?
15. ¿Cuándo saldrá el avión de la otra línea aérea?
16. Por la mañana ¿qué se vió en el lejano oriente?

---

31 algodón *cotton*
32 de vez en cuando *from time to time*

33 barquito de juguete *little **toy** boat*

17. ¿Por dónde volaba el gran pájaro de acero?
18. ¿Qué parecían las nubes?
19. ¿Qué parece un transatlántico visto desde las alturas?
20. ¿Se contraen con rapidez las amistades en un viaje en avión?

B. REPORT.

Tell in Spanish about the plane trip: the take-off, the view from the plane, the stopover, the flight over the ocean.

C. DRILL.

1. *Read the following lists of related expressions.*
1. viaje, vuelo, navegación aérea, línea aérea; aeropuerto, aeródromo, avión, aeroplano, aparato, altavoz, pista, motor, asiento, correa, uniforme.   2. viajero, pasajero; capitán, piloto, radiógrafo, revisora (camarera, azafata); nervioso, tranquilo, contento; joven, galán, gracioso, atractivo. 3. funcionar, vibrar, arrancar, deslizarse, despegar (de tierra), levantar el vuelo, volar, aterrizar; subir, ajustarse las correas, cambiar de avión.   4. ruido, peligro, seguridad, altura, hermosura, encanto; veloz, firme, sereno, impaciente, infatigable, poderoso, frágil, minúsculo.   5. ciudad, pueblecillo, casita de muñecas, valle, montaña, río, lago, mar, océano, transatlántico, barquito de juguete; nube, abismo, rayos del sol, luz dorada, salida del sol; clarear, surgir.

2. *Complete by supplying appropriate ideas.*
1. La navegación aérea significa los viajes en ____.
2. Los aviones despegan y aterrizan en ____.
3. Se oyen anunciar los vuelos en ____.
4. En el primer viaje por avión algunos viajeros se sienten ____.
5. El personal de un aeroplano lo forman ____.
6. Los pilotos parecen muy galanes en su ____.

7. Las azafatas siempre son muy _____.
8. Antes de arrancar hay que ajustarse _____.
9. El aeroplano vibra cuando comienzan a funcionar _____.
10. El avión se desliza por _____.
11. Los pasajeros se sienten tranquilos cuando el vuelo es

_____.
12. Durante el viaje se ven abajo _____.
13. Desde un avión, una ciudad se ve como _____.
14. Visto desde las alturas, un transatlántico parece _____.
15. Cuando empieza a clarear el día, se ve en el oriente

_____.

3. *Make sentences using the following ideas.* 1. ir al aeródromo. 2. anunciar en el altavoz. 3. subir al avión. 4. ajustarse las correas. 5. despegar de tierra. 6. divisar valles y ríos. 7. sentirse tranquilo. 8. aterrizar en un aeropuerto. 9. cambiar de avión. 10. ver la salida del sol.

D. TRANSLATION.

1. Airplanes look like big steel birds.
2. I like to watch them land and take off.
3. When the motors begin running, the plane seems impatient to take flight.
4. It starts moving with a great roar of motors.
5. Then it glides along the runway to take off.
6. Within a minute it is flying over the city.
7. How much can be seen from an airplane!
8. A big city is seen as little doll houses.
9. In a single instant we make out valleys, rivers, and mountains.
10. An ocean liner, seen from the heights, looks like a little toy boat.
11. I remember that on my first trip I was a little nervous.

12. Some twenty passengers were waiting at the airport.
13. Soon we heard the flight announced over the loud-speaker.
14. I saw the pilots and radio operator get on the plane.
15. The hostess who greeted us was charming and attractive.
16. While I was fastening the safety belt, I did not feel very calm.
17. The plane started moving and glided along the runway.
18. When it took off, I didn't notice.
19. The flight was steady and smooth.
20. I soon felt at home on the plane.

E. CONVERSATION AND COMPOSITION.

Topics: 1. A plane trip.   2. The best ways to travel.
3. Your most interesting trip.

El libro que más me ha impresionado

Es una novela. Su título, *Don Quijote.* Su autor,
Miguel de Cervantes. Libros hermosos hay muchos, en
prosa y en verso. Grandes obras maestras,[1] reconocidas
como tales en todo tiempo y en todo país, ésas son muy
5 pocas. Entre ellas está mi novela. De un maestro de la
novela se dice en todas partes: «¡Es un Cervantes!» De
un hombre idealista se dice: «¡Es un Quijote!»

¿Por qué *un Cervantes?* Porque en él culminan las
dotes[2] del supremo artista. Porque las poseyó[3] todas, y
10 la misma maestría tiene al describir que al narrar o dialogar; porque lo mismo nos da la esencia de un paisaje[4]
que la de un carácter; tan bien inventa una fábula como
crea un personaje; es tierno[5] y patético, es cómico y
trágico; y su pluma[6] es tan feliz en lo uno como en lo
15 otro. Tiene todas las dotes del novelista, y cada una de
ellas la posee en grado[7] eminente; que tal es la marca de
un gran maestro.

¿Por qué se dice *es un Quijote?* Porque es un personaje generoso hasta la excentricidad. Pretende[8] cambiar
20 por sí solo el orden del mundo. Tiene fe[9] en la justicia,
fe en los más nobles ideales, fe en la ayuda[10] de Dios.
Y por su amor al orden ideal que se ha forjado[11] en la

1 obras maestras *masterpieces*	7 grado *degree*
2 dotes *talents, gifts*	8 pretende *he tries, he seeks*
3 poseyó *he possessed*	9 fe *faith*
4 paisaje *landscape*	10 ayuda *aid, help*
5 tierno *tender*	11 forjado *forged*
6 pluma *pen*	

mente[12] y en el corazón está Don Quijote siempre dispuesto al sacrificio, y sufre con la naturaleza[13] de un mártir las burlas[14] y los golpes del mundo. Es un loco en las acciones y un sabio[15] en los pensamientos; cómico desde el punto de vista práctico; trágico, aun sublime, 5 desde el punto de vista ideal. Nos hace reír con sus actos extravagantes, y despierta al par[16] en nosotros la más humana simpatía y admiración.

¿Y por qué es el libro que más me ha impresionado? Por todo lo dicho arriba, y por muchas cosas más. Leyén- 10 dolo, va mi ánimo[17] en una ondulación constante de la realidad a la fantasía, de la risa a la pena,[18] de lo ridículo a lo sublime. Me siento unas veces en presencia de la vida de todos los días, de esas escenas familiares del campo o la ciudad, tan animadas y exactas; y otras veces lo que 15 veo es tan insólito,[19] tan extraño,[20] y sin embargo,[21] tan posible y verdadero, que mi ánimo fluctúa entre el ensueño[22] y la realidad. En ocasiones me río hasta soltar la carcajada, y otras siento tristeza,[23] y aun otras me pongo a pensar. A veces se junta todo ello en la misma página,[24] 20 en un mismo instante, y siento la sonrisa en el semblante[25] y la emoción en el corazón, una cosa agridulce,[26] un regocijo[27] melancólico y reflexivo. De modo que estas páginas tan ricas, de interés siempre renovado, me dan pasto[28] a la imaginación y al sentimiento, a la reflexión y al en- 25 sueño. Y me recreo en la lectura,[29] y al par siento como

12 mente *mind*
13 naturaleza *nature*
14 burlas *jests*
15 sabio *wise man*
16 al par *equally, at the same time*
17 ánimo *spirit, mind*
18 pena *sorrow*
19 insólito *unusual*
20 extraño *strange*

21 sin embargo *nevertheless*
22 ensueño *dream, illusion*
23 tristeza *sadness*
24 página *page*
25 semblante *countenance*
26 agridulce *bittersweet*
27 regocijo *gaiety*
28 pasto *nourishment, food*
29 lectura *reading*

si mi alma se fuese enriqueciendo[30] o creciendo[31] en capacidad.

¡Tesoro[32] de sentimientos, tesoro de fantasías, rico tesoro del espíritu es este libro de mi predilección!

EXERCISES

A. QUESTIONS.

1. ¿Quién es el autor de *Don Quijote?*
2. ¿En qué forma está escrito el libro?
3. ¿Son muchas o pocas las grandes obras maestras?
4. ¿De quién suele decirse que es *un Quijote?*
5. ¿Cuáles son las dotes de un gran novelista?
6. ¿Cuál es la marca del gran maestro?
7. ¿Hasta qué punto es generoso Don Quijote?
8. ¿Qué pretende hacer por sí solo?
9. ¿En qué cosas tiene fe Don Quijote?
10. ¿Por qué está siempre dispuesto al sacrificio?
11. ¿Qué es lo que él sufre como mártir?
12. ¿Cuál es la diferencia entre sus acciones y sus pensamientos?
13. ¿Desde qué punto de vista parece cómico o trágico?
14. ¿Cuáles son los sentimientos que despierta Don Quijote en el lector?
15. ¿En qué consiste la gran variedad de este libro?
16. ¿Cómo son las escenas familiares del *Quijote?*
17. ¿Qué efectos produce la lectura del *Quijote?*
18. ¿Qué emociones se juntan a veces?
19. ¿A qué dan pasto sus páginas tan ricas?
20. ¿Qué tesoros hay en esta gran obra maestra?

---

30 se fuese enriqueciendo *were being enriched*   31 creciendo *growing*   32 tesoro *treasure*

B. REPORT.

Tell in Spanish why *Don Quijote* is a great masterpiece: its artistry, theme, pictorial variety, and fusion of emotional experiences.

C. DRILL.

1. *Read the following lists of related expressions.*
1. prosa, verso; libro, novela, obra (maestra); autor, novelista, artista, maestro. 2. pluma, dote, maestría; página, título, fábula, personaje, carácter, paisaje, escena; escribir, inventar, crear, describir, narrar, dialogar. 3. animado, exacto, verdadero, familiar, insólito, extraño, posible; rico, humano, reflexivo, tierno, patético, trágico, cómico, melancólico, agridulce; recrearse (en la lectura), reírse (hasta soltar la carcajada), sentir tristeza, ponerse a pensar. 4. ánimo, alma, espíritu, mente, corazón; realidad, fantasía, ensueño, imaginación, reflexión, pensamiento, interés, sentimiento, emoción; pena, tristeza, risa, sonrisa, regocijo, admiración, simpatía. 5. fe, ideal, justicia, amor, sacrificio; idealista, generoso, sabio, sublime; loco, extravagante, ridículo.

2. *Complete by supplying appropriate ideas.*
1. Un libro puede estar escrito en prosa o en ____.
2. Las obras más importantes se llaman ____.
3. Los que escriben libros se llaman ____.
4. Los autores de novelas son ____.
5. Para escribir una novela hay que inventar una fábula y crear ____.
6. Los grandes novelistas saben narrar, dialogar y ____.
7. Las escenas familiares del *Quijote* son ____.
8. Cuando el libro es trágico, el lector siente ____.
9. Nos reímos cuando la escena que leemos es ____.
10. Decimos que las emociones se sienten en ____.

11. Entre las emociones que sentimos figuran ____.
12. Cuando uno siente regocijo, aparece en su semblante ____.
13. Un hombre dispuesto al sacrificio nos parece ____.
14. Los hombres idealistas tienen fe en ____.
15. Los actos de los locos son ____.

3. *Make sentences using the following ideas.* 1. ser una obra maestra. 2. poseer las dotes de un supremo artista. 3. inventar una fábula. 4. crear un personaje. 5. recrearse en la lectura. 6. reírse hasta soltar la carcajada. 7. sentir tristeza. 8. despertar simpatía y admiración. 9. tener fe en. 10. estar dispuesto al sacrificio.

D. TRANSLATION.

1. There are not many great masterpieces.
2. Few works are recognized as such in every time and in every country.
3. A master of the novel must possess all the gifts of the supreme artist.
4. He has the same mastery when describing as when narrating or dialoguing.
5. He can give us the essence of a landscape or of a character.
6. He invents a plot as well as he creates a character.
7. A true masterpiece awakens many emotions in the reader.
8. The book may be tender and pathetic; it may be comic or tragic.
9. Its scenes may be animated and exact or unusual and strange.
10. A masterpiece gives food to the imagination, to feeling, and to reflection.

11. Reading *Don Quijote,* the mind fluctuates between illusion and reality.
12. This masterpiece is a treasure of human emotions.
13. The book makes us laugh, and it also makes us feel sorrow.
14. Often several emotions are joined on a single page, in a single instant.
15. The bittersweet feeling is a gaiety that is melancholy and thoughtful.
16. All the characters of the *Quijote* are very human.
17. Don Quijote is not always ridiculous.
18. At times he seems mad, and other times he seems wise.
19. He is almost always idealistic and generous.
20. The book and its characters give us a panorama of human life.

E. CONVERSATION AND COMPOSITION.

Topics: 1. Your favorite authors.   2. The artistry of the masters.   3. Some reader reactions.

PART II

ARTICLES

FORMS

	SINGULAR			PLURAL	
	MASC.	FEM.	NEUTER	MASC.	FEM.
DEFINITE ARTICLE	el¹	la (el)²	lo³	los	las
INDEFINITE ARTICLE	un	una (un)²		unos	unas

1 A + el = al; de + el = del.
2 El and un replace la and una before nouns beginning with stressed a- or ha-.
3 Neuter lo is used with adjectives, adverbs, or phrases to refer to ideas.

USAGE

1. Definite Article.

(a) The main use of the definite article is to indicate particular identified persons or things.

Los dos muchachos están en **la** esquina de **la** calle.	*The two boys are on the street corner.*
La estación ABC tiene programas interesantes.	*Station ABC has interesting programs.*
No llegó **el** señor Martín.	*Mr. Martin did not arrive.*
Aguardé toda **la** mañana.	*I waited all morning.*
Nos veremos **el** mes que viene.	*We'll see each other next month.*

(b) Since the identification may indicate the owner of something, the definite article sometimes shows possession.

Yo voy a cepillar **el** abrigo.	*I'm going to brush my overcoat.*
Ahí tienes una percha para **el** sombrero.	*There you have a hatrack for your hat.*

(c) The definite article is also used to indicate the whole of any type or group of persons or things.

Son apasionados **del** cine.	*They're very fond of the movies.*
Los dibujos de muñecos encantan a **los** niños.	*The animated cartoons delight children.*
Las chicas se destacan en **el** tenis.	*Girls are outstanding in tennis.*
El otoño es **lo** mejor **del** año.	*Fall is the best part of the year.*
¡Qué hermosura es **la** salida del sol visto desde **las** alturas!	*What a thing of beauty is the sunrise seen from the heights!*

(d) Without an expressed noun, the definite article may serve as an unstressed pronoun.

Éste es **el** restaurán que te decía, **el** de los buenos alimentos.	*This is the restaurant that I was telling you about, the one with the good food.*
Tú no eres de **los** que necesitan píldoras de vitamina.	*You aren't one of those who need vitamin pills.*

2. Indefinite Article.

The indefinite article is used to indicate one or some of a type or group.

Tome **un** cigarrillo.	*Have a cigarette.*
Cogí **una** indigestión.	*I got (a case of) indigestion.*
Fueron **unas** vacaciones deliciosas allá en el campo.	*It was a delightful vacation there in the country.*
Son **unos** vecinos, **un** matrimonio del barrio.	*They are some neighbors, a couple from my neighborhood.*

3. Nouns without Articles.

(a) No article is used in prepositional phrases which form adjectival or adverbial units. The noun is not visualized as a separate entity (specific, general, or indefinite).

Tráigame unas chuletas **de cerdo.**	*Bring me some pork chops.*
Por fortuna llegaron temprano.	*Fortunately they arrived early.*
Ayer paseamos **en canoa** por el lago.	*Yesterday we went canoe riding on the lake.*
Tengo al Decano **de profesor de Historia.**	*I have the Dean as (my) history professor.*

(b) Sometimes, for the same reason, the object of a verb has no article, the verb + noun forming a unit.

Pasa **lista** todos los días.	*He calls (the) roll every day.*
Creo que hablan **español**.	*I think that they speak Spanish.*
Tomen ustedes **asiento**.	*Have a seat.*
Todos daban **gritos**.	*They were all shouting.*
Aquí no hay **propinas**.	*There's no tipping here.*
Voy a pedirle **aumento** de sueldo.	*I'm going to ask him for a raise in salary.*

(c) Similarly, predicate nouns used adjectivally, to classify by type, have no article.

No es **curso** obligatorio.	*It's not a required course.*
El profesor es **hombre** de sabiduría y bondad.	*The professor is a learned and kindly man.*
Usted es **andaluz** ¿no?	*You're an Andalusian, aren't you?*

(d) Nouns used for direct address, exclamations, or simple enumerations rarely have an article.

Buenas tardes, **señoras**.	*Good afternoon, ladies.*
¡Linda **muchacha**!	*A pretty girl!*
Venga el menú: **sopas, asados, pescados, ensaladas, legumbres**...	*Let's see the menu: soups, meats, fish, salads, vegetables...*

DRILL EXERCISES

1. *Supply the proper form of the definite article.* (*Example:* chico — el chico.) 1. chica. 2. hermano. 3. madre. 4. hombres. 5. mujeres.

2. *Supply the proper form of the indefinite article.* (*Example:* muchacho — un muchacho.) 1. muchacha. 2. novio. 3. vecinos. 4. señores. 5. señoras.

3. *Use a and de with each of the following.* (*Example:* el cine — al cine, del cine.) 1. el garaje. 2. la iglesia. 3. el baile. 4. los partidos. 5. las montañas.

4. *Use the indefinite article instead of the definite.* *(Example:* el traje de baño — un traje de baño.) 1. el vestido de noche. 2. la luna de miel. 3. el equipo de futbol. 4. los billetes de galería. 5. las colecciones de pintura.

5. *Indicate a specific reference, by using the definite article.* *(Example:* mes próximo — el mes próximo.) 1. lunes pasado. 2. 15 de abril. 3. Museo de Artes. 4. señor Martín. 5. capitán Brentano.

6. *Indicate a general reference, by using the definite article.* *(Example:* radio — la radio.) 1. natación. 2. educación. 3. realidad. 4. fantasía. 5. imaginación.

7. *Indicate a reference to an idea, by using the neuter definite article.* *(Example:* bueno — lo bueno.) 1. mejor. 2. malo. 3. mismo. 4. dicho. 5. de ayer.

COMPREHENSION EXERCISE

See if you understand the meaning of the nouns as used with or without an article.

1. Yo perdí **la mañana** arreglando **el programa** de **asignaturas.**
2. Buenos días, **señores.**
3. Tráigame **un bisté** y **una ensalada** de **lechuga.**
4. Ya llegamos **al Centro.**
5. Estacionaremos **el auto** en **un garaje.**
6. Tengamos **cuidado** al cruzar **la calle.**
7. Tenemos **unos modelos** primorosos, y a **precio** razonable.
8. Cogeremos así mejor **asiento.**
9. Es **una película** con **argumento** interesante.
10. Créame no fué **cosa** muy divertida.

11. Lo mismo nos toca **un vals** que **una rumba.**
12. Son **juegos** que ustedes **los norteamericanos** nos han llevado allá.
13. Llovió también aquí todo **el día.**
14. Es **un museo** de **arte,** no de perversas **excentricidades.**
15. De **un maestro** de **la novela** se dice: «¡Es **un Cervantes!**»

COMPLETION EXERCISE

Complete by using the noun given, supplying an article if necessary. (The gender is shown by the abbreviations m. *and* f.)

1. (alcoba *f.*)   De vuelta en _____, acaba de vestirse.
2. (zapatos *m.*)   Yo voy a dar betún a _____.
3. (sábanas *f.*)   ¿Qué, dormilón, se te pegaron _____?
4. (señora *f.*)   Que usted lo pase bien, _____.
5. (verano *m.*)   ¿Qué tal pasaste _____?
6. (fila *f.*)   Dos horas estuve haciendo _____.
7. (Química *f.*)   Mi consejero quería que tomase _____.
8. (lenguas *f.*)   Estoy especializando en _____ modernas.
9. (apetito *m.*)   Pues adentro, que vengo con _____.
10. (pollo *m.*)   El arroz con _____ es un plato suculento.
11. (mujer *f.*)   Delante de mí había _____ con dos chiquillos.
12. (programa *m.*)   A esta hora hay _____ interesante.
13. (tarde *f.*)   Aguardaron toda _____.
14. (iglesia *f.*)   Jacinto vendrá para acompañarnos a _____.
15. (sábado *m.*)   ¿Sabes lo que hicieron _____?
16. (mes *m.*)   Piensan volver _____ próximo.
17. (excursión *f.*)   Un día, a cazar; otro, de _____ al Picacho.

18. (nacionalidades *f.*)   Están representadas todas ____.
19. (navegación *f.*)   ¡Es un encanto ____ aérea!
20. (conocimiento *m.*)   Había hecho ____ con varios pasajeros.

NOUNS AND ADJECTIVES

USUAL ENDINGS

	MASCULINE		FEMININE	
	SINGULAR	PLURAL	SINGULAR	PLURAL
NOUNS	-o[1]	-os	-a[2]	-as
	-e	-es	-e	-es
	(consonant)	+ es[3]	(consonant)[4]	+ es[3]
ADJECTIVES	-o[5]	-os	-a	-as
	-e[5]	-es	-e[5]	-es
	(consonant)	+ es[3]	(consonant)[6]	+ es[3]

1 A few nouns ending in -o are feminine (e.g., mano; also some abbreviated forms like radio).

2 A few nouns ending in -a are masculine (e.g., clima, día, drama, guardarropa, panorama, piyama, telegrama, tema, tranvía); words ending in -ista are both masculine and feminine (artista, bañista, comentarista, novelista, pianista, violinista, etc.).

3 Spelling changes according to the rules of spelling: z > c before adding -es (e.g., vez, veces; feliz, felices); addition or omission of a written accent (joven, jóvenes; alemán, alemanes; francés, franceses).

4 Some common feminine endings: -ción, -dad, -tad, -tud.

5 A few adjectives have a shortened form when used before the noun (e.g., masculine singular: buen, mal, algún, ningún; masculine or feminine singular: gran; numerals—masculine: primer, tercer, un, veintiún, etc.; masculine or feminine: cien).

6 Words of nationality add -a in the feminine (e.g., inglés, inglesa; español, española).

[98]

USAGE

1. Agreement.

Adjectives agree in gender and number with the nouns (or pronouns) that they modify. The masculine plural is used to include two or more forms of different gender.

El **pavimento** está **resbaladizo.**	*The pavement is slippery.*
La **mañana** está **fresca.**	*The morning is cool.*
Esas **colecciones** de pintura **son dignas** de verse.	*Those collections of painting are worth seeing.*
(**Ellos**) parecen **simpáticos.** ¿Son novios, no?	*They seem pleasant. They're sweethearts, aren't they?*

2. Position.

(*a*) Qualifying adjectives usually follow the nouns that they modify.

Seguiré dos cursos **electivos:** sintaxis **francesa** y literatura **española.**	*I will take two elective courses: French Syntax and Spanish Literature.*
Tengo un consejero **hábil** y **diligente.**	*I have an able and diligent adviser.*

(*b*) When used before the noun, the adjectives express subjective attitudes, without distinguishing force. For some adjectives (**bueno, malo, grande**) this is the usual position.

Son **buenos** artistas.	*They are good artists.*
Hace **mal** tiempo.	*The weather is bad.*
Aquí están los **grandes** establecimientos comerciales.	*Here are the big commercial establishments.*

3. Personal *a*.

(*a*) Before noun objects (direct or indirect) referring to persons or personified things, the preposition **a** is used.

No vi **a María.**	*I didn't see Mary.*
Acaso molestemos **a tu madre.**	*We may bother your mother.*

(*b*) Personal **a** is not used when the reference is indefinite or general.

Los andaluces dan los mejores jugadores de tenis.	*The Andalusians produce the best tennis players.*

(c) Personal **a** is not used with the verb **tener** except when the meaning is limited by some other idea in the sentence. Compare:

Tengo un profesor exigente.	*I have a strict teacher.*
Tengo al Decano de profesor.	*I have the Dean as my teacher.*

4. Possessive Form.

Possession is indicated by the use of the preposition **de.**

Jacinto es sobrino de Doña Soledad.	*Jacinto is Doña Soledad's nephew.*

5. Adjective Phrases.

Prepositional phrases modifying nouns function as adjectives.

¡Lindos trajes de baño!	*Pretty bathing suits!*
Compré un billete de ida y vuelta.	*I bought a round-trip ticket.*

6. Adjectives Used as Substantives.

Adjectives may serve as nouns or pronouns.

Hasta luego, hermosa.	*See you later, beautiful.*
Conocí a algunos más.	*I met several others.*
¡La muy fresca!	*The impudent creature!*

7. Comparisons.

(a) Comparisons of equality are expressed by the use of **tan...como.** When there is no term of comparison, **tan** merely indicates a high degree.

Su pluma es **tan** feliz en **lo uno como** en lo otro.	*His pen is as happy in the one as in the other.*
Usted siempre **tan** galante.	*You're always so gallant.*

(b) Comparisons of inequality are usually expressed by the use of **más...que** or **menos...que.** The term of comparison is frequently omitted. After a superlative, phrases indicating category are introduced by **de.**

Desde allí la vista es aun **más** hermosa (**que** desde aquí).	*From there the view is even more beautiful (than from here).*

Aquí están las tiendas **más lujo**	*Here are the most luxurious*
sas **de** la ciudad.	*stores in the city.*

(c) There are very few irregular comparative or superlative forms: **mucho—más, poco—menos, bueno—mejor, malo— peor, grande—mayor, pequeño—menor.**

¿Cuáles son los **mejores** asientos?	*Which are the best seats?*

(d) The ending **-ísimo,** though derived from a superlative form, now expresses merely a high degree of a quality.

¡Hermoso, **hermosísimo!**	*Beautiful! Very beautiful!*

DRILL EXERCISES

1. *Use the masculine definite article with each noun.* (*Example:* tiempo — el tiempo.) 1. verano. 2. avión. 3. director. 4. comentarista. 5. programa.

2. *Use the feminine definite article with each noun.* (*Example:* sala — la sala.) 1. taquilla. 2. estación. 3. conversación. 4. ciudad. 5. amistad.

3. *Change the article and noun to the plural.* (*Example:* el cepillo de cabeza — los cepillos de cabeza.) 1. la maquinilla de afeitar. 2. el traje de baño. 3. el jugador de tenis. 4. el cuartito de pruebas. 5. la píldora de vitaminas.

4. *Change the noun and its modifiers to the plural.* (*Example:* una mesa vacía — unas mesas vacías.) 1. un plato suculento. 2. una buena lista de platos. 3. un gran establecimiento comercial. 4. **un buen artista.** 5. una gran obra maestra.

5. *Use* **Conozco a** *before each noun.* (*Example:* el violinista — Conozco al violinista.) 1. la pianista. 2. el cantante. 3. la actriz. 4. el jefe. 5. la taquígrafa.

6. *Use the comparative form of the adjective.* *(Example:* una vista hermosa — una vista más hermosa.) 1. un drama interesante. 2. una cara bonita. 3. un cantante célebre. 4. una escena romántica. 5. un personaje generoso.

7. *Change to the feminine.* *(Example:* el mejor — la mejor.)* 1. el peor. 2. el más difícil. 3. el más pobre. 4. los dos mayores. 5. los dos menores.

COMPREHENSION EXERCISE

See if you understand the meaning of each adjective and adjective phrase.

1. ¿Y el cepillo **de dientes** y la pasta **dentífrica?** ¡Ah, sí, aquí están!
2. **Primer** día **de clase,** y el despertador **descompuesto.**
3. Ese arroz **con pollo** es una **magistral** obra **culinaria.**
4. Tráigame un pastel **de manzana** y café **con leche.**
5. Ahora, **libres** ya del coche, vamos a la Central **de Correos.**
6. **Buena** escena **romántica, lindo** el título.
7. Cogeremos así **mejor** asiento.
8. Yo creo que la aptitud y vocación **deportivas** dependen principalmente del factor **regional.**
9. El tiempo no puede ser **peor.**
10. ¡Cuándo vendrá **el buen** tiempo y se acabarán las nevadas!
11. Para mí, en **cuanto** a estación, la **deliciosa** primavera con sus días **apacibles,** su sol y sus flores.
12. La telefonista ya nos deja **tranquilos.**
13. No he visto a la **velocísima** pareja desde el día de **la** boda.

14. El Monumento es una estatua **ecuestre** de **cierto famoso** general.
15. Tal es la marca de un **gran** maestro.

COMPLETION EXERCISE

Complete by using the proper form of the adjective given.

1. (delicioso) Ya verá usted qué ____ vacaciones pasamos aquí.
2. (bueno) Este restaurán tiene ____ alimentos.
3. (fresco) Prefiero fruta ____, no en conserva.
4. (español) Puse la radio para escuchar música ____.
5. (primero) Éste es el ____ momento de descanso que tengo.
6. (hermoso) ¡Qué ____ edificios!
7. (blanco) No es aquí muy cara la ropa ____, ¿verdad?
8. (verdadero) Es una ____ ganga.
9. (bueno) No lo hacen de muy ____ gana.
10. (dulce) ¡Lisonjero! ¡siempre con palabritas ____!
11. (mayor) Las Universidades de Madrid y Barcelona son las dos ____ de España.
12. (mejor) Los estudiantes de Medicina dan los ____ equipos de rugby.
13. (nuevo) Tengo algunos discos ____.
14. (horrible) Los exámenes fueron ____.
15. (bueno) Ahora hace ____ tiempo.
16. (precioso) La ciudad tiene un Museo de Artes ____.
17. (bello) El edificio es de ____ arquitectura.
18. (grande) Arrancó el avión con ____ ruido de motores.
19. (noble) Don Quijote tiene fe en los más ____ ideales.
20. (práctico) Es cómico desde el punto de vista ____.

PERSONAL PRONOUNS

FORMS

Subject	Indirect Object	Direct Object	Reflexive Object	Object of Preposition
yo, *I*	me	me	me	mí[1]
tú, *you* (familiar)	te	te	te	ti[1]
usted,[2] *you* (polite)	le (se)[3]	le, lo (m.) / la (f.)	se	usted (sí)[4]
él, *he*[5]	le (se)[3]	le, lo[6]	se	él (sí)[4]
ella, *she*[5]	le (se)[3]	la	se	ella (sí)[4]
ello, *it* (neuter)[7]	le	lo	se	ello
nosotros, -as, *we*	nos	nos	nos	nosotros, -as
vosotros, -as, *you*[8]	os	os	os	vosotros, -as
ustedes,[2] *you*[8]	les (se)[3]	los (m.) / las (f.)	se	ustedes (sí)[4]
ellos, *they*[5] (m.)	les (se)[3]	los	se	ellos (sí)[4]
ellas, *they*[5] (f.)	les (se)[3]	las	se	ellas (sí)[4]

1 Con + mí = conmigo; con + ti = contigo.
2 Abbreviations of usted, ustedes are: V., VV.; Vd., Vds.; Ud., Uds.
3 Se replaces le or les before lo, la, los, las.
4 Sí replaces the 3rd person prepositional forms when the meaning is reflexive; con + sí = consigo.
5 Subject pronouns very rarely refer to things.
6 For masculine things lo is the usual direct object form.
7 Neuter forms refer to ideas; ello is of limited use.
8 The plural forms for *you* in Spain are: vosotros, -as (familiar), ustedes (polite); in Spanish America: ustedes (familiar or polite).

USAGE

1. Subject Pronouns.

(a) Subject pronouns are used mainly for stress. **Usted** and **ustedes** are also used for politeness.

Y tú, hijo, abrígate.	*And you, son, wrap up.*
Eso dicen **ellos** también.	*They say that, too.*
Tome **usted** asiento.	*Have a seat.*

(b) Neuter **ello** is occasionally used to sum up an idea.

A veces se junta todo **ello** en la misma página.	*Sometimes all of it is combined on the same page.*

2. Position of Object Pronouns.

(a) Indirect and direct object pronouns usually precede the verb. The indirect precedes the direct.

Te felicito.	*I congratulate you.*
No **los** he visto.	*I haven't seen them.*
Ahora mismo **se lo** traigo.	*I'll bring it to you right away.*
Cuando **me lo** dijeron, me quedé de una pieza.	*When they told me ("said it to me"), I was dumbfounded.*

(b) Object pronouns follow and are attached to the infinitive and the present participle. But when used with a phrase considered as a unit, the pronouns may precede the whole phrase.

Tengo ganas de **conocerlo.**	*I want to meet him.*
Nos gusta ir **parándonos** cada cuatro pasos.	*We like to go along stopping every few steps.*
Bien **lo** puedes decir.	*You are quite right.*
Parece que **me** está haciendo un examen.	*You seem to be giving me an exam.*

(c) Object pronouns are usually attached to wish or command forms, except after **no** or **que.**

Escríbeme prontito.	*Write to me quite soon.*
No **me** asuste.	*Don't frighten me.*
Que usted **lo** pase bien.	*Good-by. ("May you fare well.")*

3. Special Uses of Object Pronouns.

(a) The indirect object frequently indicates possession.

No **me** han limpiado bien el traje.	*They didn't clean my suit very well.*

(b) Prepositional forms are used, in addition to the regular object pronouns, for stress or clarity (and often in the case of **usted, ustedes,** for politeness). When the verb is omitted, only the prepositional form is used.

A mí me gustaría ver esa película. ¿Y **a ti?**	*I would like to see that picture. And you?*
Este vestido **le** sentará **a usted** divinamente.	*This dress will be wonderfully becoming to you.*

(c) The same type of redundant construction may be used with a noun object, especially if the noun precedes the verb.

Híncale el diente **al** bisté.	*Sink your teeth into the beefsteak.*
A esta explanada la llaman el Mirador.	*This esplanade is called ("they call") the Mirador.*

(d) Neuter **lo** may be used as a predicate complement, standing for an idea previously expressed by a noun, an adjective, or a phrase.

¿Son novios, no?—**Lo** son.	*They're sweethearts, aren't they? —They are.*
Conque ¿apasionado del cine, eh?—**Lo** soy.	*So you're very fond of the movies, eh?—I am.*

4. Reflexive objects.

(a) The reflexive objects may be direct or indirect. They precede any other object pronoun, whether direct or indirect.

Se secó con la toalla.	*He dried himself with the towel.*
Me eché la bata encima.	*I threw on my bathrobe.*
Se me ha corrido un punto en la media.	*I've got a run in my stocking.*

(b) The plural forms may have a reciprocal meaning (*each other, one another*).

Después **nos** veremos.	*We'll see each other later.*

(c) Many verbs have come to have special meanings when used reflexively.

Levántate.	*Get up. ("Lift yourself.")*
Yo me marché.	*I left. ("I walked myself.")*

(d) A reflexive form may convey a passive meaning when the subject is a thing or an idea (not a living being). In other cases **se** may serve as an indefinite subject.

Desde aquí **se ven** las luces de la ciudad.	*From here can be seen the lights of the city.*
De un hombre idealista **se dice:** «¡Es un Quijote!»	*About an idealistic man it is said: "He is a Don Quixote!"*
Se suda y se corren los polvos.	*You sweat (One sweats) and the powder runs down.*

DRILL EXERCISES

1. *Use an appropriate subject pronoun for stress or clarity. (Example:* Me voy. — Yo me voy.*)*   1. Me quejo del frío.   2. Se siente tranquilo.   3. Se destacan en el tenis.   4. Nos vemos todos los días.   5. Se marchan al hotel.

2. *Change the indirect object pronoun to the plural. (Example:* Me gusta mucho. — Nos gusta mucho.*)*   1. Te parece interesante.   2. Me agrada el actor.   3. Le amargó la velada.   4. Trabajillo me va a costar.   5. Que le vaya bien.

3. *Change the direct object pronoun to the plural. (Example:* Lo tienen ya. — Los tienen ya.*)*   1. La quieren tomar.   2. Lo vieron ayer.   3. Te felicitan todos.   4. Me conocen bien.   5. Me vendrán a buscar esta noche.

4. *Add a prepositional form to stress or clarify the object pronoun. (Example:* Me es igual. — A mí me es igual.*)*   1. Me gusta esto.   2. Nos parece magnífico.   3. Le sentará bien el vestido.   4. Le duele soltar los cuartos.   5. Les cansa este ajetreo.

5. *Add an appropriate prepositional form to clarify the indirect object.* *(Example:* Se lo dije. — Se lo dije a usted *or* a él, a ella, a ustedes, a ellos, a ellas.) 1. Se lo pregunté. 2. Se lo mostré. 3. Se lo di. 4. Se lo pedí. 5. Se lo devolví.

6. *Change to the negative.* *(Example:* Hágalo. — No lo haga.)   1. Cómalos.   2. Escríbale.   3. Táchelo.   4. Mírelos.   5. Apresúrese.

7. *Substitute a pronoun for the noun object.* *(Example:* He visto a esa muchacha. — La he visto.)   1. Conozco a esos muchachos.   2. Recibí la carta.   3. Conocí a tu novio. 4. Vimos el monumento.   5. Están mirando los cuadros.

COMPREHENSION EXERCISE

See if you can understand the meaning of each personal pronoun.

1. También **yo** perdí la mañana.
2. Verá **usted** cómo **le** gusta esto.
3. ¡Dichosos los ojos que **la** ven, Maruja!
4. **Nos** presentaron a un Alberto no sé qué.
5. Estoy bien, gracias. Y **a ti,** Alfonso, ¿cómo **te** va?
6. Mira cómo **se** ríen esos del grupo.
7. Quiero hablar con**tigo** sola.
8. Sus amigos preguntaron por **usted** esta mañana.
9. ¡Oh! ¡**le** digo **a usted** que pasé un ratito!
10. ¡Bah, no **se** apure **usted**!
11. Que **usted lo** pase bien.
12. **Se** ve el Picacho desde aquí.
13. Vuélvase, mír**e**lo allá, lejos.
14. Mi amigo Fernando vendrá a buscar**me**.
15. Oye ¿**me** quieres acompañar a la librería?

COMPLETION EXERCISE

Complete by supplying an appropriate personal pro-noun.

1. ¡Pasen, señores! Allí al fondo tienen ____ una mesa vacía.
2. ¡Graciosa muchacha! Me parece que ____ he visto antes.
3. Muy bien, señores. Ahora mismo ____ lo traigo.
4. Y a éste ¿qué ____ damos de propina?
5. Yo ____ recreo en la lectura del libro.
6. También me gusta a ____ ese programa.
7. Compré un billete de ida y vuelta para aprovechar____ al volver esta tarde.
8. También ____ tengo que comprar sellos y tarjetas postales.
9. ¡Adelante! Pase ____.
10. A ella se ____ cayó el pañuelo.
11. Él ____ bajó a recogerlo.
12. No pudimos resistir más y ____ marchamos.
13. Me alegro, Maruja, de conocer____.
14. Ellas ____ destacan en el tenis.
15. Ahora ____ quejamos del calor.
16. No encuentro la baraja porque mi hermano anduvo anoche con ____.
17. ¡Enriqueta!, el teléfono; es para ____.
18. A mí ____ gustaría una luna de miel más larga.
19. El museo tiene algunas colecciones de pintura dignas de ver____.
20. Si a usted ____ parece, nos llegaremos al hotel.

POSSESSIVES AND DEMONSTRATIVES

4

FORMAL PRACTICE

	ONE POSSESSOR	TWO OR MORE POSSESSORS
UNSTRESSED ADJECTIVES	**mi, mis** *my* **tu, tus** *your* (familiar) **su, sus** { *your, his, her, its*	**nuestro, -a, -os, -as** *our* **vuestro, -a, -os, -as** *your* **su, sus** { *your, their*
STRESSED ADJECTIVES	**mío, -a, -os, -as** *mine* **tuyo, -a, -os, -as** *yours* (fam.) **suyo, -a, -os, -as**[1] { *yours, his, hers, its*	**nuestro, -a, -os, -as** *ours* **vuestro, -a, -os, -as** *yours* **suyo, -a, -os, -as**[1] { *yours, theirs*
PRONOUNS	**el mío, la mía,** etc. (article + stressed adjective)	

1 For clarity: **de usted, de él, de ella, de ustedes, de ellos, de ellas.**

DEMONSTRATIVE FORMS

	SINGULAR		PLURAL		MEANING
	MASC.	FEM.	MASC.	FEM.	
ADJECTIVES	**este** **ese** **aquel**	**esta** **esa** **aquella**	**estos** **esos** **aquellos**	**estas** **esas** **aquellas**	*this, these* *that, those* *that, those*
PRONOUNS	**éste, ésta,** etc. (adjective forms with written accents) Also, neuter forms: **esto, eso, aquello.**				

USAGE

1. Possessive Adjectives and Pronouns.

(a) The possessive adjectives agree in gender and number with the nouns that they modify.

Anoche estuvimos en un baile de **nuestra** Hermandad.	*Last night we went to a dance given by our Sorority.*
Me gusta la primavera, con **sus** días apacibles, **su** sol y **sus** flores.	*I like spring, with its calm days, its sunshine, and its flowers.*

(b) The stressed adjectives are either separated from the nouns (as predicate adjectives) or follow the nouns (in direct address, exclamations, or indefinite references).

El gusto es **mío**.	*The pleasure is mine.*
Feliz viaje, amigo **mío**.	*Bon voyage, my friend.*
¡Dios **mío**, si perderé también este tren!	*Good Lord! Will I miss this train, too!*
Un novio **tuyo** no puede dejar de ser simpático.	*A sweetheart of yours can't fail to be likable.*

(c) The possessive pronouns stand for a noun + a possessive.

Durillo es este colchón.—Tampoco es muy blando **el mío**.	*This mattress is a little hard.— Mine isn't very soft, either.*

2. Demonstrative Adjectives and Pronouns.

(a) The demonstrative adjectives agree in gender and number with the nouns that they modify.

Este encendedor no funciona.	*This lighter isn't working.*
Esta música se baila sola.	*This music is made for dancing.*

(b) The demonstrative **ese** indicates proximity, in a literal or figurative sense (near you, known to you, etc.); **aquel** indicates remoteness (over there, not near us, etc.).

¡Y **ese** tranvía sin venir!	*And that trolley still not here.*
También me gusta a mí **esa** emisora.	*I also like that broadcasting station.*

¡Hollywood, Hollywood! ¡Cómo fascina **ese** nombre en el mundo!	*Hollywood, Hollywood! How that name fascinates throughout the world!*
¡Quién visitara **aquellos** estudios!	*I surely would like to visit those studios!*
Allí, entre **aquellos** pinares, tenemos el hotel.	*There, among those pine groves, we have the hotel.*

(c) The masculine and feminine pronouns refer to persons or things.

Éste es mi amigo Antonio Martín.	*This is my friend Antonio Martín.*
Estas camisas son más caras que **aquéllas.**	*These shirts are more expensive than those.*

(d) The neuter pronouns sum up ideas or situations.

Me gusta **esto.** Todo está limpio y bien cuidado.	*I like this. Everything is clean and well kept.*
Algo he oído de **eso.**	*I've heard something about that.*
Duró **aquello** del pañolito media hora.	*That business of the little handkerchief lasted half an hour.*

DRILL EXERCISES

1. *Express with more than one possessor. (Example:* mi país — nuestro país.) 1. tu tierra.   2. mi oficina.   3. tu pueblo.   4. mi amigo Luis.   5. mis deportes favoritos.

2. *Change the noun and adjective to the plural. (Example:* mi primo — mis primos.) 1. mi hermano.   2. tu amigo.   3. su vecino.   4. nuestro viaje.   5. su excursión.

3. *Give the form of the possessive pronoun corresponding to each of the following. (Example:* mi bolso — el mío.) 1. mi casa.   2. tu coche.   3. su abrigo.   4. mi marido.   5. nuestras primas.

4. *Give the form of the demonstrative pronoun corresponding to each of the following. (Example:* este peine

—éste.) 1. este cepillo. 2. esta toalla. 3. esos zapatos.
4. estos calcetines. 5. aquellos pañuelos.

5. *Use the proper form of* **este** *with each of the following. (Example:* tren — este tren.) 1. calle. 2. piso.
3. vestidos. 4. música. 5. páginas.

6. *Use the proper form of* **ese** *with each of the following. (Example:* libro — ese libro.) 1. autor. 2. novela.
3. escenas. 4. pintores. 5. modernistas.

7. *Change the noun and adjective to the plural. (Example:* este sello — estos sellos.) 1. este paquete. 2. esta
camisa. 3. ese colchón. 4. esa estación. 5. aquel edificio.

COMPREHENSION EXERCISE

See if you understand the meaning of the possessives and demonstratives.

1. **Mi** talla es del treinta y cuatro.
2. ¡Qué carreras, amiga **mía!**
3. Enriqueta está hablando con **su** novio.
4. ¡Vaya si he reconocido **tu** voz!
5. Pepe dice que han llegado **sus** amigos.
6. Juega bien el equipo de **nuestra** universidad.
7. ¿Cuáles son **sus** deportes favoritos?
8. A **esta** hora tienen un programa interesante.
9. Más gracia deben tener **esos** del grupo.
10. Para sal, la de **aquella** que entra ahora.
11. También a **mí** me gusta **esa** novela.
12. **Estas** medias tan finas son una lata.
13. **Éste** es el teatro que te decía.
14. En uno de **aquellos** lagos vimos un barquito de juguete.
15. Razón tenía usted: ¡**esto** es la gloria del mundo!

COMPLETION EXERCISE

Complete with the idea indicated.

1. *(mine)* El gusto es ____.
2. *(her)* Juana dice que ____ amigos vendrán a buscarla.
3. *(his)* Era una escena entre un galán y ____ dama.
4. *(its)* Me gustaría ver uno de esos estudios y ____ estrellas.
5. *(mine)* El marido no va de muy buena gana... Lo mismito que ____ cuando lo traigo de tiendas.
6. *(your)* Tú decías ayer que ____ corazón era una hojilla en blanco ¿no?
7. *(their)* No tienen aquí ____ coche.
8. *(our)* Estuvimos en un baile de ____ Hermandad.
9. *(your)* ¿Decía usted que ____ viaje es más largo?
10. *(my)* Ya me sentía en el avión como en ____ casa.
11. *(This)* ____ es la tienda que te decía.
12. *(these)* Mire ____ precios.
13. *(This)* ____ da gusto.
14. *(Those)* ____ músicos tocan bien.
15. *(That)* ____ dicen ellos.
16. *(this)* Ya hemos visto bastante nieve ____ invierno.
17. *(that)* Fué una verdadera fiesta ____ fin de semana con ustedes.
18. *(this)* El Monumento está en ____ loma.
19. *(this)* Tiempo tendremos de contemplar todo ____.
20. *(those)* Grandes obras maestras, reconocidas como tales en todo tiempo y en todo país, ____ son muy pocas.

NEGATIVES, ADVERBS, AND PREPOSITIONS

1. Negatives.

(*a*) If a negative is expressed or implied, negative forms are used throughout the clause (for indefinite words, adverbs, and conjunctions).

No ha llamado **nadie.**	*Nobody has called.*
No hace **ni** frío **ni** calor.	*It's neither hot nor cold.*
Hacía un mes que **no** íbamos a **ningún** baile.	*For a month we hadn't gone to any dance.*

(*b*) The word **no is not** used when some other negative form precedes the verb.

Aquí **nadie** escucha.	*Here nobody is listening.*
Nunca hay tiempo para **nada.**	*There is never time for anything.*

(*c*) After comparative forms there is felt to be an implied negation.

El año pasado vinieron más veraneantes que **nunca.**	*Last year more vacationists came here than ever before.*

2. Adverbs.

(*a*) Many adverbs of manner are formed by adding **-mente** to the feminine singular forms of adjectives.

El examen fué **sencillamente** horrible.	*The exam was simply horrible.*

(*b*) Adverbial ideas are often expressed by prepositional phrases.

El día empieza **con calma.**	*The day begins calmly.*
Entré, **al cabo,** en el despacho del jefe.	*Finally I entered the boss's office.*

(c) Comparisons are usually expressed by the use of **tan,** **más,** or **menos.** The term of comparison is frequently omitted. Before numerals **más de** or **menos de** is used. The irregular comparative and superlative forms are: **mucho** (or **muy)**—**más,** **poco**—**menos, bien**—**mejor, mal**—**peor.**

Tan bien inventa una fábula como crea un personaje.	*He invents a plot as well as he creates a character.*
Hasta **más** tarde, Maruja.	*See you later, Maruja.*
Aguardé **más de** tres cuartos de hora.	*I waited more than three quarters of an hour.*

(d) The meanings of **aquí, ahí,** and **allí** are comparable to those of the demonstratives **(este, ese, aquel): aquí,** *here* (near me); **ahí,** *there* (near you, known to you, etc.); **allí,** *there* (over there, not near us, etc.).

Aquí viene Emilio.	*Here comes Emile.*
¿Cree usted que terminaron **ahí** las calamidades?	*Do you think the calamities ended there?*
Desde **allí** la vista es aun más hermosa.	*From there the view is even more beautiful.*

(e) The adverbs **acá** and **allá** are less precise than **aquí** and **allí.** They indicate direction or general location.

Les gusta ir de **acá** para **allá.**	*They like to go here and there.*
Mírelo **allá,** lejos.	*Look at it over there, in the distance.*

3. Prepositions.

Several of the most common prepositions vary considerably in meaning according to the context.

A (direction) *to, into;* (separation) *from, off;* (position or time) *at, on;* (manner) *by, with, in, on,* etc.

Luego iremos **al** restaurán.	*Later we'll go to the restaurant.*
Voy a quitar el barro **a** los chanclos de goma.	*I'm going to get the mud off my overshoes.*
Allí **al** fondo tienen ustedes una mesa vacía.	*There at the back you have an empty table.*
Aprovecharé el billete **al** volver esta tarde.	*I'll use the ticket on ("at the") returning this afternoon.*
Será mejor ir **a** pie.	*It will be better to go on foot.*

De (ownership, origin, content, etc.) *of, from, by;* (topic) *of, about;* (kind or purpose) *of, for, as;* (manner) *with, in, on,* etc.

El avión es **de** otra línea aérea.	*The plane belongs to ("is of") another airline.*
El museo tiene muchos cuadros **de** pintores modernos.	*The museum has many pictures by modern painters.*
Algo he oído **de** eso.	*I've heard something about that.*
Necesito un cepillo **de** dientes.	*I need a toothbrush ("brush for teeth").*
¿Qué le damos **de** propina?	*What shall we give him as a tip?*
Eso les pone **de** mal humor.	*That puts them in a bad mood.*

Para (destination, use, point of comparison) *for;* (purpose) *to, in order to;* (terminal point in time) *by, for;* (proximity of action) *about to.*

Ahí tienes una percha **para** el sombrero.	*There you have a hat rack for your hat.*
Mala noche hace **para** salir.	*It's a bad night for going out.*
Pepe vendrá **para** acompañarnos a la iglesia.	*Pepe will come by to go to church with us.*
Tengo un par de lecciones difíciles **para** mañana.	*I have a couple of difficult lessons for tomorrow.*
El tren está **para** partir.	*The train is about to leave.*

Por (agent or means) *by;* (reason, desire, or concern) *because of, for, to, about;* (duration of time) *during, in, for;* (direction) *along, through, on, in;* (equivalence, exchange, benefit) *for.*

Pretende cambiar **por** sí solo el orden del mundo.	*He seeks to change by himself the order of the world.*
El avión parecía impaciente **por** levantar el vuelo.	*The plane seemed impatient to take flight.*
El amo preguntó **por** usted.	*The boss asked about you.*
Basta **por** hoy, porque los libros me esperan.	*That's enough for today, since the books are waiting for me.*
Me da miedo guiar el automóvil **por** estas calles.	*It frightens me to drive the car on these streets.*
¡La palabra tiene gracia: *ball-foot* **por** *foot-ball*!	*The word is funny: "ballfoot" for "football"!*

DRILL EXERCISES

1. *Change to the negative.* *(Example:* Tienen algo que hacer. — No tienen nada que hacer.) 1. Ha llamado alguien. 2. Tomaron algo en el ambigú. 3. Se llevó alguno de los libros. 4. Siempre hay tiempo por la mañana. 5. Me gusta el verano y también el invierno.

2. *Give the comparative form.* *(Example:* tarde — más tarde.) 1. temprano. 2. pronto. 3. lejos. 4. abajo. 5. arriba.

3. *Make adverbs by adding* *-mente* *to the feminine singular of the adjective.* *(Example:* sencillo — sencillamente.) 1. feliz. 2. divino. 3. ligero. 4. preciso. 5. principal.

4. *Form adverbial phrases by using the preposition* *con.* *(Example:* calma — con calma.) 1. tranquilidad. 2. frecuencia. 3. cuidado. 4. gracia. 5. naturalidad.

5. *Form adverbial phrases by using the preposition* *a.* *(Example:* pie — a pie.) 1. el lado. 2. veces. 3. la derecha. 4. medias. 5. el fin.

6. *Form adjectival or adverbial phrases by using the preposition* *de.* *(Example:* pie — de pie.) 1. prisa. 2. noche. 3. verdad. 4. mal humor. 5. muy buena gana.

7. *Indicate destination or terminal point by using the preposition* *para.* *(Example:* Hay ____ todos los gustos. — Hay para todos los gustos.) 1. Buena lista de platos ____ un gastrónomo. 2. Figúrese la sorpresa que fué ____ todos. 3. No hay tiempo ____ nada. 4. Tienen concertada la boda ____ junio. 5. Tengo un par de lecciones difíciles ____ mañana.

8. *Indicate general direction by using the preposition* ***por.*** *(Example:* Andaban ____ la calle. — Andaban por la calle.)* 1. Entró ____ esa puerta. 2. Pasearon en canoa ____ el lago. 3. El avión se deslizó ____ la pista. 4. El billete no aparecía ____ ninguna parte. 5. Había coches ____ delante y ____ detrás.

COMPREHENSION EXERCISE

See if you understand the meaning of the negatives, adverbs, and prepositions.

1. **No** dijeron **nada.**
2. **No** me gusta **ni** es curso obligatorio.
3. Cuando el avión despegó **de** tierra **nunca** lo notamos.
4. El año pasado la playa estaba **más** animada que **nunca.**
5. Mira quién viene **por allí.**
6. Fueron una vacaciones deliciosas **allá en** el campo.
7. Hazme el favor **de** la pimienta.—**Ahí** va.
8. **Allá** tiene usted la ciudad, **a** la derecha, **al cabo de** la bahía.
9. Ahora **a** la Central **de** Correos, que está **ahí mismo.**
10. **De** taxis, **no** hay que hablar; **con** la lluvia, **ninguno** libre.
11. El fotógrafo pedía que cambiasen **ligeramente de** posición **para** enfocarlos **mejor.**
12. **En** los partidos **de** pelota ganan **con** frecuencia los vascongados.
13. ¿Quién entenderá **aquí en** mi tierra eso **de** *rugby* dicho **a** la española?
14. Bien **de** madrugada, **al** avión **de** nuevo.
15. El museo tiene unos pocos dibujos **al** lápiz **de** un pintor francés.

COMPLETION EXERCISE

Use a positive or negative form, as required by the context.

1. (algo, nada) ¿Tienen ustedes ____ que hacer esta tarde?
2. (y, ni) No hacía ni frío ____ calor.
3. (siempre, nunca) José está ____ muy galante.
4. (algún, ningún) Hacía un mes que no íbamos a ____ baile.
5. (también, tampoco) No es muy caro.—Ni barato, ____.

Use the adverb indicated by the context.

6. (acá, aquí) ____ tienen, señores, el servicio.
7. (acá, aquí) Me cansa ir siempre de ____ para allá.
8. (ahí, allí) ____ tienes la razón.
9. (ahí, allí) ¿Dónde queda el hotel?—Está ____, entre aquellos pinares.
10. (allí, allá) ¿Qué deportes cultivan ____ en su país?

Use the preposition required by the context (a, de, por, para).

11. Le hablé ____ teléfono.
12. ____ mí comenzaron los trabajos ayer.
13. El Monumento está ____ la derecha.
14. El billete no aparecía ____ ninguna parte.
15. Luego iremos a la casa ____ huéspedes.
16. Un amigo está preguntando ____ usted.
17. Hoy andan ____ mal humor.
18. ____ seguros, los fósforos.
19. Valiente es usted ____ conducir.
20. Iremos al museo ____ pie.

IDIOMATIC VERB USAGE

6

FORMAL
PRACTICE

1. Infinitive.

(a) The infinitive is the only Spanish verb form used as a noun.

Será mejor **almorzar** en el restaurán.	*It will be better to have lunch in the restaurant.*
Quiero **hablar** contigo.	*I want to talk with you.*
Lo hizo antes de **salir**.	*He did it before leaving.*

(b) Before a complementary infinitive a connecting word may be required, depending on the governing expression.

Ahora empieza **a** llover.	*Now it is beginning to rain.*
Acabó **de** vestirse.	*He finished getting dressed.*
Tengo **que** comprar sellos.	*I have to buy some stamps.*

2. Elliptical Constructions.

In conversational style, phrases or clauses often serve as complete statements.

Ahora **a trabajar**.	*Now to get to work.*
Un día, **a cazar**; otro, **de excursión** al Picacho.	*One day (we'll go) hunting; another day, (we'll go) on an excursion to the Peak.*
Y el revisor **diciendo** que no podía ser.	*And the conductor (kept) saying that it was impossible.*
El pícaro despertador **que no ha sonado**.	*The darned alarm clock didn't go off.*

3. Uses of *estar*.

(a) **Estar** is used with adverbial expressions to indicate location or condition.

¡Eh, Antonio, aquí **estamos**!	*Hey, Antonio, here we are!*
¿Cómo **estás**?—Bien, gracias.	*How are you?—Fine, thanks.*

[121]

(b) **Estar** is also used with present participles to express action in progress, and with past participles to express resultant condition.

Están esperando.	*They are waiting.*
El pavimento **está** mojado.	*The pavement is wet.*
El despertador **estaba** descompuesto.	*The alarm clock was broken.*

(c) Occasionally **estar** is used with adjectives to indicate variable conditions.

La mañana **está** fresca.	*The morning is cool.*
La playa **estaba** muy animada.	*The beach was very gay.*
Ahora **estamos** listos.	*Now we are ready.*
Aquí todo **está** siempre limpio · y bien cuidado.	*Here everything is always clean and well kept.*

4. Reflexive Forms.

(a) Many transitive verbs are used reflexively with intransitive meanings.

¡Y él a **divertirse** y yo a sufrir!	*And he'll have fun (enjoy himself) and I'll suffer!*
El anunciador **se pone** un poco pesado.	*The announcer gets ("puts himself") a little boring.*

(b) Many intransitive verbs are used reflexively to stress or clarify the subject's interest or rôle in the action.

¡Mira cómo **se ríen**!	*Look how they're laughing!*
Emilio **se quedó** en la taquilla del guardarropa.	*Emile stopped by the check-room.*

(c) Some verbs can only be used as reflexives.

No **me atrevo** a hacerlo.	*I don't dare do it.*
Ahora **nos quejamos** del frío.	*Now we're complaining of the cold.*

5. Passive Voice.

(a) The true passive (**ser** + a past participle) is little used in Spanish. It usually belongs to a somewhat formal style.

Sus delicadas atenciones no podrán **ser olvidadas**.	*Your thoughtful attentions cannot be forgotten.*

(b) Most passive ideas are expressed by reflexive or indefinite forms.

Aquí **se dió** una batalla en la guerra civil.	*A battle was fought here in the civil war.*
De un maestro de la novela **se dice:** «¡Es un Cervantes!»	*Of a master of the novel it is said (one says): "He is a Cervantes!"*

6. Wish or Command Forms.

(a) The traditional imperative forms are used for affirmative requests or commands corresponding to **tú** and **vosotros, -as.**

Toma un cigarrillo.	*Have a cigarette.*
Mirad quién viene por allí.	*Look who is coming over there.*

(b) Forms derived from the present subjunctive are used for all other wishes, requests, or commands (including the negative forms for **tú** and **vosotros**). Indirect wishes or commands are usually introduced by **que.**

¡No me **digas!**	*Don't tell me!*
Cuente usted, Rosario.	*Tell about it, Rosario.*
Tengamos cuidado.	*Let's be careful.*
Que le **vaya** bien.	*Good-by. ("May it go well with you.")*

(c) The verb **ir** has a special form, **vamos**, *let's go,* for affirmative wishes.

¿Vamos dentro?—**Vamos.**	*Shall we go in?—Let's go.*

(d) The form **vamos a** is used with infinitives to express wishes concerning actions to be carried out immediately. The governing verb may be omitted, leaving **a** + the infinitive.

Vamos a ver.	*Let's see.*
Ahora **a bailar.**	*Now let's dance.*

(e) Sometimes an adverb, a present participle, or a present indicative may express a wish or command.

¡**Adelante!**	*Come in! ("Forward!")*
Pues, **andando.**	*Well, let's get going.*
Cuando te duermas, me **avisas.**	*When you go to sleep, let me know.*

DRILL EXERCISES

1. *Complete the meaning by supplying the appropriate form of* **estar** *in the present tense.* (*Example:* ¡Qué animada _____ la tienda! — ¡Qué animada está la tienda!) 1. Los muchachos _____ en la Universidad.   2. El salón _____ muy animado.   3. Las pobres chicas _____ a régimen.   4. El amo _____ preguntando por usted.   5. Estas camisas no _____ muy bien planchadas.

2. *Express with a reflexive object, to stress or clarify the rôle of the subject.* (*Example:* Todos ríen. — Todos se ríen.)   1. Ahora callan.   2. Pararon aquí un momento. 3. Van a su casa.   4. ¡Ojalá vengan pronto a vernos! 5. Quedaron en el hotel.

3. *Express as a passive idea, using the reflexive form.* (*Example:* Aquí dieron una batalla. — Aquí se dió una batalla.)   1. No vemos el lago desde aquí.   2. En mi país cultivan todos los deportes conocidos.   3. Aquí practicamos el gran arte de comer.   4. A veces junta todo ello en la misma página.   5. Desde el avión veíamos valles, ríos y montañas.

4. *Change to the familiar imperative.* (*Example:* Oiga. — Oye.)   1. Pase.   2. Encienda.   3. Mire.   4. Cuente.   5. Dispense.

5. *Change to the polite form.* (*Example:* Figúrate. — Figúrese.)   1. ¡No me digas!   2. Vuélvete.   3. No te apresures.   4. Levántate.   5. Hazme el favor.

6. *Express without using* **vamos.** (*Example:* Ahora, vamos a trabajar. — Ahora, a trabajar.)   1. ¡Ea!, vamos a bailar.   2. Pues vamos adentro.   3. Vamos adelante. 4. Ahora vamos a estudiar.   5. Luego, vamos a corretear.

COMPREHENSION EXERCISE

See if you understand the meaning of these verb forms.

1. **Me alegro** de **conocerle.**
2. Le cansa este ajetreo de **ir** de acá para allá.
3. Su percha debía yo de **parecer.**
4. Y el hombrecito **empeñado** en **bailar** conmigo cuantos bailes podía.
5. Sí, **lloviendo** también aquí toda la tarde.
6. Tornaron a **ensayar,** y tampoco ahora **estaba** bien.
7. La mujer era muy gorda y **estaba** muy azorada.
8. Parecía que nunca iba a **acabar** de **subir.**
9. Y el revisor que **mete** prisa y el tren que **está** para partir.
10. **Levántate,** hijo, que ya es tarde.
11. **Oye,** no me **pongas** más tu impermeable encima del abrigo.
12. **Paremos** aquí un momento.
13. **Pasen, pasen,** señores.
14. Adiós, que ustedes **sigan** bien.
15. Pues, **andando,** y luego iremos al restaurán.

COMPLETION EXERCISE

Use an appropriate form of the verb given.

1. (conocer)   Tengo ganas de _____ a tu novio.
2. (probarse)   A las mujeres nos gusta _____ algunas **cosas.**
3. (pasar)   Haga usted el favor de _____ al cuartito de pruebas.
4. (casarse)   David y Rosita _____ la semana pasada.
5. (contemplar)   Tiempo tendremos de _____ todo **esto.**

6. (juntarse) Cielo, tierra y mar ____ en tanta hermosura.

7. (estar) El Monumento ____ en aquella loma.

8. (estar) Le digo a usted que aquí ____ en mis glorias.

9. (estar) Parece que me ____ usted haciendo un examen.

10. (sentirse) Después de un rato todos ____ tranquilos.

11. (bajarse) Repiten la misma acción: el galán ____ a recoger el pañuelo.

12. (reírse) Me hizo tanta gracia que ____ hasta soltar la carcajada.

13. (correr) Pero, Emilio, no ____ tanto, que parece que vuelas.

14. (dispensar) ____, prima, un momento.

15. (apresurarse) Anda, anda. No ____ en volver.

16. (bailar) ¡Ea!, a ____ ese tango que están tocando.

17. (apurarse) ¡Bah, no ____ usted!

18. (oír) ____, camarero, tráigame esta sopa de hierbas.

19. (ir) Adiós, que le ____ felizmente.

20. (conservarse) Que ____ usted bueno.

TENSES OF THE INDICATIVE

1. Present Indicative.

(a) The present tense usually indicates present actions or states.

Ya **termino.**	*I'm finishing now.*
Éste **es** el primer momento de descanso que **tengo.**	*This is the first peaceful moment I've had ("am having").*

(b) The present tense may also indicate a graphic view of past actions or states.

Tuve que aguardar una hora... Por fin **viene** el tren...mucha gente en el andén...y el revisor que **mete** prisa...

I had to wait an hour...The train finally arrived...a lot of people on the platform ...and the conductor hurrying things up...

(c) The present tense may also indicate immediate, or definite, future actions or states.

¿**Vamos** dentro?	*Shall we go in?*
Verá usted cómo le **gusta** esto.	*You'll see how you'll like this.*

2. Imperfect Indicative.

The imperfect tense indicates an incomplete view of past actions or states. It is a descriptive tense which presents attendant circumstances.

Eran ya las ocho.	*It was already eight o'clock.*
Llovía y **hacía** frío.	*It was rainy and cold.*
El autobús que **salía** entonces **iba** llenito hasta los topes.	*The bus that was leaving then was jam-packed.*
Allí **quería** meterse una mujer con dos maletas.	*A woman was trying to get in there with two suitcases.*
La tienda **estaba** bien iluminada.	*The store was well lighted.*
Hacía un mes que no **íbamos** al Centro.	*We hadn't been ("weren't going") downtown for a month.*

[127]

3. Preterite Indicative.

The preterite tense indicates a complete view of past actions or states. It is a narrative tense which reports events.

Quise tomar un taxi.	*I tried to take a taxi.*
Llegué tarde a la oficina.	*I got to the office late.*
Ensayaron la misma escena diez veces.	*They rehearsed the same scene ten times.*
Yo no **pude** resistir más, y **me marché.**	*I couldn't stand it any longer and I left.*
Anoche **estuvimos** en un baile.	*Last night we went to a dance.*
Alberto **bailó** mucho con María.	*Albert danced a lot with Mary.*

4. Future Indicative.

(*a*) The future tense usually indicates future actions or states.

Traeré la baraja.	*I'll bring the deck of cards.*
Ya **ajustaremos** cuentas.	*We'll settle accounts later.*

(*b*) The future tense may also indicate a feeling of uncertainty with regard to present actions or states, thus serving as a modal form.

En broma lo **dirás.**	*You're probably joking.*
Será él quien llama ahora.	*It must be he who is at the door now.*

5. Conditional.

(*a*) The conditional tense may indicate futurity within past sequences.

Dijo que **traería** la baraja.	*He said he would bring the deck.*

(*b*) The conditional (as a modal form) may indicate uncertainty with regard to past actions or states.

En broma lo **dirían.**	*They were probably joking.*

(*c*) More often the conditional (used as a mode) indicates the conclusions to unreal if-clauses, which are usually implied rather than expressed.

Me **gustaría** ver esos estudios.	*I would like to see those studios.*
Desearía un traje estilo sastre.	*I would like a tailored suit.*

6. Progressive Forms.

The use of **estar** (or some other verb, like **ir**) with a present participle stresses or clarifies the idea of action in progress.

Dos horas **estuvimos haciendo** fila.	*We spent two hours standing in line.*
Les gusta **ir parándose** ante los mostradores.	*They like to go along stopping before the counters.*

7. Perfect Tenses.

The use of **haber** with a past participle indicates an action or state completed prior to the time of the corresponding simple tense.

Me parece que lo **he visto** antes.	*I believe I have seen it before.*
Fuí a tomar el tren y **habían cambiado** el horario.	*I went to take the train and they had changed the schedule.*

DRILL EXERCISES

1. *Change to refer to past situations or circumstances, by using the imperfect. (Example:* Son ya las siete. — Eran ya las siete.) 1. Empieza el día. 2. Hace un tiempo hermoso. 3. El despertador está descompuesto. 4. Todos están en el comedor. 5. Les queda poco tiempo para desayunarse.

2. *Change to refer to past events, by using the preterite. (Example:* Se levanta a las siete. — Se levantó a las siete.) 1. Acaba de vestirse. 2. Entra en el comedor. 3. Desayuna de prisa. 4. Toma el autobús. 5. Llega a la oficina.

3. *Express with a feeling of uncertainty, by changing the present to future or the past to conditional. (Example:* ¿Qué hora es? — ¿Qué hora será?) 1. Ya son las diez. 2. ¿Dónde están sus amigos? 3. Están en casa. 4. ¿A qué hora llegaron? 5. Llegaron a las ocho.

4. *Use each statement as a dependent clause in the conditional, after* **Dijo que.** *(Example:* Estará aquí. — Dijo que estaría aquí.) 1. Vendrá a las ocho. 2. Irá con nosotros. 3. Tendrá poco tiempo. 4. Saldrá temprano. 5. Volverá a las once.

5. *Express as the conclusion to an implied unreal if-clause, by using the conditional. (Example:* Voy al cine. — Iría al cine.) 1. Escucho la radio. 2. Juego al tenis. 3. Echamos una partida de naipes. 4. Vamos de tiendas. 5. Deseo un traje estilo sastre.

6. *Change to refer to the past, by using the imperfect of* **estar.** *(Example:* Está lloviendo. — Estaba lloviendo.) 1. Están charlando. 2. Estamos escuchando. 3. Está granizando. 4. Estoy terminando. 5. Están haciendo fila.

7. *Change to the corresponding past perfect form. (Example:* Lo he oído. — Lo había oído.) 1. Lo he visto. 2. Lo ha dicho. 3. No hemos salido. 4. No han llegado. 5. Lo han cambiado.

COMPREHENSION EXERCISE

See if you understand the meaning of these verb forms.

1. ¿Me **quieres** acompañar al Centro?
2. Yo **vengo** en un instante con el vestido y con la modista.
3. Hombre, **parece** que lo **estás saboreando;** con tanto gusto lo **dices.**
4. **Llego** aquí y **pregunto** al botones del ascensor si **ha llegado** el jefe.
5. **Se casaron** el sábado, y los dos **tenían** que volver a clases el lunes.
6. Yo **creí** que nos **quedábamos** en mitad de la cuesta.
7. Allí **estuve** una vez viendo impresionar una película.

8. Tan graciosa y atractiva **era** la joven, que yo no **dejé** de contemplarla mientras me **ajustaba** las correas del asiento.
9. ¡Cuándo **vendrá** el buen tiempo y se **acabarán** las nevadas!
10. ¿Qué? No oigo bien...Será la Central, que **estará** escuchando.
11. Nos **gustaría** hacer la excursión a la playa.
12. Pepe dijo que **vendría** a buscarnos.
13. **Estuve esperando** tu llamada toda la tarde.
14. ¡Ah, pues sí que **han sido** calamidades!
15. ¡Ya **podía haber facturado** el equipaje!

COMPLETION EXERCISE

Complete by using an appropriate form of the verb given.

1. (desear)   ¿Qué postre ____ los señores?
2. (conversar)   Unos entran, otros salen, muchos ____ en grupos.
3. (suplantar)   A ver cuándo riñen ustedes y yo ____ a Emilio.
4. (ser)   Notaron que la muchacha ____ graciosa y atractiva.
5. (dar)   Mientras jugaban, ____ gritos y golpetazos.
6. (estar)   El año pasado ____ la playa muy animada.
7. (acabar)   Parecía que la mujer nunca ____ de subir.
8. (vibrar)   Cuando los motores comenzaron a funcionar, ____ el aeroplano.
9. (ser)   El examen que tuve ayer ____ horrible.
10. (poder)   Acaban de llegar ahora. No ____ tomar el tren de las dos.

11. (coger)   Ayer comí tanto que ____ una indigestión.
12. (tomar)   Después nos veremos y ____ algo en el ambigú.
13. (ver)   Es un plato delicioso. Pruébelo y ____.
14. (tener)   Lo siento, hombre, ya ____ más cuidado.
15. (sacar)   Mañana ____ en limpio mi tema.
16. (hacer)   Sentimos no poder ir con ustedes. ¡Con cuánto gusto ____ el viaje!
17. (estar)   Bien venido, Fernando. Pasa, que Alfonso ____ terminando.
18. (estar)   No quisieron bailar el tango que ____ tocando.
19. (haber)   Parece que ____ terminado la sección.
20. (haber)   Lo dijo una señora que yo ____ visto antes entrar en el aeroplano algo nerviosa.

USES OF THE SUBJUNCTIVE

1. Indicative and Subjunctive.

(a) The indicative expresses ideas visualized as real. These ideas may be affirmative, negative, or interrogative. They may be true or false, or they may be mere suppositions accepted as a basis for conclusions.

Aquí todos **hablan** y nadie **escucha**.	*Here everybody is talking and nobody is listening.*
¿No te **parece** que **es** hora de meterse en la cama?	*Don't you think that it's time to get to bed?*
Si usted **quiere, subiremos** al segundo piso.	*If you wish, we will go up to the second floor.*

(b) The subjunctive expresses ideas which, for varying reasons, are visualized as unreal or hypothetical. These ideas are abstractions which are subordinated to some governing idea of attitude. The attitude is usually one of emotion or uncertainty.

Ojalá **tengamos** pronto el gusto de que se **vengan** ustedes a pasar con nosotros unos días.	*I hope that we may soon have the pleasure of your coming to spend a few days with us.*
Como **quieras**, pero acaso **molestemos** a tu padre.	*As you wish, but we may bother your father.*

2. Subjunctive of Emotion or Volition.

(a) The subjunctive may depend on any type of expression of emotion or volition (joy, sorrow, wish, request, etc.).

Es lástima que no me **atreva** con el arroz con pollo.	*It's too bad that I don't dare have the chicken and rice.*
Ojalá no **haya** estática y la recepción **sea** clara.	*I hope there won't be any static and the reception will be clear.*
El fotógrafo pedía que **cambiasen** de posición.	*The photographer was asking them to change position.*

(b) The subjunctive may depend on an expression of purpose (which implies volition).

Apresúrese, que no le **tomen** el   *Hurry, so they won't get your*
puesto.   *place.*

3. Subjunctive of Uncertainty or Disbelief.

(a) The subjunctive may depend on an expression of doubt or disbelief. If no uncertainty is felt, the indicative is used. Compare:

Parece mentira que **seas** con-   *It seems impossible that you*
migo tan dura de corazón.   *should be so hard-hearted*
                                     toward me. (Doubt)
No es que le **duela** soltar los   *It's not that he minds spending*
cuartos.   *the money.* (Disbelief)
No parece que él **va** de buena   *He doesn't seem to be going will-*
gana.   *ingly.* (No feeling of uncer-
                                     tainty)

(b) The subjunctive may indicate a type of thing (not known to exist), rather than an actual thing. Compare:

Tráigame cualquier fruta que   *Bring me any fruit that you may*
tengan.   *have.* (Type of thing)
Éste es el restaurán que más me   *This is the restaurant that I like*
gusta.   *best.* (Actual thing)

(c) The subjunctive may express a concession based on a supposition or hypothetical situation, rather than a stated fact. Compare:

Tienes gracia, aunque me **llames**   *You're funny, even though you*
embustero.   *may be calling me a liar.*
                                      (Hypothetical situation)

Los dos son famosos, aunque me   *Both are famous, though I like*
agrada la actriz más que el   *the actress better than the*
actor.   *actor.* (Stated fact)

(d) The subjunctive may refer to indefinite time or manner. Compare:

Apaga cuando **quieras.**   *Turn out the lights whenever*
                                     you wish. (Indefinite time)

Cuando me lo **dijeron,** me que-   *When they told me, I was dumb-*
dé de una pieza.   *founded.* (Definite time)

| Bueno, como usted **guste**. | *Well, as you please.* (Indefinite manner) |
| Así, de repente, como quien **se bebe** un vaso de agua. | *Just like that, as casually as one drinking a glass of water.* (Definite manner) |

(e) The past subjunctive may refer to remote possibilities or contrary-to-fact conditions. Compare:

| Si te **parece**, haremos un ratito de limpieza. | *If it seems all right with you, we'll do a little cleaning.* (Accepted possibility) |
| Nos sentíamos tan tranquilos como si no **hubiese** peligro alguno. | *We felt as calm as if there were no danger at all.* (Contrary-to-fact condition) |

4. Infinitive and Subjunctive.

The infinitive, rather than a dependent clause, is used with expressions of emotion, volition, or purpose when the main verb and the dependent verb have the same subject. Compare:

¿Quieres **poner** la radio?	*Do you want to turn on the radio?* (Same subject)
¿Quieres que **ponga** la radio?	*Do you want me to turn on the radio?* (Different subject)
Vamos a Correos para **certificar** una carta.	*We're going to the postoffice to register a letter.* (Same subject)
Luego iremos al Banco para **que cobre** usted el cheque.	*Then we'll go to the bank so that you can cash the check.* (Different subject)

5. Sequence of Tenses with the Subjunctive.

If the main verb is in a past tense (preterite, imperfect, past perfect, conditional, or conditional perfect), the dependent verb is also in a past tense (past or past perfect).

| Mi consejero quería que **tomase** la Física. | *My advisor wanted me to take physics.* |
| David me dijo que se iba a casar tan pronto como **encontrara** un piso. | *David told me that he was going to get married as soon as he could find an apartment.* |

DRILL EXERCISES

1. *Express as an exclamatory wish, using* **ojalá.** *(Example:* Que se diviertan. — ¡Ojalá que se diviertan!) 1. Que se apresuren. 2. Que se vean pronto. 3. Que vayan al baile. 4. Que tengan cuidado. 5. Que saquen buenas notas.

√ 2. *Express with* **Quieren** *instead of* **Me piden.** *(Example:* Me piden que vaya al Centro. — Quieren que vaya al Centro.) 1. Me piden que vaya a su casa. 2. Me piden que llegue temprano. 3. Me piden que tome un taxi. 4. Me piden que compre sellos. 5. Me piden que vuelva esta tarde.

3. *Express with* **Espero** *instead of* **Es posible.** *(Example:* Es posible que estén terminando ahora. — Espero que estén terminando ahora.) 1. Es posible que trabajen más. 2. Es posible que tengan algunos discos nuevos. 3. Es posible que nos acompañen al lago. 4. Es posible que hagan la excursión. 5. Es posible que tomen el tren de las dos.

4. *Answer using* **pocos** *instead of* **muchos.** *(Example:* ¿Habrá muchos que hagan rabona? — Habrá pocos que hagan rabona.) 1. ¿Habrá muchos que sean mejores? 2. ¿Habrá muchos que necesiten libros? 3. ¿Habrá muchos que saquen buenas notas? 4. ¿Habrá muchos que se especialicen en lenguas modernas? 5. ¿Habrá muchos que se atrevan a hacerlo?

5. *Change to refer to the future. (Example:* Lo hacemos cuando hay tiempo. — Lo haremos cuando haya tiempo.) 1. Me paga cuando cobra los cheques. 2. Lo conciertan cuando se ven. 3. Se ponen de mal humor cuando pierden la mañana. 4. Le damos una propina cuando nos

deja la cuenta.   5. Se acostumbran cuando llevan aquí algún tiempo.

6. *Express with* **Será preciso** *instead of* **Será mejor.** *(Example:* Será mejor almorzar en el restaurán. — Será preciso almorzar en el restaurán.)   1. Será mejor subir al segundo piso.   2. Será mejor buscar los saldos.   3. Será mejor mandar un telegrama.   4. Será mejor tomar el tren.   5. Será mejor facturar el equipaje.

7. *Change to refer to the past. (Example:* Quieren que vayamos a su casa. — Querían que fuéramos a su casa.)   1. Desean que lleguemos temprano.   2. Esperan que hagamos la excursión.   3. Quieren que los acompañemos al baile.   4. Desean que compremos discos.   5. Esperan que trabajemos menos.

COMPREHENSION EXERCISE

See if you understand the meaning of these verb forms.

1. Siento no **haber** podido escribirte antes.
2. Quieren que **vayamos** a su casa de campo.
3. ¿Le parece que **aguardemos** a que **termine** esta sección?
4. Parece que ella **lleva** el marido a remolque.
5. Bastará con que yo **garantice** el cheque con mi firma.
6. Buena lista de platos para un gastrónomo...y envidia del que **esté** a régimen.
7. Cuando el camarero nos **deje** la cuenta y **acabemos** de almorzar, le damos un *¡Adiós, gracias!* y a pagar a la cajera.
8. Será ella quien **llama** ahora.
9. Cuando te **duermas,** me avisas.
10. Yo tengo un tío que vaya si nos **avisa** cuando se **duerme.**
11. Cómetela a ella con los ojos si **quieres.**

12. ¡Qué lástima que no **sea** maestra de verdad!
13. ¡Ah, pues sí que han sido calamidades! ¡Ni que las **estuviera** usted inventando!
14. Traeré la baraja, si **es** que la **encuentro**.
15. Leyendo esta novela, siento como si mi alma se **fuese** enriqueciendo.

COMPLETION EXERCISE

Complete by using the indicative or subjunctive form, according to the context.

1. (es, sea)   ¡Ojalá ____ pronto!
2. (llegamos, lleguemos)   Por fortuna ____ temprano.
3. (viene, venga)   En la bocacalle que ____ torcemos a la derecha.
4. (lleva, lleve)   Ya se acostumbrará usted cuando ____ aquí algún tiempo.
5. (traigo, traiga)   Lo mismo que mi marido cuando lo ____ de tiendas.
6. (vale, valga)   Créame que este vestido ____ muchísimo más.
7. (gusta, guste)   Parece mentira que les ____ esto.
8. (ven, vean)   Ya lo concertarán cuando se ____ el mes próximo.
9. (hacen, hagan)   Así habrá menos estudiantes que ____ rabona.
10. (encuentran, encuentren)   Se van a casar tan pronto como ____ un piso.
11. (remite, remita)   Vamos a Correos para que usted ____ ese paquete.
12. (acompañamos, acompañemos)   Pepe quiere que le ____ a la estación.

13. (estuvieron, estuvieran)   Sentí que sus amigos no _____ en el baile.

14. (he, haya)   Me parece que lo _____ visto antes.

15. (ha, haya)   Es posible que _____ terminado la sección.

16. (falta, falte)   No es que les _____ tiempo para hacerlo.

17. (cansa, canse)   Es que les _____ este ajetreo.

18. (podía, pudiera)   Allí estaba el jefe en su butaca, como si nada _____ hacer sin mí.

19. (parece, parezca)   Si a usted le _____, nos llegaremos al hotel.

20. (eran, fuesen)   Por entre las nubes, como si _____ islas del cielo, divisábamos valles, ríos y montañas.

APPENDIX

A. REGULAR

(Conjugation of three model verbs:

INFINITIVE [Cf. Pt. II, unit 6, §1]	tomar	
PRESENT INDICATIVE [7:1]	tomo tomas toma	tomamos tomáis toman
PRESENT SUBJUNCTIVE [8:1-4]	tome tomes tome	tomemos toméis tomen
IMPERATIVE [6:6]	toma	tomad
FUTURE INDICATIVE [7:4]	tomaré tomarás tomará	tomaremos tomaréis tomarán
CONDITIONAL [7:5]	tomaría tomarías tomaría	tomaríamos tomaríais tomarían
IMPERFECT INDICATIVE [7:2]	tomaba tomabas tomaba	tomábamos tomabais tomaban
PRETERITE INDICATIVE [7:3]	tomé tomaste tomó	tomamos tomasteis tomaron
PAST SUBJUNCTIVE [8:5] — -ra Form	tomara tomaras tomara	tomáramos tomarais tomaran
PAST SUBJUNCTIVE [8:5] — -se Form	tomase tomases tomase	tomásemos tomaseis tomasen
PRESENT PARTICIPLE [7:6]	tomando	
PAST PARTICIPLE [6:5; 7: 7]	tomado	
PERFECT TENSES [7:7]	(*Appropriate tenses* *of* haber + tomado)	

an -ar, an -er, and an -ir verb)

comer		vivir	
como	comemos	vivo	vivimos
comes	coméis	vives	vivís
come	comen	vive	viven
coma	comamos	viva	vivamos
comas	comáis	vivas	viváis
coma	coman	viva	vivan
come	comed	vive	vivid
comeré	comeremos	viviré	viviremos
comerás	comeréis	vivirás	viviréis
comerá	comerán	vivirá	vivirán
comería	comeríamos	viviría	viviríamos
comerías	comeríais	vivirías	viviríais
comería	comerían	viviría	vivirían
comía	comíamos	vivía	vivíamos
comías	comíais	vivías	vivíais
comía	comían	vivía	vivían
comí	comimos	viví	vivimos
comiste	comisteis	viviste	vivisteis
comió	comieron	vivió	vivieron
comiera	comiéramos	viviera	viviéramos
comieras	comierais	vivieras	vivierais
comiera	comieran	viviera	vivieran
comiese	comiésemos	viviese	viviésemos
comieses	comieseis	vivieses	vivieseis
comiese	comiesen	viviese	viviesen
comiendo		viviendo	
comido		vivido	
(*Appropriate tenses* *of* haber + comido)		(*Appropriate tenses* *of* haber + vivido)	

	PRESENT INDICATIVE		PRESENT SUBJUNCTIVE	
ORTHOGRAPHIC CHANGES			saque	saquemos
models: sacar (*qu*)			saques	saquéis
coger (*j*)			saque	saquen
leer (*í, y*)				
spelling equivalents:	cojo	cogemos	coja	cojamos
c g z gu j + a, o	coges	cogéis	cojas	cojáis
qu gu c gü {j/g} + e, i	coge	cogen	coja	cojan
a, e, o + {í (*stressed*) / y (*unstressed*)}				
RADICAL CHANGES	cuento	contamos	cuente	contemos
models: contar (*ue*)	cuentas	contáis	cuentes	contéis
dormir (*ue, u*)	cuenta	cuentan	cuente	cuenten
pedir (*i*)				
-ar, -er, -ir verbs	duermo	dormimos	duerma	durmamos
o > ue	duermes	dormís	duermas	durmáis
e > ie } *when stressed*	duerme	duermen	duerma	duerman
e > i				
-ir verbs	pido	pedimos	pida	pidamos
o > u} *unstressed before*	pides	pedís	pidas	pidáis
e > i} -a-, -ie-, -ió	pide	piden	pida	pidan
RADICAL + ORTHOGRAPHIC	empiezo	empezamos	empiece	empecemos
	empiezas	empezáis	empieces	empecéis
models: empezar (*ie; c*)	empieza	empiezan	empiece	empiecen
reñir (*i*)				
i, ñ, ll + {ie > e / ió > ó}	riño	reñimos	riña	riñamos
	riñes	reñís	riñas	riñáis
	riñe	riñen	riña	riñan
OTHER IRREGULAR PATTERNS	conozco	conocemos	conozca	conozcamos
models: conocer (*zc*)	conoces	conocéis	conozcas	conozcáis
conducir (*zc; -uj-*)	conoce	conocen	conozca	conozcan
guiar (*í*)				
infinitives:	conduzco	conducimos	conduzca	conduzcamos
-ecer, -ocer: c > zc	conduces	conducís	conduzcas	conduzcáis
	conduce	conducen	conduzca	conduzcan
-ucir: {c > zc / -uj- *in pret., etc.*}				
-iar: i > í} *when stem is*	guío	guiamos	guíe	guiemos
-uar: u > ú} *stressed*	guías	guiáis	guíes	guiéis
	guía	guían	guíe	guíen

verbs with fixed patterns)

IMPERATIVE SINGULAR	PRETERITE INDICATIVE		PAST SUBJUNCTIVE	PARTICIPLES: PRESENT PAST
	saqué sacaste sacó	sacamos sacasteis sacaron		
	leí leíste leyó	**leímos** **leísteis** **leyeron**	**leyera,** *etc.* *or* **leyese,** *etc.*	leyendo leído
cuenta				
duerme	dormí dormiste **durmió**	dormimos dormisteis **durmieron**	**durmiera,** *etc.* *or* **durmiese,** *etc.*	**durmiendo** dormido
pide	pedí pediste **pidió**	pedimos pedisteis **pidieron**	**pidiera,** *etc.* *or* **pidiese,** *etc.*	**pidiendo** pedido
empieza	**empecé** empezaste empezó	empezamos empezasteis empezaron		
riñe	reñí reñiste **riñó**	**reñimos** **reñisteis** **riñeron**	**riñera,** *etc.* *or* **riñese,** *etc.*	**riñendo** reñido
	conduje **condujiste** **condujo**	**condujimos** **condujisteis** **condujeron**	**condujera,** *etc.* *or* **condujese,** *etc.*	
guía				

INFINITIVE	PRESENT INDICATIVE		PRESENT SUBJUNCTIVE		IMPERATIVE SINGULAR
andar					
caer	caigo	caemos	caiga	caigamos	
	caes	caéis	caigas	caigáis	
	cae	caen	caiga	caigan	
dar	doy	damos	dé	demos	
	das	dais	des	deis	da
	da	dan	dé	den	
decir	digo	decimos	diga	digamos	
	dices	decís	digas	digáis	di
	dice	dicen	diga	digan	
estar	estoy	estamos	esté	estemos	
	estás	estáis	estés	estéis	está
	está	están	esté	estén	
haber	he	hemos	haya	hayamos	
	has	habéis	hayas	hayáis	
	ha	han	haya	hayan	
hacer	hago	hacemos	haga	hagamos	
	haces	hacéis	hagas	hagáis	haz
	hace	hacen	haga	hagan	
ir³	voy	vamos	vaya	vayamos	
	vas	vais	vayas	vayáis	ve
	va	van	vaya	vayan	
oír	oigo	oímos	oiga	oigamos	
	oyes	oís	oigas	oigáis	oye
	oye	oyen	oiga	oigan	
poder	puedo	podemos	pueda	podamos	
	puedes	podéis	puedas	podáis	
	puede	pueden	pueda	puedan	

¹ COMPOUND FORMS not included:

    contraer, like traer
    entretener, like tener
    exponer, like poner
    sobresalir, like salir

² PAST PARTICIPLES not included:

    abrir: abierto
    describir: descrito
    devolver: devuelto
    escribir: escrito
    volver: vuelto

FUTURE IND. AND CONDITIONAL	PRETERITE INDICATIVE		PAST SUBJUNCTIVE	PARTICIPLES: PRESENT PAST[2]
	anduve	anduvimos	anduviera, *etc.* *or* anduviese, *etc.*	
	anduviste	anduvisteis		
	anduvo	anduvieron		
	caí	caímos	cayera, *etc.* *or* cayese, *etc.*	cayendo caído
	caíste	caísteis		
	cayó	cayeron		
	di	dimos	diera, *etc.* *or* diese, *etc.*	
	diste	disteis		
	dió	dieron		
diré, *etc.* diría, *etc.*	dije	dijimos	dijera, *etc.* *or* dijese, *etc.*	diciendo dicho
	dijiste	dijisteis		
	dijo	dijeron		
	estuve	estuvimos	estuviera, *etc.* *or* estuviese, *etc.*	
	estuviste	estuvisteis		
	estuvo	estuvieron		
habré, *etc.* habría, *etc.*	hube	hubimos	hubiera, *etc.* *or* hubiese, *etc.*	
	hubiste	hubisteis		
	hubo	hubieron		
haré, *etc.* haría, *etc.*	hice	hicimos	hiciera, *etc.* *or* hiciese, *etc.*	haciendo hecho
	hiciste	hicisteis		
	hizo	hicieron		
	fuí	fuimos	fuera, *etc.* *or* fuese, *etc.*	yendo ido
	fuiste	fuisteis		
	fué	fueron		
	oí	oímos	oyera, *etc.* *or* oyese, *etc.*	oyendo oído
	oíste	oísteis		
	oyó	oyeron		
podré, *etc.* podría, *etc.*	pude	pudimos	pudiera, *etc.* *or* pudiese, *etc.*	pudiendo podido
	pudiste	pudisteis		
	pudo	pudieron		

[3] IMPERFECT of **ir**:

iba	íbamos
ibas	ibais
iba	iban

INFINITIVE	PRESENT INDICATIVE		PRESENT SUBJUNCTIVE		IMPERATIVE SINGULAR
poner	pongo pones pone	ponemos ponéis ponen	ponga pongas ponga	pongamos pongáis pongan	pon
querer	quiero quieres quiere	queremos queréis quieren	quiera quieras quiera	queramos queráis quieran	quiere
saber	sé sabes sabe	sabemos sabéis saben	sepa sepas sepa	sepamos sepáis sepan	
salir	salgo sales sale	salimos salís salen	salga salgas salga	salgamos salgáis salgan	sal
ser[4]	soy eres es	somos sois son	sea seas sea	seamos seáis sean	sé
tener	tengo tienes tiene	tenemos tenéis tienen	tenga tengas tenga	tengamos tengáis tengan	ten
traer	traigo traes trae	traemos traéis traen	traiga traigas traiga	traigamos traigáis traigan	
valer	valgo vales vale	valemos valéis valen	valga valgas valga	valgamos valgáis valgan	val
venir	vengo vienes viene	venimos venís vienen	venga vengas venga	vengamos vengáis vengan	ven
ver[5]	veo ves ve	vemos veis ven	vea veas vea	veamos veáis vean	ve

[4] IMPERFECT of ser:

era   éramos
eras erais
era   eran

FUTURE IND. AND CONDITIONAL	PRETERITE INDICATIVE		PAST SUBJUNCTIVE	PARTICIPLES: PRESENT PAST
pondré, *etc.* pondría, *etc.*	puse pusiste puso	pusimos pusisteis pusieron	pusiera, *etc.* *or* pusiese, *etc.*	poniendo puesto
querré, *etc.* querría, *etc.*	quise quisiste quiso	quisimos quisisteis quisieron	quisiera, *etc.* *or* quisiese, *etc.*	
sabré, *etc.* sabría, *etc.*	supe supiste supo	supimos supisteis supieron	supiera, *etc.* *or* supiese, *etc.*	
saldré, *etc.* saldría, *etc.*				
	fuí fuiste fué	fuimos fuisteis fueron	fuera, *etc.* *or* fuese, *etc.*	
tendré, *etc.* tendría, *etc.*	tuve tuviste tuvo	tuvimos tuvisteis tuvieron	tuviera, *etc.* *or* tuviese, *etc.*	
	traje trajiste trajo	trajimos trajisteis trajeron	trajera, *etc.* *or* trajese, *etc.*	trayendo traído
valdré, *etc.* valdría, *etc.*				
vendré, *etc.* vendría, *etc.*	vine viniste vino	vinimos vinisteis vinieron	viniera, *etc.* *or* viniese, *etc.*	viniendo venido
				viendo visto

[5] IMPERFECT of **ver:**

veía	veíamos
veías	veíais
veía	veían

VOCABULARIES

NOTES ON THE VOCABULARIES

NOUNS. Gender is indicated by the abbreviations *m.* and *f.*

ADJECTIVES. The singular forms are given for each adjective.

VERBS. In the Spanish-English Vocabulary each irregular stem used in the text is represented by one form with a cross reference to the infinitive. In the English-Spanish Vocabulary verbs with orthographic, radical, or other changes according to fixed patterns have these changes shown in parentheses. Model verbs of each type are given on pp. 144-145. Other irregular verbs are marked with an asterisk (*). These verbs are given on pp. 146-149.

IDIOMATIC PHRASES. Entries are made under the main words, with preference being given to nouns and adjectives.

FORMS AND USAGE. In the English-Spanish Vocabulary forms requiring special analysis have a reference to the appropriate unit in Part II (pp. 92-139).

ABBREVIATIONS

adj.	adjective	*n.*	neuter
adv.	adverb	*obj.*	object
conj.	conjunction	*part.*	participle
dim.	diminutive	*pl.*	plural
f.	feminine	*prep.*	preposition
indef.	indefinite	*pres.*	present
inf.	infinitive	*pron.*	pronoun
m.	masculine	*rel.*	relative
mf.	m. + f.	*vb.*	verb

SPANISH—ENGLISH VOCABULARY

A

a to, into; from, off; at, on; for; by, with, in, on; *sign of personal object; (+ inf.)* let's
abajo down, below
abanico *m.* fan
abismo *m.* abyss
abonar to pay
abono *m.* subscription; **billete de abono** commutation ticket
abrazar to embrace; **te abraza** affectionately yours
abrazo *m.* embrace
abrigarse to wrap up
abrigo *m.* overcoat
abril *m.* April
abrir to open, to open the door
aburrir to bore
acá here, around here; **ir de acá para allá** to go here and there
acabar to finish; **acabarse** to end; **acabar de** *(+ inf.)* to finish, to have just
académico, -a academic
acaso maybe, perhaps
acción *f.* action
acera *f.* sidewalk
acerca de about, concerning
acero *m.* steel
acompañar to accompany, to go with
acontecer to happen
acostarse to go to bed
acostumbrarse to become accustomed, to get used (to it)
acto *m.* act
actor *m.* actor
actriz *f.* actress
actualidad *f.* current event; account
Adela Adele

adelantar to advance, to move up
¡adelante! come in!, (let's) go in!
Adelita *dim. of* Adela
además besides, moreover
adentro inside; **¡adentro!** (let's) go in!
adiós good-by; hello
admiración *f.* admiration
adolescente *mf.* adolescent
¿adónde? where?
adorada *f.* darling, flame
aéreo, -a aerial; airy; **línea aérea** airline; **navegación aérea** flying
aeródromo *m.* airport, airfield
aeroplano *m.* airplane
aeropuerto *m.* airport
afecto, -a fond; **su afectísimo, -a** sincerely yours, cordially yours
afeitarse to shave
aficionado, -a *mf.* enthusiast, fan
agitación *f.* excitement
agosto August
agradar to please; **(me) agrada (I)** like
agradecer to be grateful, to thank; **se agradece** thank you
agradecimiento *m.* gratitude, thanks
agridulce bittersweet
agua *f.* water; **hacérsele a uno la boca agua** to make one's mouth water
aguardar to wait; **aguardar a que** to wait until; **aguarda que te aguarda** waiting and waiting
agudo, -a sharp
¡ah! ah!, oh!
ahí there; **ahí mismo** right over there; **ahí va** here it is
ahora now; **ahora mismo** right now
ajetreo *m.* bustle, bustling about

ajustar to arrange; to adjust, to fasten; **ajustar cuentas** to settle accounts
al (= a + el) to the, at the; *(+ inf.)* on, when
Alberto Albert
alcoba *f.* bedroom
alegrarse to be glad
alemán, -ana German
Alfonso Alphonso
álgebra *f.* algebra
algo something; *adv.* somewhat, rather
algodón *m.* cotton
alguien somebody
algún, alguno, -a some, one, *pl.* some, a few, several; **no...alguno, -a** not...at all, no...whatsoever
alimento *m.* food
all- *see below, after* **alu-**
alma *f.* soul
almorzar to eat lunch, to have lunch
altavoz *m.* loudspeaker
alto, -a high, tall; *m.* high place; **en voz alta** aloud, loudly
altura *f.* height; summit
alumno, -a *mf.* pupil, student
allá there, out there, over there
allí there; **por allí** over there
amable amiable, kind; dear
amapola *f.* poppy
amargar to spoil *(a party, etc.)*
ambigú *m.* refreshment counter
americana *f.* coat *(of a man's suit)*
amigo, -a *mf.* friend
amistad *f.* friendship
amo *m.* boss
amor *m.* love
anciano, -a *mf.* elderly person
Andalucía Andalusia
andaluz, -uza *mf.* Andalusian
andar to walk, to go; to be; **andar con** to use *(to handle);* **¡anda!** come on!, go ahead!, go on!; **pues, andando** well, let's get going

andén *m.* (railroad) platform
anduve *see* **andar**
animado, -a animated, gay
ánimo *m.* spirit, mind, heart
anoche last night
ansia *f.* anguish
ante before, in front of
antes before, sooner, earlier; **antes de** before
antiguo, -a old; former
Antonio Anthony
anunciador, -ora *mf.* announcer
anunciar to announce
año *m.* year
apacible calm, mild
apagar to turn off, to turn out (the lights)
aparato *m.* plane
aparecer to appear, to turn up, to be (found)
apasionado, -a very fond
apellido *m.* surname, last name, family name
apenas hardly, scarcely
apetito *m.* appetite
apresurarse to hurry
aprovechar to profit by, to make use of
aptitud *f.* aptitude
apurarse to worry
aquel, aquella that; **aquellos, -as** those; **aquel que** that one who; **aquél, aquélla,** *etc.* that (one), those; **aquello** that *(idea, situation, etc.)*
aquí here; **aquí...** this is...(speaking); **aquí tienes** here is
arboleda *f.* grove
argumento *m.* plot *(of a play, etc.)*
arquitectura *f.* architecture
arrancar to start moving
arreglar to arrange
arriba up; above; **¡arriba!** (get) up!
arroz *m.* rice; **arroz con pollo** chicken and rice

arte *m. or f.* art; **bellas artes** fine arts; **museo de artes** art museum
artículo *m.* article
artista *mf.* artist
as *m.* ace
asado *m.* roast meat; **asado de cordero** roast lamb
ascensor *m.* elevator
asearse to groom oneself
aseo *m.* neatness; grooming
así thus, (in) that way, (just) like that
asiento *m.* seat
asignatura *f.* course, subject, study
asturiano, -a *mf.* Asturian
Asturias Asturias
asunto *m.* subject; matter, business
asustar to frighten
atardecer: al atardecer in the late afternoon
atención *f.* attention, courtesy
atender to attend to, to look after
aterrizar to land *(in a plane)*
atletismo *m.* athletics, track *(track and field events)*
atractivo, -a attractive
atragantarse to choke
atreverse to dare; **atreverse con** to dare have
aumento *m.* increase; **aumento de sueldo** raise in salary
aun even, still
aún still, yet
aunque although, (even) though
auto *m.* auto, car
autobús *m.* bus
automóvil *m.* automobile
autor, -ora *mf.* author
aviador, -ora *mf.* aviator; **capitán aviador** flight captain
avión *m.* plane, airplane
avisar to inform, to let know
¡ay! oh!, alas!
ayer yesterday
ayuda *f.* aid, help
ayudar to help

azafata *f.* hostess, stewardess
azorado, -a excited, upset
azul blue

B

¡bah! bah!
bahía *f.* bay
bailar to dance
baile *m.* dance
bajarse to stoop down
bajo, -a low; *m.* low place; **bajo** *prep.* under, beneath
balompié *m.* football, soccer
baloncesto *m.* basketball
banco *m.* bank
bandeja *f.* tray
bañista *mf.* bather
baño *m.* bath; swim; **cuarto de baño** bathroom; **traje de baño** bathing suit
baraja *f.* deck (of cards)
barato, -a cheap, inexpensive; **barato** *adv.* cheaply; **baratísimo, -a** very cheap
Barcelona Barcelona
barco *m.* boat; **barquito de juguete** (little) toy boat
barrio *m.* district, neighborhood
barro *m.* mud
bastante enough
bastar to suffice, to be enough; **bastar con que** to be only necessary that
basto *m. (playing card)* club
bata *f.* bathrobe
batalla *f.* battle; **dar una batalla** to fight a battle
beber to drink
bello, -a beautiful; **bellas artes** fine arts
beso *m.* kiss
betún *m.* shoe polish; **dar betún a** to polish *(shoes)*
bien well; fine, all right; very, quite; **bien venido** welcome; **más bien** rather

billete bill *(bank note)*; ticket
bisté *m.* beefsteak
blanco, -a white; **en blanco** blank; **ropa blanca** linen
blando, -a soft
bobo *m.* simpleton; **ese bobo de** that silly
boca *f.* mouth
bocacalle *f.* intersection
boda *f.* wedding
bolso *m.* bag, purse
bomba *f.* bomb
bondad *f.* kindness; **(hombre) de bondad** kindly (man)
bonito, -a pretty
botones *m.* bellhop; **botones del ascensor** elevator boy
boxeo *m.* boxing
brillar to shine
brocha *f.* brush
broma *f.* joke; **en broma** jokingly
bromista *mf.* joker
buen, bueno, -a good; **bueno** *adv.* well, fine, all right; **muy buenas (tardes)** good afternoon; **otra buena me esperaba** there was more to come
bull- *see below, after* **bult-**
bulto *m.* bundle, package; **bulto de mano** piece of hand luggage
bullicio *m.* hubbub, noise
burla *f.* jest
buscar to look for; **venir a buscar** to come by for
butaca *f.* armchair, easy chair; orchestra seat, main floor seat

C

¡ca! oh no!, no, indeed!
caballo *m.* *(playing card, with figure of horse and rider)* queen
cabeza *f.* head; **cepillo de cabeza** hairbrush
cabo *m.* end; **al cabo** at last, finally; **al cabo de** at the end of

cada each, every
caer to fall, to drop; **dejar caer to** drop *(let fall)*
café *m.* coffee
caja *f.* box; cash box, safe
cajero, -a *mf.* cashier
calamidad *f.* calamity
calcetín *m.* sock
calidad *f.* quality
call- *see below, after* **calo-**
calma *f.* calm; **con calma** calmly
calor *m.* heat; **hacer calor** to be warm *or* hot (weather)
callar(se) to be silent, to quiet down
calle *f.* street
cama *f.* bed
camarero, -a *mf.* waiter, waitress; steward, stewardess
cambiar to change; **cambiar de avión** to change planes
camisa *f.* shirt
campeón, -ona *mf.* champion
campeonato *m.* championship
campo *m.* field; country
canoa *f.* canoe; **pasear(se) en canoa** to go canoeing, to go canoe riding
cansar to tire
cantante *mf.* singer
capacidad *f.* capacity
capitán *m.* captain
capricho *m.* caprice
cara *f.* face
carácter *m.* character
¡caramba! gracious!, confound it!
carcajada *f.* outburst of laughter; **soltar la carcajada** to roar with laughter; **buenas carcajadas sueltan** they're really roaring with laughter
cariño *m.* affection, love; **con mucho cariño** affectionately yours
carne *f.* meat
caro, -a expensive
carrera *f.* run, race; **¡qué carreras!** what rushing around!
carta *f.* letter

cartel *m.* show bill
casa *f.* house; home; **casa de huéspedes** boarding house; **casita de muñecas** (little) doll house; **sentirse como en su casa** to feel quite at home
casarse (con) to marry, to get married
casi almost
castellano, -a *mf.* Castilian
Castilla Castile
catedrático -a *mf.* professor
catorce fourteen
cayó *see* caer
cazar to hunt *(for game)*, to go hunting
célebre famous
centavo *m.* cent
central *f.* central *(operator)*; main office; **central de correos** (main) post office
centro *m.* business district, down town
cepillar to brush
cepillo *m.* brush; **cepillo de cabeza** hairbrush; **cepillo de dientes** toothbrush
cerdo *m.* pig; **chuleta de cerdo** pork chop
cereal *m.* cereal
certificar to register *(a letter)*
Cervantes, Miguel de (1547-1616)
ch- *see below, after* cu-
cielo *m.* sky; heaven
cien, ciento (a, one) hundred
cierto, -a (a) certain
cigarrillo *m.* cigarette
cinco five
cincuenta fifty
cine *m.* cinema, movies
cinematografía *f.* cinematography
circulación *f.* traffic
ciudad *f.* city
civil civil
clarear to (begin to) dawn
claro, -a clear; **claro es** of course

clase *f.* class; kind
clima *m.* climate
cobrar to collect; to cash *(a check)*
coche *m.* coach, car
coger to catch, to get
cola *f.* queue, line; **hacer cola** to wait in line
colchón *m.* mattress
colección *f.* collection
coloquio *m.* conversation
comedia *f.* comedy, play
comedor *m.* dining room
comentarista *mf.* commentator
comenzar to commence, to begin
comer to eat; **comerse con los ojos** to stare, to feast one's eyes
comercial commercial
cómico, -a comic, comical
como as, like, however; since
¿cómo? how?; ¿cómo no...? how could I fail to...?
compañía *f.* company
completo, -a complete
compra *f.* purchase; **de compras** shopping
comprar to buy
común common; **por lo común** commonly, usually
con with; and; to, toward; **con tal que** provided that
concertar to arrange, to set
concierto *m.* concert; *vb., see* concertar
concurrencia *f.* crowd *(gathering)*
conducir to drive *(a car)*
conga *f.* conga
conmigo (= con + mí) with me, with myself; toward me
conocer to know; to meet; to recognize, to perceive, to see
conocimiento *m.* acquaintance; **hacer conocimiento** to become acquainted
conozco *see* conocer
conque so then, (and) so
consejero, -a *mf.* adviser

conserva *f.* preserves; **en conserva** preserved, canned
conservarse to keep *(remain)*
consigo (= **con** + **sí**) with himself, herself, itself, oneself, themselves, yourself, yourselves; with him, her, it, one, them, you *(used reflexively)*
consistir en to consist of
constante constant
contar to tell *(relate)*; **cuente usted** tell about it
contemplar to contemplate, to look at
contento, -a contented, happy, glad, pleased
contestar to answer
contigo (= **con** + **ti**) with you, with yourself
contraer to contract, to acquire
contrario, -a opposite
conversación *f.* conversation
conversar to converse
copa *f.* *(playing card, representing a goblet)* heart
corazón *m.* heart; **duro de corazón** hard-hearted
cordero *m.* lamb
cordillera *f.* mountain range
coro *m.* chorus; **a coro** in chorus
correa *f.* strap, belt; **correa (de seguridad)** safety belt; **correa del asiento** seat belt
correo *m.* mail; **central de correos** (main) post office; **en correos** at the post office
correr to run; to go fast; **correrse** to run (down); **de prisa y corriendo** very quickly, on the run
corresponder to return (love, *etc.*)
corretear to go from place to place
corriente current, common
cortar to cut, to cut off; to fly through
corto, -a short
cosa *f.* thing; **una cosa, alguna cosa**

something; **no fué cosa muy divertida** it wasn't very amusing
costar to cost
costumbre *f.* custom
crear to create
crecer to grow
creer to believe, to think
cruzar to cross
cuaderno *m.* notebook
cuadro *m.* picture
¿cuál? which?, which one?; **¿cuál es...?** which is...?, what is...?
cualquier any, some
cuando when, whenever; **de vez en cuando** from time to time
¿cuándo? when?
cuanto, -a as much as, *pl.* as many as, all the; **en cuanto a** as to, as for, with regard to
¿cuánto, -a? how much?, *pl.* how many?
¡cuánto, -a! how much!, *pl.* how many!
cuarenta forty
cuarto *m.* quarter; room; *pl.* cash, money; **cuarto de baño** bathroom; **soltar los cuartos** to spend the money
cuatro four; few
cuenta *f.* account; bill; **darse cuenta** to be aware, to notice
cuento *see* **contar**
cuesta *f.* slope, hill
cuidado *m.* care; **¡cuidado!** careful!, look out!, watch out!; **con cuidado** carefully; **tener cuidado** to be careful
cuidar to take care of; **bien cuidado** well kept
culinario, -a culinary
culminar to culminate
cultivar to cultivate
cura *f.* cure, treatment
curso *m.* course; school year; **de medio curso** midyear

CH

chanclo *m.* overshoe; **chanclo de goma** overshoe, rubber
charla *f.* chat
charlar to chat
cheque *m.* check
chico, -a small; *m.* boy, fellow, *f.* girl; **chiquito, -a** very small, tiny
chimenea *f.* smokestack
chinela *f.* house slipper
chiquillo, -a *mf.* child, kid
¡chist! sh!
chuleta *f.* chop

D

dama *f.* leading lady *(theatre)*
dar to give; to produce
David David
de of, from; off; by; about; for, as; with, in, on; than
debajo underneath
deber to be obliged (must, ought, should); **deber de** must
decano, -a *mf.* dean
decir to say; **digo** I mean; **que digamos** *(after negative)* we might say; **bien puedes decirlo** you're quite right; **querer decir** to mean; **todo lo dicho arriba** all that has been said above
dejar to leave; to let; **dejar caer** to drop *(let fall)*; **dejar de** *(+ inf.)* to stop, to fail to
del (= **de** + **el**) of the
delante ahead, in front; **delante de** in front of; **por delante** ahead
delicado, -a delicate, considerate, thoughtful
delicioso, -a delicious, delightful
demasiado, -a too much, *pl.* too many; **demasiado** *adv.* too, too much
dentífrico, -a: pasta dentífrica toothpaste

dentro inside, within; **dentro de** within
depender to depend
dependiente, -ta *mf.* (store) clerk
deporte *m.* sport
deportivo, -a sports, for sports
derecho, -a straight; right; **derechos** *m.pl.* fees; **derechito, -a** right straight; **a la derecha** (to the) right
desayunar(se) to eat breakfast
desayuno *m.* breakfast
descanso *m.* rest, peace
descompuesto, -a broken *(out of order)*
describir to describe
desde from
desear to desire, to wish; **desearía** I would like
deslizarse to slide, to glide
despacho *m.* office, study
despedirse to take leave, to say good-by
despegar (de tierra) to take off, to leave the ground
despertador *m.* alarm clock
despertar to awaken
despierto *see* **despertar**
después afterwards, later, then; **después de** after
destacarse to stand out, to be distinguished
detrás *or* **por detrás** behind
devolver to return, to give back
di *see* **dar**
día *m.* day; **buenos días** good morning; **de todos los días** everyday
dialogar to dialogue
diálogo *m.* dialogue
dibujo *m.* sketch, drawing; **dibujo de muñecos** cartoon *(movies)*
dice *see* **decir**
dich- *see below, after* **dici-**
diciembre *m.* December
diciendo *see* **decir**
dicho *see* **decir**

dichoso, -a happy, lucky; **dichosos los ojos que ven a usted** it's surely good to see you again
diente *m.* tooth; **cepillo de dientes** toothbrush; **hincar el diente** to sink one's teeth
dieron *see* **dar**
diez ten; **diez y seis** sixteen, **diez y siete** seventeen, *etc.*
diferencia *f.* difference
diferenciarse to differ
difícil difficult, hard
diga *see* **decir**
digno, -a worthy; **digno de verse** worth seeing
digo *see* **decir**
dije *see* **decir**
diligente diligent
dinero *m.* money
dió *see* **dar**
Dios God; **con Dios** good-by; **¡Dios mío!** Good Lord!, for goodness' sake!; **¡por Dios!** for heaven's sake!
diré *see* **decir**
dirección *f.* direction
director *m.* director
disco *m.* disc, record
discutir to discuss
dispensar to pardon, to excuse; **dispensa** pardon me, excuse me
dispuesto, -a disposed, ready
distante distant
distinguirse to distinguish oneself, to be outstanding
divertido, -a amusing, entertaining
divertir to amuse; **divertirse** to enjoy oneself, to have a good time, to have fun; **¡sí que está usted divertido!** you really are in a predicament!
dividir to divide
divinamente divinely, wonderfully
divisar to descry, to make out
doce twelve
docena *f.* dozen

doctoral doctoral, professorial
dólar *m.* dollar
doler to hurt; to bother; **no le duele** he doesn't mind
domingo *m.* Sunday
don Don; **Don Quijote** Don Quixote
donde where
¿dónde? where?
doña Doña
dorado, -a golden
dormilón, -ona *mf.* sleepyhead
dormir to sleep; **dormirse** to go to sleep
dos two; **los dos** both
dotes *f. pl.* talents, gifts
drama *m.* drama
duele *see* **doler**
duermo *see* **dormir**
dulce sweet
durar to last
duro, -a hard; **durillo, -a** a little hard; **duro con** hard on; **duro de corazón** hard-hearted

E

e and *(used before i- or hi-)*
¡ea! come on!, let's get going!
ech- *see below, after* **ecu-**
ecuestre equestrian
echar to throw; to play; **echarse (encima)** to throw on, to put on
edificio *m.* building
educación *f.* education
efecto *m.* effect; **en efecto** indeed, that is right
¿eh? eh?, right?; **¡eh!** hey!
ejercicio *m.* exercise
el the; *pron.* the one, that
él he; him, it
electivo, -a elective
Elena Helen
ella she; her, it
ellos, -as they; them
embargo: sin embargo nevertheless

embustero, -a *mf.* liar
Emilia Emily
Emilio Emile
eminente eminent
emisora *f.* (broadcasting) station
emoción *f.* emotion
empeñarse to persist; empeñado en determined to, persisting in, insisting on
empezar to begin
empiezo *see* empezar
empleado, -a *mf.* employee
empujón *m.* shove
en in, into; at; on; over
encantado, -a delighted
encantar to enchant, to delight
encanto *m.* delight
encendedor *m.* lighter
encender to light; encienda have a light
encerrar to inclose; to contain
enciendo *see* encender
encierro *see* encerrar
encima above, on top, on; encima de above
encontrar to find; encontrarse con to meet *(come across)*
encuentro *m.* encounter; *vb., see* encontrar
endosar to endorse
enero *m.* January
enfocar to focus
enlazar to link
Enrique Henry
enriquecer to enrich
Enriqueta Henrietta
ensalada *f.* salad
ensayar to try; to rehearse
ensueño *m.* dream, illusion
entender to understand
entero, -a entire, whole
entiendo *see* entender
entonces then
entrar (en) to enter, to go in
entre between, among; por entre through, between

entretendré *see* entretener
entretenerse to entertain oneself
entusiasta *mf.* enthusiast
envidia *f.* envy
equipaje *m.* baggage, luggage
equipo *m.* team
era *see* ser
eres *see* ser
es *see* ser
esa, ésa *see* ese
escándalo *m.* scandal
escandaloso, -a scandalous, shocking
escaparate *m.* show window
escena *f.* scene; setting
escribir to write
escrito *see* escribir
escuchar to listen (to)
escultura *f.* sculpture
ese, esa that; esos, -as those;ése, ésa, *etc.* that (one), those; eso that *(idea, situation, etc.)*
esencia *f.* essence
esmeralda *f.* emerald
eso *see* ese
espacio *m.* space
espada *f. (playing card, representing a sword)* spade
España *f.* Spain
español, -ola Spanish; *mf.* Spaniard; *m.* Spanish *(language);* a la española in the Spanish way
españolizar to make Spanish, to give a Spanish form to
especialice *see* especializar
especializar(se) to specialize, to major
espejo *m.* mirror
esperar to await, to wait (for)
espíritu *m.* spirit
espiritual spiritual
esquina *f.* corner
esta, ésta *see* este
está *see* estar
establecimiento *m.* establishment
estación *f.* station; season
estacionar to park *(a car)*

estar to be; to spend *(time);* **estar para** *(+ inf.)* to be about to
estática *f.* static
estatua *f.* statue
estatura *f.* stature
este, esta this; **estos, -as** these; **éste, ésta,** *etc.* this (one), these, the latter; **esto** this *(idea, situation, etc.)*
esté *see* **estar**
estilo *m.* style; **estilo sastre** tailored
esto *see* **este**
estoy *see* **estar**
estrella *f.* star
estribación *f.* spur *(of a mountain range)*
estudiante *mf.* student
estudiar to study
estudio *m.* studio
estuve *see* **estar**
eterno, -a eternal
exacto, -a exact
examen *m.* exam, examination; **andar de exámenes** to be having exams; **hacer un examen** to examine, to give an examination
excentricidad *f.* eccentricity
exclamación *f.* exclamation
exclamar to exclaim, to announce
excursión *f.* excursion, trip
exigente strict *(demanding)*
explanada *f.* esplanade
exponer to display
expresar to express
expresión *f.* expression
expreso, -a express *(train, etc.)*
extenso, -a extensive
extraño, -a strange
extravagante extravagant, odd

F

fábula *f.* fable, story, plot
fácil easy
factor *m.* factor
facturar to check *(baggage)*

facultad *f.* faculty; school *(university division)*
faltar to be lacking
familiar familiar
famoso, -a famous
fantasía *f.* fantasy
fascinar to fascinate
fatiga *f.* fatigue
favor *m.* favor; **hacer el favor de** to please (pass *or* give)
favorito, -a favorite
fe *f.* faith
febrero *m.* February
fecha *f.* date
felicitar to congratulate
Felisa Felicia
feliz happy; felicitous; ¡**feliz viaje!** bon voyage!, have a pleasant trip!
felizmente happily; **que le vaya felizmente** good luck to you
feo, -a ugly
Fernando Ferdinand
festonear to festoon
fiesta *f.* festival, party
figurar to figure; **figurarse** to imagine; **me lo figuro** I (can) imagine
fila *f.* row, line; **hacer fila** to stand in line
filosofía *f.* philosophy; **filosofía y letras** liberal arts
fin *m.* end; **fin de semana** weekend; **al fin, por fin** finally, at last; **un sin fin de** no end of
fino, -a fine; of good quality; sheer *(thin)*
finura *f.* courtesy
firma *f.* signature
firmar to sign
firme firm, steady
física *f.* physics
flor *f.* flower
fluctuar to fluctuate
fondo *m.* back, background; **al fondo** at the back, in the background
forjar to forge

forma *f.* form
formar to form
fortuna *f.* fortune; **por fortuna** fortunately
fósforo *m.* match
fotógrafo *m.* photographer
fox-trot *m.* foxtrot
fracturar to fracture; **fracturarse** to get fractured
frágil fragile
francés, -esa French; *mf.* Frenchman, Frenchwoman; *m.* French *(language)*
franqueo *m.* postage
frase *f.* phrase
frecuencia *f.* frequency; **con frecuencia** frequently
fresco, -a cool; fresh; impudent
frío, -a cold; *m.* cold; **hacer frío** to be cold (weather)
frito, -a fried
frondoso, -a leafy, luxuriant
fruta *f.* fruit
fué *see* **ir** *and* **ser**
fuego *m.* fire; **pegar fuego** to set fire
fuerte strong; heavy
fuí *see* **ir** *and* **ser**
fumar to smoke
funcionar to function; to work, to run
futbol *m.* football, soccer
futurista *mf.* futurist

G

galán, -ana elegant, dashing; *m.* leading man *(theatre)*
galante gallant
galería *f.* gallery, balcony
gallego, -a *mf.* Galician
gana *f.* desire; **de buena gana** willingly; **tener ganas de** (+ *inf.*) to want to *(feel like)*
ganar to win
ganga *f.* bargain

garaje *m.* garage
garantice *see* **garantizar**
garantizar to guarantee
gastrónomo, -a *mf.* gourmet
general *adj. and m.* general; **en general** in general, generally
género *m.* kind, sort; cloth, material
generoso, -a generous
gente *f.* people
gloria *f.* glory; **estar en sus glorias** to be in one's glory
glotón, -ona *mf.* glutton
gobernar to govern
gobierno *see* **gobernar**
golpe *m.* blow; **golpetazo** big blow, bang
goma *f.* rubber
gordo, -a fat
gracia *f.* grace, charm; wit; **gracias** thanks, thank you; **con gracia** gracefully; **hacer gracia** to amuse; **tener gracia** to be clever, to be funny
gracioso, -a charming, attractive
grado *m.* degree
gramófono *m.* phonograph
gran, grande large, big, great; **gran ópera** grand opera
granizar to hail
grave grave
gritar to shout, to call out
grito *m.* shout; **dar gritos** to shout
grupo *m.* group
guardarropa *m.* checkroom
guerra *f.* war
guiar to drive *(a car)*
gustar to please; **(me) gusta** (I) like it; **como usted guste** as you wish, just as you please
gusto *m.* taste; pleasure; preference; **dar gusto** to be a pleasure; **el gustito que nos da** the fun it is for us; **ser del gusto de** to be to the liking of; **tanto gusto** it's a pleasure (to know you)

H

ha *see* haber
haber to have *(done something);*
hay, había, *etc.* there is (are),
there was (were), *etc.;* haber de
(+ inf.) to be going to, to be supposed to; ¡cómo ha de ser! what
can you expect!; hay que *(+ inf.)*
one must, it is necessary to; ¡hay
que ver! isn't that something!; no
hay de qué you're welcome
hábil able *(competent)*
hablar to talk
habré *see* haber
hacer to make; to do; hace (un
mes) for (a month), it has been
(a month)
haga *see* hacer
hallar to find
han *see* haber
haré *see* hacer
has *see* haber
hasta up to; until; even; hasta
(luego) see you (later)
hay *see* haber
haya *see* haber
haz *see* hacer
he *see* haber
hecho *see* hacer
hemos *see* haber
hermandad *f.* sorority
hermano, -a *mf.* brother, sister
hermoso, -a beautiful; hermosísimo,
-a very beautiful
hermosura *f.* beauty; thing of beauty
hice *see* hacer
hierba *f.* herb; sopa de hierbas
(Spanish) vegetable soup
hijo, -a *mf.* son, daughter
hincar to stick, to sink
historia *f.* history
hizo *see* hacer
hogar *m.* home
hoja *f.* sheet *(of paper);* hojilla en
blanco blank piece of paper

¡hola! hello!, hi!
holandés, -esa Dutch
hombre *m.* man; hombrecito little
man
hora *f.* hour; time (of day)
horario *m.* schedule
horrible horrible
hospitalidad *f.* hospitality
hotel *m.* hotel
hoy today
hubiera *see* haber
hubiese *see* haber
huésped, -eda *mf.* guest; casa de
huéspedes boarding house
huevo *m.* egg
humano, -a human
humor *m.* humor, mood; de mal
humor in a bad mood

I

iba *see* ir
ida *f.* going; de ida y vuelta round-
trip
ideal *adj. and m.* ideal
idealista idealistic
iglesia *f.* church
igual equal; me es igual it's all the
same to me
iluminar to light *(illuminate)*
imaginación *f.* imagination
impaciente impatient
impermeable *m.* raincoat
importante important
importar to matter
importe *m.* amount
impresión *f.* shooting *(of a film)*
impresionar to impress; to shoot *(a
film)*
incluso including
indicar to indicate
indigestión *f.* indigestion; coger una
indigestión to get (a case of) indigestion
infatigable untiring
informar to inform

inglés, -esa English; *mf.* Englishman, Englishwoman; *m.* English *(language)*
inmenso, -a immense
insólito, -a unusual
instante *m.* instant, moment; **en un mismo instante** at the same time, in a single instant
interés *m.* interest
interesante interesting
interesar to interest
interior interior; **ropa interior** underclothes, underwear
invención *f.* invention; **¡para invenciones estoy yo!** I'm in a fine mood for making things up!
inventar to invent, to make up
invierno *m.* winter
ir to go; to be; **irse** to go (away), to leave; **ir** (+ *pres. part.*) to be gradually; **ir a** (+ *inf.*) to go to, to be going to; **ir bien** to suit, to look well on; **ahí va** here it is; **¿cómo te va?** how goes it with you?; **que le vaya bien** good luck, good-by; **¡vamos!** let's go!, come now!; **vamos al asunto** let's get to the subject; **¡vaya!** well!, why!; **¡vaya si...!** certainly...!, of course...!; really...!; **ya voy** I'm on my way
isla *f.* island
italiano, -a Italian
izquierdo, -a left

J

jabón *m.* soap
¡ja, ja! ha, ha!
Jacinto Hyacinth
jefe *m.* boss
¡je, je! he, he!
¡ji, ji! he, he!; te-hee!
José Joseph
joven young; *mf.* young man, young woman; **jovencito, -a** youngish

Juana Jane
juego *m.* game; *vb., see* **jugar**
jueves *m.* Thursday
jugador, -ora *mf.* player
jugar to play (*a game*)
jugo *m.* juice
juguete *m.* toy
Julia Julia
julio *m.* July
junio *m.* June
juntar to join, to combine; **juntarse** to join, to meet, to come together
junto a near, next to, beside
justicia *f.* justice

K

kimono *m.* kimono, housecoat

L

la the; *pron.* the one, that; her, it, you; **a la una** at one o'clock; **es la una** it is one o'clock
lado *m.* side; **al lado** next door; **al lado de** beside; **al otro lado de** on the other side of
lago *m.* lake
lamentar to regret, to be sorry
lápiz *m.* pencil
largo, -a long
las the; *pron.* the ones, those; them, you; **a las (dos)** at (two) o'clock; **son las (dos)** it is (two) o'clock
lástima *f.* pity; **es lástima** it's too bad
lata *f.* nuisance
lavandero, -a *mf.* laundryman, laundress
lavar to wash; **lavarse** to wash (oneself)
le *m.* him, you; *mf.* (to) him, her, it, you
lección *f.* lesson
lech- *see below, after* **lect-**
lector, -ora *mf.* reader

lectura *f.* reading
leche *f.* milk
lechuga *f.* lettuce
leer to read
legumbre *f.* vegetable
lejano, -a distant, far
lejos far, far off, far away
lengua *f.* language
les (to) them, you
letra *f.* letter *(of the alphabet);* **letrica** little letter; **cuatro letras** a few lines; **filosofía y letras** liberal arts
levantar to lift; **levantarse** to get up
leyendo *see* **leer**
libre free; **libre de** free from, rid of
librería *f.* bookstore
libro *m.* book
ligeramente lightly, slightly
limpiar to clean
límpido, -a limpid
limpieza *f.* cleanliness; cleaning
limpio, -a clean; **sacar en limpio** to make a clean copy of
lindo, -a pretty
línea *f.* line; **línea aérea** airline
lisonjero, -a *mf.* flatterer
lista *f.* list; roll; **lista de platos** bill of fare, menu; **pasar lista** to call the roll
listo, -a ready
literatura *f.* literature
ll- *see below, after* **lu-**
lo *n.* the; that *(idea, situation, etc.); pron.* it, so; *m.* it, you; one, any
localidad *f.* seat *(theatre)*
loco, -a crazy, mad; *m.* madman
lograr to attain
loma *f.* (long, low) hill
los the; *pron.* the ones, those; them, you
lucha *f.* wrestling
luego then, next, later
lugar *m.* place
Luis Louis

lujoso, -a luxurious
luminoso, -a luminous
luna *f.* moon; moonlight; **luna de miel** honeymoon; **hay luna** the moon is shining
lunes *m.* Monday
luz *f.* light

LL

llamada *f.* call
llamar to call; to knock, to ring
llanura *f.* plain
llegar to arrive; to come; **llegarse a** to approach, to move along to
llenar to fill; **llenarse de** to stuff oneself with
lleno, -a full; **iba llenito hasta los topes** it was jam-packed
llevar to carry; to take; to wear; to have been *(a certain length of time)*
llover to rain
lluvia *f.* rain

M

madre *f.* mother
Madrid Madrid
madrugada *f.* dawn; **de madrugada** at dawn; **bien de madrugada** in the early dawn
maestría *f.* mastery
maestro, -a *adj. and m.* master; *mf.* teacher; **obra maestra** masterpiece
magistral masterly
magnífico, -a magnificent, wonderful
mal, malo, -a bad; **mal** *adv.* badly, bad; **menos mal** fortunately
maleta *f.* suitcase
mancha *f.* spot, stain
mandar to send
manga *f.* sleeve
mano *f.* hand
Manuel Manuel
manzana *f.* apple

mañana *f.* morning; *adv.* tomorrow;
¡**qué mañanita!** what a morning!
maquinilla *(f.)* **de afeitar** safety
razor
mar *m. or f.* sea
maravilla *f.* marvel
marca *f.* mark, stamp
marcharse to go (away), to leave
María Mary
marido *m.* husband
martes *m.* Tuesday
mártir *mf.* martyr
Maruja *dim. of* **María**
Marujilla *dim. of* **Maruja**
marzo *m.* March
más more, most; **más bien** rather;
nada más only, just; **no...más** no
longer, not...any longer, not...
again; **no...más que** only; **(poco)
más o menos** more or less
masa *f.* mass
matrícula *f.* matriculation
matricularse to matriculate, to enroll
matrimonio *m.* married couple
mayo *m.* May
mayor larger, largest
me me, to me; myself
mecanógrafo, -a *mf.* typist
media *f.* stocking
medicina *f.* medicine; **alumno de
medicina** medical student
medio, -a (a, one) half; **a medias**
half-and-half; **(la una) y media**
half past (one)
mejor better, best; **lo mejor** the best
part
melancólico, -a melancholy
menor less, lesser
menos less, fewer
mensajero *m.* messenger boy
mente *f.* mind
mentir to lie *(tell lies)*
mentira *f.* lie; **parece mentira** it
seems unbelievable
menú *m.* menu

menudo, -a small
mes *m.* month
mesa *f.* table
meter to put (in); **meterse (en)** to
get (in, into)
mi my
mí me; myself
miedo *m.* fear; **dar miedo** to fright-
en; **con un poquito de miedo** just
a little afraid
miel *f.* honey; **luna de miel** honeymoon
miembro *m.* member
mientras while
miércoles *m.* Wednesday
Miguel Michael
minúsculo, -a very small, tiny
minuto *m.* minute
mío, -a mine, of mine; **el mío** mine
mirador *m.* lookout
mirar to look (at), to watch; **mirar
de reojo** to look out of the corner
of one's eye
misa *f.* mass *(service);* **a misa de diez**
to ten o'clock mass
mismo, -a same, very (same); *adv.*
right, even; **ahí mismo** right over
there; **ahora mismo** right now,
right away; **lo mismito** the very
same thing, exactly the same; **lo
mismo que** the same as, as well as
mitad *f.* half; middle; **en mitad de**
halfway through, halfway up
moda *f.* fashion; **de moda** in fashion, fashionable
modelo *m.* model
modernista *mf.* modernist
moderno, -a modern
modista *f.* dressmaker; fitter
modo *m.* way, manner; **de modo
que** so that, so then
mojado, -a wet
molestar to bother, to disturb
momento *m.* moment
montaña *f.* mountain
monumento *m.* monument

mostrador *m.* counter *(in a store)*
mostrar to show
motor *m.* motor
movimiento *m.* movement, traffic
mozo *m.* waiter
muchacho, -a *mf.* boy, girl
mucho, -a much, a lot of, *pl.* many;
  mucho *adv.* much, a lot; muchísimo very much
mujer *f.* woman
mundo *m.* world
muñeca *f.* doll; casita de muñecas
  (little) doll house
muñeco *m.* puppet; dibujo de muñecos cartoon *(movies)*
museo *m.* museum
música *f.* music
musical musical
músico *m.* musician
muy very

N

nacional national
nacionalidad *f.* nationality
nada nothing, (not) anything; nada
  más only, just; de nada you're
  welcome
nadie nobody
naipe *m.* (playing) card
naranja *f.* orange
nariz *f.* nose
narrar to narrate
natación *f.* swimming
naturaleza *f.* nature
naturalidad *f.* naturalness; con
  naturalidad in a natural way
navegación *f.* navigation; navegación aérea flying
necesitar to need
nervioso, -a nervous
nevada *f.* snowfall
nevar to snow
ni neither, nor, not even; ni...ni
  neither...nor; ¡ni que...! one
  might think that...!

nieve *f.* snow
ningún, ninguno, -a no, not any,
  none
niño, -a *mf.* child
no no; not; ¿no? right?
noble noble
noche *f.* evening, night; buenas noches good evening; mala noche
  hace it's a bad night
nombre *m.* name
norteamericano, -a American
nos us, to us; ourselves; one another, each other
nosotros, -as we; us; ourselves
nota *f.* grade, mark
notar to note, to notice
noticia *f.* news (item); *pl.* news
noticiario *m.* newscast, newsreel
novela *f.* novel
novelista *mf.* novelist
noventa ninety
noviembre *m.* november
novio, -a *mf.* sweetheart
nube *f.* cloud
nuestro, -a our; ours, of ours; el
  nuestro ours
nueve nine
nuevo, -a new; de nuevo anew,
  again
número *m.* number
nunca never, (not) ever; más que
  nunca more than ever (before)

O

o or
obligatorio, -a required
obra *f.* work, production; obra
  maestra masterpiece
observar to observe
ocasión *f.* occasion
och- *see below, after* oct-
océano *m.* ocean
octubre *m.* October
ochenta eighty
ocho eight

oficina *f.* office

oficinista *mf.* office worker

¡oh! oh!

oigo *see* oír

oír to hear; to listen (to); **como usted lo oye** that's right

ojalá I hope

ojo *m.* eye; **comerse con los ojos** to stare, to feast one's eyes on; **dichosos los ojos que ven a usted** it's surely good to see you again

óleo *m.* oil; **cuadro al óleo** oil painting

olivar *m.* olive grove

olvidar to forget

once eleven

onda *f.* wave

ondulación *f.* undulation, wave

ópera *f.* opera; **gran ópera** grand opera

opinión *f.* opinion

orden *m.* order

oriente *m.* east

oro *m. (playing card, representing a gold coin)* diamond

orquesta *f.* orchestra

os you, to you; yourselves; one another, each other

otoño *m.* autumn, fall

otro other, another

oye *see* oír

P

padecer to suffer, to endure

padre *m.* father

pagar to pay

página *f.* page

país *m.* country

paisaje *m.* landscape

pájaro *m.* bird

pajarraco *m.* bird, sneaky fellow

palabra *f.* word; words *(speech);* **palabrita** little word

pálido, -a pale

palo *m.* suit *(in cards)*

palpar to feel *(touch)*

panorama *m.* panorama

pantalón *m.* trousers, pants

pantalla *f.* screen

pañuelo *m.* handkerchief; **pañolito** little handkerchief

papá *m.* papa, dad

paquete package, parcel; **paquete postal** parcel

par *m.* pair, couple; **al par** equally, at the same time

para for; to, in order to; by; about to; **para que** in order that, so that

parada *f.* stop; **hacer parada** to stop

paraje *m.* place, spot

parar(se) to stop

parecer to seem, to appear, to be like, to look like; to seem all right, to seem best; **al parecer** seemingly, apparently; **¿qué le parece?** how does it seem to you?

pareja *f.* couple

parezco *see* parecer

parte *f.* part; place; **en todas partes** everywhere; **por ninguna parte** nowhere

partida *f.* game *(of cards);* **echar una partida** to play a game

partido *m.* game, match

partir to depart, to leave

pasado, -a past, last

pasajero, -a *mf.* passenger

pasar to pass; to spend *(time);* to happen; to come in, to go in; to get by; to call *(roll);* **que usted lo pase bien** good-by; **ya se le pasará** he'll get over it

pasear(se) to take a walk; to take a ride, to go riding

paso *m.* step

pasta *f.* paste

pastel *m.* pastry, pie

pasto *m.* nourishment, food

patata *f.* potato

patético, -a pathetic

pavimento *m.* pavement
pedir to request, to ask (for); to order
pegar to stick; to set *(fire)*
peinarse to comb one's hair
peine *m.* comb
película *f.* film, picture, movie
peliculero, -a *mf.* movie actor, movie actress
peligro *m.* danger
pelmazo *m.* bore *(boring person)*
pelota *f.* pelota *(Basque ball game)*
pena *f.* sorrow
pensamiento *m.* thought
pensar to think; to intend
peor worse
Pepe Joe
pequeño, -a small, little
percha *f.* clothes tree, hat rack
perder to lose; to waste; to miss
perfección *f.* perfection
periódico *m.* newspaper
pero but
persona *f.* person; **personita** little person; **mala persona** scoundrel, rascal
personaje *m.* personage, character
personal *m.* personnel
pertenecer to belong to, to go to
perverso, -a perverse
pesado, -a dull, boring
pescado *m.* fish
pianista *mf.* pianist
picacho *m.* peak
pícaro, -a rascally, darned; *m.* rascal
pido *see* pedir
pie *m.* foot; **a pie** on foot; **de pie** standing
pienso *see* pensar
pierdo *see* perder
pierna *f.* leg
pieza *f.* piece; **quedarse de una pieza** to be dumbfounded
píldora *f.* pill
piloto *m.* pilot
pimienta *f.* pepper

pinar *m.* pine grove
pintamonas *mf.* dauber
pintor, -ora *mf.* painter
pintura *f.* painting
piso *m.* floor; apartment
pista *f.* runway
piyama *m.* pajamas
placer *m.* pleasure
planchar to iron
plantarse to stand *(take a stand);* **plantado, -a** standing
plata *f.* silver
plática *f.* chat
plato *m.* plate; dish; **lista de platos** bill of fare, menu
playa *f.* shore, beach
pluma *f.* pen
pobre poor
poco, -a little, *pl.* few; **poco** *adv.* (a) little; **poco más o menos** more or less; **un poquito** a little (bit); **unos pocos** a few
poder to be able (can, may)
poderoso, -a powerful
podré *see* poder
policiaco, -a detective *(story, film)*
poll- *see below, after* polv-
polvo *m.* powder; *pl.* powder *(cosmetic)*
pollo *m.* chicken
poner to put; to write; to turn on *(a radio, etc.);* **ponerse** to put on, to wear; to become, to get; **ponerse a** *(+ inf.)* to begin to
pongo *see* poner
poquito *see* poco
por by; because of, about, for, to; in, during, on, along, across, through
porque because, for
portarse to behave, to conduct oneself
poseer to possess
poseyó *see* poseer
posible possible
posición *f.* position

postal postal; **paquete postal** parcel; **tarjeta postal** post card
postre *m.* dessert
practicar to practice
práctico, -a practical
precio *m.* price; **rebaja de precios** price reduction
precioso, -a precious, lovely
precisamente precisely
predilección *f.* predilection, choice
preferible preferable
preferir to prefer
prefiero *see* preferir
preguntar to ask, to inquire
prenda (de vestir) *f.* garment
preparar to prepare
presencia *f.* presence
presentar to present, to introduce
pretender to try, to seek
primavera *f.* spring
primer, primero, -a first; **primero** *adv.* first
primo, -a *mf.* cousin
primoroso, -a exquisite, lovely
principalmente principally, mainly
principio *m.* beginning
prisa *f.* haste; **de prisa** quickly; **de prisa y corriendo** very quickly, on the run; **meter prisa** to hurry things up; **¡qué de prisita!** how quickly!
probar to test, to try (out); **probarse** to try on
producir to produce
profesor, -ora *mf.* professor
programa *m.* program
pronto soon; **prontito** quite soon; **de pronto** suddenly
pronunciación *f.* pronunciation
propina *f.* tip; **aquí no hay propinas** there's no tipping here
prosa *f.* prose
protestar to protest
próximo, -a next
proyectar to project

prueba *f.* test; fitting; **cuartito de pruebas** fitting room
pruebo *see* probar
pude *see* poder
pueblo *m.* town; **pueblecillo** little town
puedo *see* poder
puerta *f.* door
pues since *(because)*, then *(therefore)*; well, why; *often used for emphasis*
puesto *m.* place; *vb.*, *see* poner
¡pum! bang!, wham!
punta *f.* point *(tip)*
punto *m.* point; stitch; **punto de vista** viewpoint; **se me ha corrido un punto en la media** I've got a run in my stocking
puré *m.* purée; **puré de patatas** mashed potatoes
puse *see* poner

Q

que *pron.* that, which, who, whom; *conj.* that; than; as; for, since; so (that); *often used for emphasis*
¿qué? what?; what do you say?; **¿qué tal?** how?; **¿por qué?** why?; **no hay de qué** not at all, you're welcome
¡qué! what (a)!, how!
quebrantar to break
quedar to remain, to be left; to be (located); **quedarse** to remain, to stay, to stop by
quehacer *m.* chore
quejarse to complain
querer to want, to wish, to be willing; to try; **querer decir** to mean; **quisiera** (I) would like
querido, -a dear
quien who; whom; **a quien** whom
¿quién? who?; whom?; **¿a quién?** whom?

¡quién! who!; (+ *past subjunctive*)
I wish I could...!, I surely would
like to...!

quiero *see* querer

Quijote *m.* Don Quixote (*quixotic
person*)

química *f.* chemistry

quince fifteen

quise *see* querer

quitar to remove, to get off

R

rabona: hacer rabona to play
hooky, to cut class

radio *f.* radio

radiógrafo *m.* radio operator

Ramón Raymond

Ramoncete *dim. of* Ramón

rapidez *f.* rapidity, swiftness

rato *m.* little while; un rato de limpieza a little cleaning; un rato ya
largo quite a while ago; pasé un
ratito I had a time of it

rayo *m.* ray; a los rayos del sol in
the rays of the sun

razón *f.* reason; tener razón to be
right

razonable reasonable

realidad *f.* reality

rebaja *f.* reduction

recepción *f.* reception

recibir to receive

recibo *m.* receipt

recoger to pick up

reconocer to recognize

reconocimiento *m.* gratitude

recordar to recall, to remember

recrearse to delight, to take delight

recreo *m.* recreation

rector, -ora *mf.* rector, president

reemplazar to replace, to substitute

reflexión *f.* reflection

reflexivo, -a reflective, thoughtful

régimen *m.* diet; estar a régimen to
be on a diet

regional regional.

regocijo *m.* gaiety, merriment

reír(se) to laugh

religión *f.* religion

reloj *m.* clock

remitir to send (*by mail*)

remolque *m.* tow; a remolque unwillingly; llevar a remolque to
tow, to have in tow

renglón *m.* line (*of writing*)

renovar to renew

reñir to quarrel, to have a quarrel

reojo: mirar de reojo to look out
of the corner of one's eye

repantigarse to loll, to sprawl out
(*in a chair, etc.*)

repente: de repente suddenly

repetir to repeat

repito *see* repetir

representar to represent

resbaladizo, -a slippery

resistir to bear, to stand

resonar to resound, to sound loudly

respirar to breathe (*a sigh of relief*)

responder to reply, to answer

restaurán *m.* restaurant

reunirse to meet, to come together

revés *m.* reverse; pasa al revés
que... it is the reverse from what
it is...

revisar to check

revisor *m.* conductor (*on a train*)

revisora *f.* stewardess, hostess

revista *f.* revue

rey *m.* king

Ricardo Richard

rico, -a rich; delicious, tasty

ridículo, -a ridiculous

riño *see* reñir

río *m.* river; *vb., see* reír

risa *f.* laughter

robar to rob

robledal *m.* oak grove

rojizo, -a reddish

romántico, -a romantic

ronquido *m.* snore; **dar ronquidos** to snore

ropa *f.* clothing, clothes; **ropa blanca** linen; **ropa de vestir** wearing apparel; **ropa interior** underclothes, underwear

Rosa Rose

Rosalinda Rosalind

Rosario Rosary

Rosarito *dim. of* **Rosario**

Rosita *dim. of* **Rosa**

rugby *m.* rugby

ruido *m.* noise, roar

rumba *f.* rumba

S

sábado *m.* Saturday

sábana *f.* sheet; **pegársele a uno las sábanas** to get up late

saber to know; **no sé qué** something or other, some...or other

sabiduría *f.* learning; **(hombre) de sabiduría** learned (man)

sabio, -a wise; *m.* wise man

saborear to savor

sabré *see* **saber**

sabroso, -a savory, tasty

sacar to take out; to get

sacrificio *m.* sacrifice

sal *f.* salt; charm

sala *f.* (large) room; **sala de clase** classroom

saldo *m.* (clearance) sale

saldré *see* **salir**

salida *f.* coming out; **salida del sol** sunrise

salir to leave, to go out; to turn out, to prove to be

salón *m.* (large) room, hall, ballroom; **saloncillo** (small) lounge; **saloncillo de fumar** smoking lounge

saludar to greet

saludo *m.* greeting

salvar to save

saque *see* **sacar**

sastre *m.* tailor; **estilo sastre** tailored

se (to) him, her, it, them, you; himself, herself, itself, oneself, themselves, yourself, yourselves; one another, each other; *(indef. subject)* one, you

sé *see* **saber**

sea *see* **ser**

secar to dry; **secarse** to dry (oneself)

sección *f.* section; show *(showing)*

seguida: en seguida immediately, right away

seguir to follow; to continue; to take *(a course)*; **que usted siga bien** good-by

según according to

segundo, -a second

seguridad *f.* security, safety

seguro, -a sure; dependable; **de seguro** surely, of course

seis six

sello *m.* stamp; **sello de a tres (centavos)** three-cent stamp

semana *f.* week; **fin de semana** weekend

semblante *m.* countenance, face

semestre *m.* semester

sencillamente simply

sencillez *f.* simplicity

sencillo, -a simple; one-way

sensación *f.* sensation, feeling

sentar (bien) to suit, to be becoming; **sentarse** to sit down

sentimiento *m.* feeling

sentir to feel; to regret, to be sorry; **sentirse** to feel

señalar to indicate, to point out

señor *m.* gentleman; Mr.; sir; **Señor** Lord

señora *f.* lady; ma'am; **señora (de)** Mrs.

señorita *f.* young lady; Miss

señorito *m.* sir *(used by servants, etc.)*

septiembre *m.* September

ser to be
sereno, -a serene, calm, smooth
serio, -a serious
servicio *m.* service; meal, order
servir to serve, to be of service; sírvase please; para servir a usted at your service
sesenta sixty
setenta seventy
si if; whether; vaya si... certainly..., really...; ¡si...! why...!, I wonder if...!
sí yes; sí, sí yes, indeed; sí (que)... indeed..., certainly...
sí himself, herself, itself, oneself, yourself, yourselves; por sí solo all by himself
siempre always; de siempre as always, usual
siento *see* sentar and sentir
sierra *f.* sierra, mountain range
siete seven
significar to signify, to mean
sigo *see* seguir
simpatía *f.* liking, sympathy
simpático, -a likable, pleasant, nice
sin without; not; sin embargo nevertheless; un sin fin de no end of
sincero, -a sincere
sino but, except; no...sino only, not...but; sino que but
sintaxis *f.* syntax
sirvo *see* servir
sobre on, upon, above, over; about, concerning
sobresalir to excel, to stand out
sobretodo above all, especially
sobrino, -a *mf.* nephew, niece
sofocarse to become embarrassed
sol *m.* sun; sunshine; haber sol, hacer sol to be sunny
soler (+ *inf.*) to be accustomed to, usually (+ *verb*)
solitario *m.* solitaire; hacer solitarios to play solitaire
solo, -a alone, only, single; *m.* solo;

por sí solo all by himself; esta música se baila sola this music is just made for dancing
sólo only
soltar to turn loose, to let go (of); soltar la carcajada to roar with laughter
sombra *f.* shade, shadow; tener mala sombra to be unpleasant
sombrero *m.* hat
son *see* ser
sonar to sound, to ring, to go off
sonrisa *f.* smile; sonrisita little smile, smirk
sopa *f.* soup
sorpresa *f.* surprise
soso, -a dull, insipid; el soso de X that insipid X
sota *f.* *(playing card)* jack
soy *see* ser
su his, her, its, their, your
subir to go up; subir a to get on *(a train, etc.);* to come to, to amount to
sublime sublime
suculento, -a succulent
sudar to sweat
sueldo *m.* salary
suele *see* soler
suelto *see* soltar
suena *see* sonar
sufrir to suffer
superior superior, first-rate
suplantar to supplant, to displace
supremo, -a supreme
surgir to rise; to appear
surtido *m.* stock, supply
suyo, -a (of) his, hers, theirs, yours; el suyo his, hers, theirs, yours

T

tabla *f.* panel *(painting)*
tachar to erase
tal such (a); con tal que provided; ¿qué tal? how?

talla *f.* size *(clothes);* **mi talla es del 34** my size is 34
también also, too
tampoco neither, (not) either
tan so, so much, such (a); **tan... como** as...as
tango *m.* tango
tanto, -a as much, so much; **tanto** *adv.* as much, so much
taquígrafo, -a *mf.* stenographer
taquilla *f.* ticket window; **taquilla del guardarropa** checkroom (window)
taquillero, -a *mf.* ticket seller
tardar to take (long), to be long
tarde *f.* afternoon; *adv.* late; **tardecito** a little late; **buenas tardes** good afternoon
tarjeta *f.* card; **tarjeta postal** post card
taxi *m.* taxi
te you, to you; yourself
teatro *m.* theatre
técnico, -a technical
tecnicolor *m.* technicolor
telefonear to telephone
telefonista *mf.* operator *(telephone)*
teléfono *m.* telephone
telegrama *m.* telegram
tema *m.* theme
temprano early
tendré *see* **tener**
tener to have; *(+ noun)* to be *(+ adj.);* **tener que** *(+ inf.)* to have to; **aquí tiene** here is, here are
tengo *see* **tener**
tenis *m.* tennis
tercer, tercero, -a third
Teresa Theresa
terminar to finish, to end
tesoro *m.* treasure
ti you; yourself
tiempo *m.* time; weather; **hacer (buen) tiempo** to be (good) weather; **hacer un tiempo (hermoso)** to be (beautiful) weather

tienda *f.* shop, store; **de tiendas** shopping
tiene *see* **tener**
tierno, -a tender
tierra *f.* earth, land, ground; region, country
tinta *f.* ink; **sudar tinta** "to sweat blood"
tintorería *f.* dry cleaner's
tío, -a *mf.* uncle, aunt
título *m.* title
toalla *f.* towel
tocar to play *(music)*
todavía still, yet
todo, -a all, every; **todo** *pron.* everything, *pl.* all, everybody; **todos los (días)** every (day); **con todo** all the same
tomar to take; to get; to have; **¡toma!** well!, why!, of course!; **tome usted** here is, here are
tope: lleno hasta los topes jampacked
torcer to turn
tornar a *(+ inf.)* again *(+ verb)*
tostada *f.* (piece of) toast
trabajar to work
trabajo *m.* work, labor; **costar trabajo** to be hard, not to be easy
traer to bring
tragar to swallow; to eat a lot
trágico, -a tragic
traigo *see* **traer**
traje *m.* suit; **traje de baño** bathing suit
trampa *f.* trick *(cheating)*
tranquilidad *f.* calmness; **con tranquilidad** calmly, quietly
tranquilo, -a tranquil, calm, quiet; **dejar tranquilo** to leave alone, to stop bothering
transatlántico *m.* ocean liner
transeúnte *mf.* pedestrian
transparente transparent
tranvía *m.* streetcar, trolley
tratar de *(+ inf.)* to try to

trato *m.* treatment, manner
trece thirteen
treinta thirty
tren *m.* train
trepidar to shake, to vibrate
tres three
trigo *m.* wheat
trinar to rage; **está que trina** he is in a huff
tristeza *f.* sadness
tu your
tú you
tuve *see* **tener**
tuyo, -a yours, of yours; **el tuyo** yours

U

¡uf! ugh!
un, una a, an; **unos, -as** some, a few; **un, uno, -a** one; **uno** *pron.* one, *pl.* some
uniforme *m.* uniform
universidad *f.* university
uno *see* **un**
usar to use
usted you

V

va *see* **ir**
vacaciones *f. pl.* vacation
vacante vacant
vacío, -a empty
valer to be worth
valga *see* **valer**
valiente valiant, courageous
vall- *see below, after* **vals**
valor *m.* value
vals *m.* waltz
valle *m.* valley
vamos *see* **ir**
variedad *f.* variety
varios, -as various, several
vas *see* **ir**
vasco, -a Basque
vascongado, -a *mf.* Basque

vaso *m.* glass
vasto, -a vast
vaya *see* **ir**
vea *see* **ver**
vecino, -a *mf.* neighbor
veinte twenty; **veintiún, veintiuno, -a** twenty-one; **veintidós** twenty-two; *etc.*
velada *f.* evening *(activities)*
veloz swift, speedy; **velocísimo, -a** very speedy
vender to sell
vendré *see* **venir**
vengo *see* **venir**
venir to come; **¡venga!** let's have!, bring on!, let's see!; **¡bien venido (-a)!** welcome!; **el (mes) que viene** next (month)
veo *see* **ver**
ver to see; to watch; **verse** to meet; **a ver** let's see; really?; **¡hay que ver!** isn't that something!
veraneante *mf.* (summer) vacationist
verano *m.* summer
verdad *f.* truth; **¿verdad?** true?, isn't it so?, *etc.;* **de verdad** truly, really; **es verdad** it's true
verdadero, -a true, real
verso *m.* verse
vestíbulo *m.* vestibule
vestido *m.* dress; **vestido de noche** evening dress
vestir to dress; to wear; **vestirse** to get dressed; **ropa de vestir** wearing apparel
vez *f.* time; **a veces** at times, sometimes; **algunas veces** sometimes; **de vez en cuando** from time to time; **muchas veces** often; **otra vez** again; **una vez** once; **unas veces** sometimes
viaje *m.* trip; **¡feliz viaje!** bon voyage!, have a pleasant trip!
viajero, -a *mf.* traveler, passenger; **¡señores viajeros del 35, al avión!** flight number 35 now boarding!

vibrar to vibrate
vicaría *f.* vicarage
vicerrector, -ora *mf.* vice-rector, vicepresident
victoria *f.* victory
vida *f.* life
viene *see* **venir**
viernes *m.* Friday
vilo: en vilo up in the air; **levantar en vilo** to bowl over
vine *see* **venir**
violinista *mf.* violinist
visitar to visit
vista *f.* view; **hasta la vista** so long, good-by
visto *see* **ver**
vitamina *f.* vitamin
viveza *f.* liveliness, vivacity
vivir to live
vivo, -a live, living
vocación *f.* vocation, inclination
volar to fly; **parece que vuelas** you're fairly flying
volver to return; **volverse** to turn around

vosotros, -as you; yourselves
voy *see* **ir**
voz *f.* voice; tone of voice; **en voz alta** aloud, loudly
vuela *see* **volar**
vuelo *m.* flight; **levantar el vuelo** to take flight, to start flying
vuelta *f.* return; **vuelta a** back to; **de vuelta** back; **de ida y vuelta** round-trip
vuelvo *see* **volver**
vuestro, -a your; yours, of yours; **el vuestro** yours

Y

y and
ya already; now; later; *often used for emphasis;* ¡**ya, ya!** oh great!; ¡**da unos ronquidos que ya, ya!** he really snores!
yo I

Z

zapato *m.* shoe

ENGLISH—SPANISH VOCABULARY

A

a un, una [1]
able *(competent)* hábil; **to be able** poder*
about de, acerca de, sobre, por [5]; **to be about to** estar* para (+ *inf.)*
above *adv.* arriba; *prep.* sobre, encima de; **above all** sobretodo
abyss abismo *m.*
academic académico, -a
accompany acompañar
according to según
account cuenta *f.; (current event)* actualidad *f.; to settle accounts* ajustar cuentas
accustom: to become accustomed acostumbrarse; **to be accustomed to** soler *(ue) (+ inf.)*
ace as *m.*
acquaint: to become acquainted hacer* conocimiento
acquaintance conocimiento *m.*
acquire *(to contract)* contraer*
across por
act acto *m.*
action acción *f.*
actor actor *m.; movie actor* peliculero *m.*
actress actriz *f.; movie actress* peliculera *f.*
Adele Adela; *dim.* Adelita
adjust ajustar
admiration admiración *f.*
adolescent adolescente *mf.*
advance adelantar
adviser consejero, -a *mf.*
aerial aéreo, -a
affection cariño *m.*
affectionately yours con mucho cariño; te abraza
afraid con miedo; **just a little**

afraid con un poquito de miedo
after después de
afternoon tarde *f.; good afternoon* buenas tardes, muy buenas (tardes); **in the late afternoon** al atardecer
afterwards después
again otra vez, de nuevo; tornar a (+ *inf.),* vuelta a (+ *inf.); not...* **again** no...más
ah! ¡ah!
ahead (por) delante
aid ayuda *f.*
air: up in the air en vilo
airfield aeródromo *m.*
airline línea aérea *f.*
airplane aeroplano *m.,* avión *m.,* aparato *m.*
airport aeropuerto *m.,* aeródromo *m.*
airy aéreo, -a
alarm clock despertador *m.*
alas! ¡ay!
Albert Alberto
algebra álgebra *f.*
all todo, -a; *(as many as)* cuantos, -as; **all right** bien, bueno; **not... at all** no...alguno, -a; **not at all** *(you're welcome)* no hay de qué
almost casi
alone solo, -a; **to leave alone** *(not bother)* dejar tranquilo, -a
along por
aloud en voz alta
Alphonso Alfonso
already ya
also también
although aunque
always siempre; **as always** *(usual)* de siempre
American norteamericano, -a
amiable amable

among entre
amount importe *m.;* **to amount to**
subir a
amuse hacer* gracia
amusing divertido, -a
an un, una [1]
and y; e *(before* i- *or* hi-); con
Andalusia Andalucía
Andalusian andaluz, -uza *mf.*
anew de nuevo
anguish ansia *f.*
animated animado, -a
announce anunciar; exclamar (en
voz alta)
announcer anunciador, -ora *mf.*
another otro, -a; **one another** nos,
os, se [3]
answer contestar, responder
Anthony Antonio
any cualquier; *(it)* lo; **(not) any**
ningún, ninguno, -a [5]; **there
isn't any (static)** no hay (estática)
anything *(something)* algo; **(not)
anything** nada [5]
apartment piso *m.*
apparel ropa *f.;* **wearing apparel**
ropa de vestir
apparently al parecer
appear parecer *(zc); (turn up)* aparecer *(zc); (rise)* surgir *(j)*
appetite apetito *m.*
apple manzana *f.;* **apple pie** pastel
(m.) de manzana
approach *(move along)* llegarse *(gu)*
April abril *m.*
aptitude aptitud *f.*
architecture arquitectura *f.*
armchair butaca *f.*
arrange arreglar, ajustar; concertar
(ie)
arrive llegar *(gu)*
art arte *m.* or *f.;* **art museum** museo
(m.) de artes; **fine arts** bellas artes; **liberal arts** filosofía y letras
article artículo *m.*
artist artista *mf.*

as *(for)* de [5]; **as...as** tan...como
[2, 5]; **as to, as for** en cuanto a;
as well as, the same as lo mismo
que
ask *(inquire)* preguntar; *(request)*
pedir *(i);* **to ask about** preguntar
por; **to ask for** pedir *(i)*
Asturian asturiano, -a *mf.*
Asturias Asturias
at *(position or time)* a; *(location)*
en [5]
athletics atletismo *m.*
attain lograr
attend to atender *(ie)*
attention atención *f.*
attractive atractivo, -a; gracioso, -a
August agosto *m.*
aunt tía *f.*
author autor, -ora *mf.*
auto auto *m.*
automobile automóvil *m.*
autumn otoño *m.*
aviator aviador, -ora *mf.*
await esperar
awaken despertar *(ie)*
aware: **to be aware** darse* cuenta

B

back fondo *m.;* **at the back** al fondo; **back to** vuelta a *(+ inf.)*
background fondo *m.;* **in the background** al fondo
bad mal, malo, -a; *adv.* mal; **it's too
bad** es lástima
badly mal
bag *(purse)* bolso *m.*
baggage equipaje *m.*
bah! ¡bah!
balcony *(theatre)* galería *f.*
ballroom salón *m.*
bang *(blow)* golpetazo *m.;* **bang!**
¡pum!
bank banco *m.*
Barcelona Barcelona
bargain ganga *f.*

basketball baloncesto *m.;* **basketball championship** campeonato *(m.)* de baloncesto
Basque vasco, -a; vascongado, -a *mf.*
bath baño *m.*
bather bañista *mf.*
bathing suit traje *(m.)* de baño
bathrobe bata *f.*
bathroom cuarto *(m.)* de baño
battle batalla *f.;* **to fight a battle** dar* una batalla
bay bahía *f.*
be ser*; estar* [6]; quedar; ir*, andar*; **here it is** aquí lo tienes, ahí va; **it has been (a month)** hace (un mes)
beach playa *f.*
bear *(stand)* resistir
beautiful hermoso, -a; bello, -a; **very beautiful** hermosísimo, -a
beauty hermosura *f.;* **a thing of beauty** una hermosura
because porque; **because of** por
become ponerse*; **to be becoming** sentar *(ie)* bien
bed cama *f.;* **to go to bed** acostarse *(ue);* **to get to bed** *(get into the bed)* meterse en la cama
bedroom alcoba *f.*
beefsteak bisté *m.*
before *adv.* antes; *prep.* antes de; *(in front of)* ante
begin empezar *(ie; c),* comenzar *(ie; c);* ponerse* a *(+ inf.)*
beginning principio *m.*
behave portarse
behind (por) detrás
believe creer *(i, y)*
bellhop botones *m.*
belong pertenecer *(zc)*
below abajo
belt *(strap)* correa *f.;* **safety belt** correa (de seguridad); **seat belt** correa del asiento
beneath bajo
beside junto a, al lado de

besides además
best mejor; **the best part** lo mejor
better mejor; *(with* gustar*)* más
between (por) entre
big gran, grande
bill cuenta *f.;* *(bank note)* billete *m.;* **bill of fare** lista *(f.)* de platos
bird pájaro *m.;* **an ugly little bird** un pajarraco chiquito y feo
bittersweet agridulce
blank en blanco
blood: "to sweat blood" sudar tinta
blow golpe *m.;* **big blow** golpetazo *m.*
blue azul; **pale blue** azul pálido
board: flight number 35, now boarding! ¡señores viajeros del 35, al avión!
boarding house casa *(f.)* de huéspedes
boat barco *m.;* *(little)* **toy boat** barquito de juguete
bomb bomba *f.*
bon voyage feliz viaje
book libro *m.*
bookstore librería *f.*
bore *(boring person)* pelmazo *m.; vb.* aburrir
boring pesado, -a
boss amo *m.,* jefe *m.*
both los dos, las dos
bother *(disturb)* molestar; *(hurt)* doler *(ue);* **not bother** *(leave alone)* dejar tranquilo, -a
bowl over levantar en vilo
box caja *f.*
boxing boxeo *m.*
boy muchacho *m.,* chico *m.;* **elevator boy** botones *(m.)* del ascensor
break quebrantar
breakfast desayuno *m.:* **to eat breakfast, to have breakfast** desayunar(se)
breathe (a sigh of relief) respirar

bring traer*; bring on...! ¡venga...!
broadcasting station emisora f.
broken descompuesto, -a
brother hermano m.
brush cepillo m.; brocha f.; vb. cepillar; to brush one's teeth cepillarse los dientes
building edificio m.
bundle bulto m.
bus autobús m.
business (matter) asunto m.; business district centro m.; that business of eso de, aquello de
bustle or bustling around ajetreo m.
but pero; sino
buy comprar
by (agent) por, de; (point in time) para; (manner) a [5]

C

calamity calamidad f.
call llamada f.; vb. llamar; to call out (shout) gritar; to call the roll pasar lista
calm calma f.; adj. tranquilo, -a; sereno, -a; (mild) apacible
calmly con calma, con tranquilidad
calmness tranquilidad f.
can (to be able) poder*
canned en conserva
canoe canoa f.; to go canoeing, to go canoe riding pasear(se) en canoa
capacity capacidad f.
caprice capricho m.
captain capitán m.
car coche m., auto m.
card tarjeta f.; (playing card) naipe m.; post card tarjeta postal
care cuidado m.; to take care of cuidar
careful! ¡cuidado!; to be careful tener* cuidado
carefully con cuidado

carry llevar
cartoon (movies) dibujo (de muñecos) m.
cash (a check) cobrar; cash box caja f.
cashier cajero, -a mf.
Castile Castilla
Castilian castellano, -a mf.
catch coger (j)
cent centavo m.
central central f.
cereal cereal m.
certain or a certain cierto, -a
certainly... sí (que)..., vaya si...
chair: easy chair butaca m.
champion campeón, -ona mf.
championship campeonato m.
change cambiar; to change (planes) cambiar de (avión)
character carácter m.; (personage) personaje m.
charm gracia f., sal f.
charming gracioso, -a
chat charla f., plática f.; vb. charlar
cheap barato, -a; extremely cheap baratísimo, -a
cheaply barato
check cheque m.; vb. revisar; (baggage) facturar
checkroom guardarropa m.; checkroom window taquilla (f.) del guardarropa
chemistry química f.
chicken pollo m.; chicken and rice arroz (m.) con pollo
child niño, -a mf.; chiquillo, -a mf.
choice (predilection) predilección f.
choke atragantarse
chop chuleta f.
chore quehacer m.
chorus coro m.; in chorus a coro
church iglesia f.
cigarette cigarrillo m.
cinema cine m.
cinematography cinematografía f.
city ciudad f.

civil civil

class clase *f.; * **to cut class** *(play hooky)* hacer* rabona

classroom sala *(f.)* de clase

clean limpio, -a; *vb.* limpiar; **to make a clean copy of** sacar *(qu)* en limpio

cleaner's *(dry cleaner's)* tintorería *f.*

cleaning limpieza *f.;* **a little cleaning** un rato de limpieza

cleanliness limpieza *f.*

clear claro, -a

clerk *(in a store)* dependiente, -ta *mf.*

clever: **to be clever** tener* gracia

climate clima *m.*

clock reloj *m.;* **alarm clock** despertador *m.*

cloth *(material)* género *m.*

clothes ropa *f.;* **clothes tree** percha *f.*

clothing ropa *f.*

cloud nube *f.*

club *(playing card)* basto *m.*

coach coche *m.*

coat *(suit coat)* americana *f.*

coffee café *m.*

cold frío, -a; frío *m.;* **to be cold (weather)** hacer* frío

collect cobrar

collection colección *f.*

comb peine *m.;* **to comb one's hair** peinarse

combine *(join)* juntar

come venir*; *(arrive)* llegar *(gu);* **come now!** ¡vamos!; **come on!** ¡ea!, ¡ande (usted)!; **to come by for** venir* a buscar; **to come in** pasar; **come in!** ¡adelante!, ¡pase (usted)!; **coming out** salida *f.;* **to come to** *(amount to)* subir a; **to come together** *(meet)* reunirse *(ú),* *(join)* juntarse

comedy comedia *f.*

comic cómico, -a

comical cómico, -a

commence comenzar *(ie; c)*

commentator comentarista *mf.*

commercial comercial

common común; *(current)* corriente

commonly por lo común

commutation ticket billete *(m.)* de abono

company compañía *f.*

complain quejarse

complete completo, -a

concerning acerca de, sobre

concert concierto *m.*

conduct oneself portarse

conductor *(on a train)* revisor *m.*

confound it! ¡caramba!

conga conga *f.*

congratulate felicitar

considerate *(delicate)* delicado, -a

consist of consistir en

constant constante

contain *(inclose)* encerrar *(ie)*

contemplate contemplar

contented contento, -a

continue seguir *(i; g)*

contract contraer*

conversation conversación *f.,* coloquio *m.*

converse conversar

cool fresco, -a

copy: **to make a clean copy of** sacar *(qu)* en limpio

cordially yours su afectísimo, -a

corner esquina *f.;* **to look out of the corner of one's eye** mirar de reojo

cost costar *(ue)*

cotton algodón *m.*

countenance semblante *m.*

counter *(in a store)* mostrador *m.;* **refreshment counter** ambigú *m.*

country campo *m.;* país *m.,* tierra *f.*

couple pareja *f.;* *(pair)* par *m.;* *(married couple)* matrimonio *m.*

courageous valiente

course curso *m.;* *(subject)* asignatura *f.;* **of course** de seguro, claro (es);

of course! ¡toma!; of course...!
¡vaya si...!
courtesy finura *f.; (attention)* atención *f.*
cousin primo, -a *mf.*
crazy loco, -a
create crear
cross cruzar *(c)*
crowd *(gathering)* concurrencia *f.*
culinary culinario, -a
culminate culminar
cultivate cultivar
cure cura *f.*
current corriente; current event actualidad *f.*
custom costumbre *f.*
cut (off) cortar; to cut class *(play
hooky)* hacer* rabona

D

dad papá *m.*
dance baile *m.; vb.* bailar; this music is just made for dancing esta
música se baila sola
danger peligro *m.*
dare atreverse; to dare to have
atreverse con
darling adorada *f.*
darned pícaro, -a
dashing *(elegant)* galán, -ana
date fecha *f.*
dauber pintamonas *mf.*
daughter hija *f.*
David David
dawn madrugada *f.;* at dawn de madrugada; in the early dawn bien
de madrugada; to (begin to)
dawn clarear
day día *m.*
dean decano, -a *mf.*
dear querido, -a; *(amiable)* amable
December diciembre *m.*
deck (of cards) baraja *f.*
degree grado *m.*
delicate delicado, -a
delicious delicioso, -a; rico, -a

delight encanto *m.; vb.* encantar;
to delight in, to take delight in
recrearse en
delighted encantado, -a
delightful delicioso, -a
depart partir
depend depender; to depend on depender de
dependable *(sure)* seguro, -a
describe describir*
descry divisar
desire gana *f.; vb.* desear
dessert postre *m.*
detective film película policiaca *f.*
determined to empeñado (-a) en
dialogue diálogo *m.; vb.* dialogar
(gu)
diamond *(playing card)* oro *m. (gold
coin)*
diet régimen *m.;* to be on a diet
estar* a régimen
differ diferenciarse
difference diferencia *f.*
difficult difícil
diligent diligente
dining room comedor *m.*
direction dirección *f.*
director director *m.*
disc disco *m.*
discuss discutir
dish plato *m.*
displace suplantar
display exponer*
disposed dispuesto, -a
distant distante; lejano, -a
distinguish distinguir *(g);* to be distinguished distinguirse *(g),* destacarse *(qu)*
district *(neighborhood)* barrio *m.;*
business district centro *m.*
disturb *(bother)* molestar
divide dividir
divinely divinamente
do hacer*; *not expressed as auxili-
ary verb;* what did she do with
him? ¿qué hizo de él?

doctoral doctoral
doll muñeca *f.; (little) doll house* casita *(f.)* de muñecas
dollar dólar *m.*
Don don; **Don Quixote** Don Quijote
Doña doña
door puerta *f.*
down abajo; **down there** allá abajo; **down town** centro *m.*
downtown *adj.* del centro; *adv. (in town)* en el centro, *(to town)* al centro
dozen docena *f.*
drama drama *m.*
drawing dibujo *m.*
dream *(illusion)* ensueño *m.*
dress vestido *m.; vb.* vestir *(i);* **to dress (oneself), to get dressed** vestirse *(i);* **evening dress** vestido de noche
dressmaker modista *f.*
drink beber
drive *(a car)* guiar *(i),* conducir *(zc, -uj-)*
drop caer*; *(let fall)* dejar caer
dry secar *(qu);* **to dry (oneself)** secarse *(qu)*
dry cleaner's tintorería *f.*
dull *(insipid)* soso, -a; *(boring)* pesado, -a
dumbfounded: **to be dumbfounded** quedarse de una pieza
during por
Dutch holandés, -esa

E

each cada; **each other** nos, os, se [3]
earlier *(before)* antes
early temprano
earth tierra *f.*
east oriente *m.*
easy fácil; **not to be easy** costar *(ue)* trabajo
eat comer; **to eat a lot** tragar *(gu);*

to eat breakfast desayunar(se); **to eat lunch** almorzar *(ue; c)*
eccentricity excentricidad *f.*
education educación *f.*
effect efecto *m.*
egg huevo *m.*
eh? ¿eh?
eight ocho
eighteen diez y ocho
eighty ochenta
either: **(not) either** tampoco
elderly person anciano, -a *mf.*
elective electivo, -a
elegant *(dashing)* galán, -ana
elevator ascensor *m.;* **elevator boy** botones *(m.)* del ascensor
eleven once
embarrassed: **to become embarrassed** sofocarse *(qu)*
embrace abrazo *m.; vb.* abrazar *(c)*
emerald esmeralda *f.*
Emile Emilio
Emily Emilia
eminent eminente
emotion emoción *f.*
employee empleado, -a *mf.*
empty vacío, -a
enchant encantar
encounter encuentro *m.*
end fin *m.;* cabo *m.; vb.* terminar, acabarse; **at the end of** al cabo de; **no end of** un sin fin de
endorse *(a check)* endosar
endure *(suffer)* padecer *(zc)*
English inglés, -esa; *(language)* inglés *m.*
Englishman, Englishwoman inglés, -esa *mf.*
enjoy oneself divertirse *(ie, i)*
enough bastante; **to be enough** bastar; **I have enough with** me basta con; **that's enough cleaning** basta de limpieza
enrich enriquecer *(zc)*
enroll matricularse
enter entrar

entertain entretener*
entertaining divertido, -a; cosa divertida
enthusiast entusiasta *mf.; (fan)* aficionado, -a
entire entero, -a
envy envidia *f.*
equal igual
equally *(at the same time)* al par
equestrian ecuestre
erase tachar
especially sobretodo
esplanade explanada *f.*
essence esencia *f.*
establishment establecimiento *m.*
eternal eterno, -a
even aun, hasta; *(right)* mismo
evening noche *f.; (activities)* velada *f.; evening dress* vestido *(m.)* de noche
event: current event actualidad *f.*
ever: (not) ever nunca; more than ever (before) más que nunca [5]
every todo, -a; todos los, todas las; *(each)* cada
everybody todos *m. pl.*
everyday de todos los días
everything todo
everywhere en todas partes
exact exacto, -a
exam or examination examen *m.;* to give an examination hacer* un examen; to be having exams andar* de exámenes
examine hacer* un examen
excel sobresalir*
except *(but)* sino
excited *(upset)* azorado, -a
excitement agitación *f.*
exclaim exclamar
exclamation exclamación *f.*
excursion excursión *f.*
excuse dispensar
exercise ejercicio *m.*
expect: what can you expect! ¡cómo ha de ser!

expensive caro, -a
express *(train, etc.)* expreso, -a; *vb.* expresar
expression expresión *f.*
exquisite primoroso, -a
extensive extenso, -a
extravagant *(odd)* extravagante
extremely -ísimo [2]
eye ojo *m.;* to feast one's eyes on comerse con los ojos; to look out of the corner of one's eye mirar de reojo

F

fable fábula *f.*
face cara *f.; (countenance)* semblante *m.*
factor factor *m.*
faculty facultad *f.*
fail to dejar de *(+ inf.)*
faith fe *f.*
fall *(autumn)* otoño *m.; vb.* caer*
familiar familiar
family name apellido *m.*
famous famoso, -a; célebre
fan abanico *m.; (enthusiast)* aficionado, -a *mf.*
fantasy fantasía *f.*
far *adj.* lejano, -a; *adv.* lejos; far off, far away lejos
fascinate fascinar
fashion moda *f.; in fashion* de moda
fashionable de moda
fast: to go fast correr
fasten *(adjust)* ajustar
fat gordo, -a
father padre *m.*
fatigue fatiga *f.*
favor favor *m.*
favorite favorito, -a
fear miedo *m.*
feast one's eyes on comerse con los ojos
February febrero *m.*
fee *see* fees

feel sentir *(ie, i);* sentirse *(ie, i); (to touch)* palpar
feeling sentimiento *m.;* sensación *f.*
fees derechos *m. pl.*
Felicia Felisa
felicitous feliz
fellow chico *m.*
Ferdinand Fernando
festival fiesta *f.*
festoon festonear
few pocos, -as; **a few** unos (pocos), algunos, -as; **every few steps** cada cuatro pasos
fewer menos
field campo *m.*
fifteen quince
fifty cincuenta
fight a battle dar* una batalla
figure figurar
fill llenar
film película *f.*
finally al fin, al cabo, por fin
find hallar, encontrar *(ue);* **to be found** *(to appear)* aparecer *(zc)*
fine fino, -a; *adv.* bien, bueno; **fine arts** bellas artes *f.*
finish terminar, acabar; acabar de *(+ inf.)*
fire fuego *m.;* **to set fire** poner* fuego
firm firme
first primer, primero, -a; *adv.* primero
first-rate superior
fish pescado *m.*
fitter *(dressmaker)* modista *f.*
fitting prueba *f.;* **fitting room** cuartito *(m.)* de pruebas
five cinco
flame *(sweetheart)* adorada *f.*
flatterer lisonjero, -a *mf.*
flight vuelo *m.;* **to take flight** levantar el vuelo; **flight number 35, now boarding!** ¡señores viajeros del 35, al avión!

floor piso *m.;* **main floor seat** butaca *f.*
flower flor *f.*
fluctuate fluctuar *(ú)*
fly volar *(ue);* **to fly through** volar *(ue)* por, cortar; **you're fairly flying** parece que vuelas
flying navegación aérea *f.*
focus enfocar *(qu)*
follow seguir *(i; g)*
fond afecto, -a; **very fond** apasionado, -a
food alimento *m.; (nourishment)* pasto *m.*
foot pie *m.;* **on foot** a pie
football balompié *m.,* futbol *m.;* **football championship** campeonato *(m.)* de futbol
for *conj.* que, porque; *prep. (destination)* para; *(cause)* por; *(use)* de [5]; *often indirect object;* **for (a month)** hace (un mes)
forge forjar
forget olvidar
form forma *f.; vb.* formar
former antiguo, -a
fortunately por fortuna; menos mal (que)
fortune fortuna *f.*
forty cuarenta
four cuatro
fourteen catorce
foxtrot fox-trot *m.*
fracture fracturar; **to get fractured** fracturarse
fragile frágil
free libre
French francés, -esa; *(language)* francés *m.*
Frenchman, Frenchwoman francés, -esa *mf.*
frequency frecuencia *f.*
frequently con frecuencia
fresh fresco, -a
Friday viernes
fried frito, -a

friend amigo, -a *mf.*
friendship amistad *f.; to make friendships* contraer* amistades
frighten asustar, dar* miedo
from desde, de; *(with verbs of separation)* a [5]
front: in front of delante de, ante
fruit fruta *f.*
full lleno, -a
fun *(pleasure)* gusto *m.; to be fun* dar* gusto; **to have fun** divertirse *(ie, i)*
function funcionar
funny: to be funny tener* gracia
futurist futurista *mf.*

G

gaiety regocijo *m.*
Galician gallego, -a *mf.*
gallant galante
gallery galería *f.*
game juego *m.; (cards)* partida *f.; (match)* partido *m.; to play a game of cards* echar una partida de naipes
garage garaje *m.*
garment prenda (de vestir) *f.*
gay *(animated)* animado, -a
general general *adj. and m.*
generally en general
generous generoso, -a
gentleman señor *m.*
German alemán, -ana
get *(take)* tomar; *(obtain)* sacar *(qu); (catch)* coger *(j); (become)* ponerse*; **to get by** *(pass)* pasar; **to get in, to get into** meterse en; **to get off** *(remove)* quitar; **to get on** *(a train, etc.)* subir (a); **he'll get over it** ya se le pasará; **to get up** levantarse
gifts *(talents)* dotes *f. pl.*
girl muchacha *f.*, chica *f.*
give dar*; **to give back** devolver* *(ue)*

glad contento, -a; **to be glad** alegrarse
glass vaso *m.*
glide *(slide)* deslizarse *(c)*
glory gloria *f.; to be in one's glory* estar* en sus glorias
glutton glotón, -ona *mf.*
go ir*; andar*; **go ahead!, go on!** ¡ande (usted)!; **how goes it?** ¿cómo le va?; **let's get going!** ¡ea!, ¡andando!; **to go (away)** irse*, marcharse; **to go in** pasar (a), entrar (en); **(let's) go in!** ¡adentro!, ¡adelante!; **to go off** *(sound)* sonar *(ue);* **to go out** salir*; **to go to** *(belong to)* pertenecer *(zc)* a; **to be going to** ir* a, haber* de *(+ inf.);* **to go with** *(accompany)* acompañar
God Dios *m.*
golden dorado, -a
good buen, bueno, -a
good-by adiós, con Dios, hasta la vista, que le vaya bien, que usted siga bien, que usted lo pase bien; **to say good-by to** despedirse *(i)* de
goodness: for goodness' sake! ¡por Dios!
gourmet gastrónomo, -a *mf.*
govern gobernar *(ie)*
grace gracia *f.*
gracefully con gracia
gracious! ¡caramba!
grade *(mark)* nota *f.*
grand opera gran ópera *f.*
grateful: to be grateful agradecer *(zc)*
gratitude agradecimiento *m.*, reconocimiento *m.*
grave grave
great gran, grande; **oh great!** ¡ya, ya!
greet saludar
greeting saludo *m.*
groom oneself asearse
grooming aseo *m.*

ground tierra *f.;* to leave the ground *(take off)* despegar *(gu)* (de tierra)

group grupo *m.*

grove arboleda *f.;* oak grove robledal *m.;* olive grove olivar *m.;* pine grove pinar *m.*

grow crecer *(zc)*

guarantee garantizar *(c)*

guest huésped, -eda *mf.*

H

ha, ha! ¡ja, ja!

hail *(weather)* granizar *(c)*

hairbrush cepillo *(m.)* de cabeza

half mitad *f.;* (a, one) half medio, -a; half-and-half a medias; half past (eleven) (las once) y media

halfway through, halfway up a mitad de

hall *(large room)* salón *m.*

hand mano *f.;* by hand a mano; piece of hand luggage bulto *(m.)* de mano

handkerchief pañuelo *m.;* little handkerchief pañolito *m.*

happen acontecer *(zc),* pasar

happily felizmente

happy feliz; *(contented)* contento, -a; *(lucky)* dichoso, -a

hard duro, -a; *(difficult)* difícil; hard on duro con; a little hard durillo, -a

hard-hearted duro (-a) de corazón

hardly apenas

haste prisa *f.*

hat sombrero *m.*

hat rack percha *f.*

have tener*; haber* *(+ past part.); (take)* tomar; let's have...! ¡venga...!; to have just acabar de *(+ inf.);* to have to tener* que *(+ inf.)*

he él [3]

hear oír*

heart corazón *m.; (spirit)* ánimo *m.; (playing card)* copa *f. (goblet)*

heat calor *m.*

heaven cielo *m.;* for heaven's sake! ¡por Dios!; oh, heavens! ¡ay, cielos!

heavy *(strong)* fuerte

he, he! ¡je, je!, ¡ji, ji!

height altura *f.*

Helen Elena

hello! ¡hola!; ¡adiós!

help ayuda *f.; vb.* ayudar

Henrietta Enriqueta

Henry Enrique

her su [4]; el, la [1, 3]; *pron.* la; le, se; ella, sí [3]

herb hierba *f.*

here aquí, acá [5]; here is aquí tiene usted, tome usted; from here to there de acá para allá

hers suyo, -a; de ella; *pron.* el suyo, *etc.* [4]

herself se; sí, -sigo [3]

hey! ¡eh!

hi! ¡hola!

high alto, -a; high place alto *m.*

hill *(slope)* cuesta *f.;* (long, low) hill loma *f.*

him le, lo; se; él, sí [3]

himself se; sí, -sigo [3]; by himself por sí solo

his su; suyo, -a; de él; *pron.* el suyo, *etc.* [4]; el, la [1, 3]

history historia *f.*

home casa *f.,* hogar *m.;* to feel at home sentirse *(ie, i)* como en su casa

honey miel *f.*

honeymoon luna *(f.)* de miel

hooky: to play hooky hacer* rabona

hope: I hope...! ¡ojalá...!

horrible horrible

hospitality hospitalidad *f.*

hostess *(stewardess)* revisora *f.,* camarera *f.,* azafata *f.*

hot: to be hot (weather) hacer* calor
hotel hotel *m.*
hour hora *f.; a quarter of an hour* un cuarto de hora
house casa *f.; boarding house* casa de huéspedes; (little) doll house casita de muñecas
housecoat kimono *m.*
house slipper chinela *f.*
how? ¿cómo?, ¿qué tal?; how many? ¿cuántos, -as?; how much? ¿cuánto, -a?
how! ¡qué!; how many! ¡cuántos, -as!; how much! ¡cuánto, -a!
however *(as)* como
hubbub bullicio *m.*
huff: he is in a huff está que trina
human humano, -a
humor humor *m.; in a bad humor* de mal humor
hundred cien, ciento
hunt *or* go hunting cazar *(c)*
hurry apresurarse; to hurry things up meter prisa
hurt doler *(ue)*
husband marido *m.*
Hyacinth Jacinto

I

I yo [3]
ideal ideal *adj. and m.*
idealistic idealista
if si
illusion *(dream)* ensueño *m.*
imagination imaginación *f.*
imagine figurarse; I can imagine me lo figuro
immediately en seguida
immense inmenso, -a
impatient impaciente; impatient to impaciente por (+ *inf.)*
important importante
impress impresionar
impudent fresco, -a

in en; *(time, space)* por; *(manner)* a, de [5]; *(after superlative)* de [2]
inclination *(vocation)* vocación *f.*
inclose encerrar *(ie)*
including incluso
increase aumento *m.*
indeed en efecto; indeed... sí (que)...; no, indeed! ¡ca!; yes, indeed! ¡sí, sí!
indicate indicar *(qu)*, señalar
indigestion indigestión *f.; to get indigestion* coger *(j)* una indigestión
inexpensive barato, -a
inform informar
ink tinta *f.*
inquire preguntar
inside dentro, adentro
insipid soso, -a; that insipid X el soso de X
insist on empeñarse en
instant instante *m.; in a single instant* en un mismo instante
intend pensar *(ie)*
interest interés *m.; vb.* interesar
interesting interesante
interior interior
intersection bocacalle *f.*
into en; a [5]
introduce *(present)* presentar
invent inventar
invention invención *f.*
iron planchar
island isla *f.*
it lo, la; le, se; él, ella; ello [3]
Italian italiano, -a
its su [4]
itself se; sí, -sigo [3]

J

jack *(playing card)* sota *f.*
jam-packed lleno (-a) hasta los topes
Jane Juana
January enero *m.*
jest burla *f.*

Joe Pepe
join juntar; *(meet)* juntarse
joke broma *f.; you're probably joking* en broma lo dirás
joker bromista *mf.*
jokingly en broma
Joseph José
juice jugo *m.*
Julia Julia
July julio *m.*
June junio *m.*
just *(only)* nada más; **to have just** acabar de *(+ inf.)*
justice justicia *f.*

K

keep *(remain)* conservarse; **well kept** bien cuidado, -a
kid *(child)* chiquillo, -a *mf.*
kimono kimono *m.*
kind clase *f.; (sort)* género *m.; (amiable)* amable
kindly (man) (hombre) de bondad
kindness bondad *f.*
king rey *m.*
kiss beso *m.*
knock *(at the door)* llamar
know saber*; *(be acquainted with)* conocer *(zc);* **to let know** avisar

L

labor trabajo *m.*
lack: **to be lacking** faltar
lady señora *f.;* **leading lady** *(theatre)* dama *f.*
lake lago *m.*
lamb cordero *m.;* **lamb chop** chuleta *(f.)* de cordero; **roast lamb** asado *(m.)* de cordero
land tierra *f.; vb.* aterrizar *(c)*
landscape paisaje *m.*
language lengua *f.*
larger mayor, más grande
largest mayor, más grande

last pasado, -a; *vb.* durar; **at last** al fin, al cabo, por fin
late tarde; **a little late** tardecito; **to get up late** levantarse tarde, pegársele *(gu)* a uno las sábanas
later después, luego, más tarde; ya *(+ future);* **a little later** poco después
latter: **the latter** éste, ésta
laugh reír(se) *(i)*
laughter risa *f.; (burst of laughter)* carcajada *f.;* **to roar with laughter** reírse *(i)* a carcajadas, soltar *(ue)* la carcajada
laundress lavandera *f.*
laundryman lavandero *m.*
leading lady *(theatre)* dama *f.*
leading man *(theatre)* galán *m.*
leafy frondoso, -a
learned **(man)** (hombre) de sabiduría
learning sabiduría *f.*
leave dejar; *(depart)* salir*, partir; *(go away)* irse*, marcharse; **to leave alone** *(not bother)* dejar tranquilo, -a; **to leave the ground** *(take off)* despegar *(gu)* (de tierra); **to take leave** despedirse *(i)*
left izquierdo, -a; **to the left** a la izquierda
leg pierna *f.*
less menos; *(lesser)* menor
lesser menor
lesson lección *f.*
let dejar; *wish or command* [6]; **to let know** avisar; **to let go of** soltar *(ue)*
letter carta *f.; (alphabet)* letra *f.;* **little letter** letrica *f.*
lettuce lechuga *f.*
liar embustero, -a *mf.*
liberal arts filosofía y letras
lie mentira *f.; vb.* mentir *(ie, i)*
life vida *f.*
lift levantar

light luz *f.; vb.* encender *(ie); (illuminate)* iluminar; **have a light** encienda (usted)

lighter encendedor *m.*

lightly ligeramente

likable simpático, -a

like *(similar to)* como; **just like that** *(thus)* así; **to be like, to look like** *(appear)* parecer *(zc);* **I like (it)** me gusta, me agrada; **I would like** *(want)* quisiera, desearía; **I surely would like to…!** ¡quién *(+ past subjunctive)!*

liking simpatía *f.*

limpid límpido, -a

line línea *f.; (row)* fila *f.; (queue)* cola *f.; (writing)* renglón *m.;* **a few lines** unos renglones, cuatro letras; **to stand in line** hacer* fila; **to wait in line** hacer* cola

linen ropa blanca *f.*

liner: **ocean liner** transatlántico *m.*

link enlazar *(c)*

list lista *f.*

listen (to) escuchar, oír*

literature literatura *f.*

little poco, -a; *(small)* pequeño, -a; chico, -a; *(tiny)* chiquito, -a; *adv.* poco; **a little** un poco, un poquito; un poco de *(+ noun);* **a little later** poco después

liveliness viveza *f.*

living *(live)* vivo, -a

loll *(in a chair, etc.)* repantigarse *(gu)*

long largo, -a; **so long!** ¡hasta la vista!; **to take long** tardar; **to be long in** tardar en *(+ inf.)*

longer: **no longer, not…any longer** no…más

look mirar; **look out!** ¡cuidado!; **to look after** *(attend to)* atender *(ie);* **to look at** mirar, contemplar; **to look for** buscar *(qu);* **to look like** *(appear)* parecer *(zc);* **to look well on** ir* bien, sentar *(ie)* bien

lookout mirador *m.*

Lord Señor *m.;* **Good Lord!** ¡Dios mío!

lot: **a lot** *(much)* mucho; **a lot of** *(much)* mucho, -a, *(many)* muchos, -as

loudly en voz alta

loudspeaker altavoz *m.;* **over the loudspeaker** en el altavoz

Louis Luis

lounge saloncillo *m.*

love amor *m.; (affection)* cariño *m.*

lovely precioso, -a; primoroso, -a

low bajo, -a; **low place** bajo *m.*

luck: **good luck to you** que le vaya felizmente

lucky dichoso, -a

luggage equipaje *m.;* **piece of hand luggage** bulto *(m.)* de mano

luminous luminoso, -a

lunch: **to eat lunch, to have lunch** almorzar *(ue; c)*

luxuriant frondoso, -a

luxurious lujoso, -a

M

ma'am señora

mad loco, -a

madman loco *m.*

Madrid Madrid

magnificent magnífico, -a

mail correo *m.; (send)* remitir

main floor seat butaca *f.;* **main floor ticket** billete *(m.)* de butaca

main office central *f.;* **main post office** central de correos

mainly principalmente

major *(specialize)* especializar(se) *(c)*

make hacer*; **to make a clean copy of** sacar *(qu)* en limpio; **to make out** *(descry)* divisar; **to make up** *(invent)* inventar; **to make use of** aprovechar

man hombre *m.;* **leading man** *(theatre)* galán *m.;* **little man** hombrecito *m.;* **wise man** sabio *m.;* **young man** joven *m.*

manner modo *m.; (treatment)* trato *m.*

Manuel Manuel

many muchos, -as; **as many as** *(all the)* cuantos, -as; **how many?** ¿cuántos, -as?; **too many** demasiados, -as

March marzo *m.*

mark marca *f.; (grade)* nota *f.*

marry *or* **get married** casarse (con); **married couple** matrimonio *m.*

martyr mártir *mf.*

marvel maravilla *f.*

Mary María; *dim.* Maruja, Marujilla

mashed potatoes puré *(m.)* de patatas

mass masa *f.; (service)* misa *f.;* **to ten o'clock mass** a misa de diez

master maestro *m.*

masterly magistral

masterpiece obra maestra *f.*

mastery maestría *f.*

match fósforo *m.; (game)* partido *m.*

material *(cloth)* género *m.*

matriculate matricularse

matriculation matrícula *f.;* **matriculation fees** derechos *(m.)* de matrícula

matter *(business)* asunto *m.; vb.* importar

mattress colchón *m.*

may *(to be able)* poder*

May mayo *m.*

maybe acaso

me me; mí, -migo [3]

meal *(an order)* servicio *m.*

mean significar *(qu),* querer* decir; **I mean...** digo...

meat carne *f.;* **roast meat** asado *m.*

medical student alumno (-a) de medicina

medicine medicina *f.*

meet *(become acquainted)* conocer

(zc); (come across) encontrarse *(ue)* con; *(come together)* reunirse *(ú); (join)* juntarse; *(see one another)* verse*

melancholy melancólico, -a

member miembro *m.*

menu menú *m.;* lista *(f.)* de platos

merriment regocijo *m.*

messenger boy mensajero *m.*

Michael Miguel

middle mitad *f.*

midyear de medio curso

mild *(calm)* apacible

milk leche *f.*

mind mente *f.; (spirit)* ánimo *m.;* **he doesn't mind** no le duele *(+ inf.)*

mine mío, -a; *pron.* el mío, *etc.* [4]

minute minuto *m.*

mirror espejo *m.*

miss *(lose)* perder *(ie)*

Miss señorita

model modelo *m.*

modern moderno, -a

modernist modernista *mf.*

moment momento *m.,* instante *m.*

Monday lunes *m.*

money dinero *m.; (cash)* cuartos *m. pl.;* **to spend the money** soltar *(ue)* los cuartos

month mes *m.*

monument monumento *m.*

mood humor *m.;* **in a bad mood** de mal humor; **I'm in a fine mood for...!** ¡para...estoy yo!

moon luna *f.;* **the moon is shining** hay luna

moonlight luna *f.*

more más; **more or less** (poco) más o menos; **more...than** más...que [2, 5]; **more than** más que; más de *(+ numeral)*

moreover además

morning mañana *f.;* **what a morning!** ¡qué mañanita!

most más

mother madre *f.*
motor motor *m.*
mountain montaña *f.;* **mountain range** cordillera *f.,* sierra *f.*
mouth boca *f.;* **to make one's mouth water** hacérsele* a uno la boca agua
move: to start moving arrancar *(qu);* **to move along to** *(approach)* llegarse *(gu)* a; **to move up** *(advance)* adelantar
movement movimiento *m.*
movie *(film)* película *f.;* **movies** *(cinema)* cine *m.;* **movie actor, movie actress** peliculero, -a *mf.*
Mr. señor
Mrs. señora (de)
much mucho, -a; *adv.* mucho; **as much** tanto, -a; **as much as** *(all the)* cuanto, -a; **how much?** ¿cuánto, -a?; **how much!** ¡cuánto, -a!; **so much** tanto, -a; **too much** demasiado, -a; *adv.* demasiado; **very much** mucho, muchísimo
mud barro *m.*
museum museo *m.*
music música *f.*
musical musical
musician músico *m.*
must *(to be obliged)* deber; *(conjecture)* deber (de); *future or conditional* [7]; **one must** hay que *(+ inf.)*
my mi [4]; el, la [1, 3]

N

name nombre *m.;* **family name, last name** apellido *m.*
narrate narrar
national nacional
nationality nacionalidad *f.*
natural: in a natural way con naturalidad
naturalness naturalidad *f.*
nature naturaleza *f.*

navigation navegación *f.*
near *(next to)* junto a
neatness aseo *m.*
necessary: it is necessary to hay que *(+ inf.);* **to be only necessary that...** bastar con que...
need necesitar
neighbor vecino, -a *mf.*
neighborhood *(district)* barrio *m.*
neither tampoco
nephew sobrino *m.*
nervous nervioso, -a
never nunca
nevertheless sin embargo
new nuevo, -a
news *(item)* noticia *f.;* *(items)* noticias *f. pl.*
newscast noticiario *m.*
newspaper periódico *m.*
newsreel noticiario *m.*
next que viene, próximo, -a; *adv.* luego; **next door** al lado; **next to** junto a
nice *(likable)* simpático, -a
niece sobrina *f.*
night noche *f.;* **last night** anoche; **it's a bad night** hace mala noche
nine nueve
nineteen diez y nueve
ninety noventa
no no; ningún, ninguno, -a; **oh no!, no, indeed!** ¡ca!
noble noble
nobody nadie
noise ruido *m.;* *(hubbub)* bullicio *m.*
none ninguno, -a
nor ni
nose nariz *f.*
not no; sin *(+ inf.);* **not any** ningún, ninguno, -a; **not at all** *(you're welcome)* no hay de qué
note notar
notebook cuaderno *m.*
nothing nada

notice notar; *(be aware)* darse* cuenta; **I didn't notice** no lo noté
nourishment pasto *m.*
novel novela *f.*
novelist novelista *mf.*
November noviembre *m.*
now ahora; *(already)* ya; **right now** ahora mismo
nowhere por ninguna parte
nuisance lata *f.*
number número *m.*

O

oak grove robledal *m.*
obliged: to be obliged *(must, ought, should)* deber
observe observar
occasion ocasión *f.*
ocean océano *m.;* **ocean liner** transatlántico *m.*
o'clock: at one o'clock, at two o'clock, *etc.* a la una, a las dos, *etc.;* **it is one o'clock, it is two o'clock,** *etc.* es la una, son las dos, *etc.;* **the two o'clock train** el tren de las dos
October octubre *m.*
odd *(extravagant)* extravagante
of de
off *(with verbs of separation)* a [5]
office oficina *f.;* *(study)* despacho *m.;* **office worker** oficinista *mf.*
often muchas veces
oh! ¡oh!, ¡ah!, ¡ay!
oil óleo *m.;* **oil painting** cuadro *(m.)* al óleo
old *(former)* antiguo, -a
olive grove olivar *m.*
on *(location)* en, sobre; *(position or time)* a; *(direction)* por; *(manner)* a, de [5]
once una vez
one un, uno, -a; *pron.* uno, -a; se [3, 6]; *(it)* lo; **(some) one** alguno, -a; **the one** (+ *prep. or relative*)

el, la [1]; **one another** nos, os, se [3]; **I'm not one of those who...** no soy de los que...
oneself se; sí, -sigo [3]
one-way *(ticket)* sencillo
only sólo, nada más, no...más que, no...sino
open abrir*
opera ópera *f.;* **grand opera** gran ópera
operator *(telephone)* telefonista *mf.;* **radio operator** radiógrafo *m.*
opinion opinión *f.*
opposite contrario, -a
or o
orange naranja *f.;* **orange juice** jugo *(m.)* de naranja
orchestra orquesta *f.;* **orchestra seat** butaca *f.*
order orden *m.; vb.* pedir *(i);* **in order to** para; **in order that** para que
other otro, -a; **each other** nos, os, se [3]
ought *(to be obliged)* deber
our nuestro, -a [4]; el, la [1, 3]
ours nuestro, -a; *pron.* el nuestro, *etc.* [4]
ourselves nos; nosotros, -as [3]
outburst of laughter carcajada *f.*
outstanding: to be outstanding distinguirse *(g),* destacarse *(qu)*
over sobre; *(on)* en; **over there** por allí
overcoat abrigo *m.*
overshoe chanclo (de goma) *m.*

P

package paquete *m.;* *(bundle)* bulto *m.*
page página *f.*
painter pintor, -ora *mf.*
painting pintura *f.;* **oil painting** cuadro *(m.)* al óleo
pair par *m.*

pajamas piyama *m.*
pale pálido, -a
panel *(painting)* tabla *f.*
panorama panorama *m.*
pants pantalón *m.*
papa papá *m.*
paper: piece of paper hojilla *f.*
parcel paquete *m.;* postal parcel paquete postal
pardon dispensar
park *(a car)* estacionar
part parte *f.;* the best part lo mejor
party *(festival)* fiesta *f.*
pass pasar
passenger pasajero, -a *mf.;* viajero, -a *mf.*
past pasado, -a
paste pasta *f.*
pastry pastel *m.*
pathetic patético, -a
pavement pavimento *m.*
pay pagar *(gu); (fees)* abonar
peace *(rest)* descanso *m.*
peak picacho *m.*
pedestrian transeúnte *mf.*
pelota pelota (vasca) *f.*
pen pluma *f.*
pencil lápiz *m.*
people gente *f.*
pepper pimienta *f.*
perceive *(recognize)* conocer *(zc)*
perfection perfección *f.*
perhaps acaso
persist in empeñarse en *(+ inf.)*
person persona *f.;* elderly person anciano, -a *mf.;* little person personita *f.*
personage personaje *m.*
personnel personal *m.*
perverse perverso, -a
philosophy filosofía *f.*
phonograph gramófono *m.*
photographer fotógrafo *m.*
phrase frase *f.*
physics física *f.*
pianist pianista *mf.*

pick up recoger *(j)*
picture cuadro *m.; (film)* película *f.*
pie pastel *m.*
piece pieza *f.;* piece of paper hojilla *f.*
pig cerdo *m.*
pill píldora *f.*
pilot piloto *m.*
pine grove pinar *m.*
pity lástima *f.*
place lugar *m.,* paraje *m.; (position)* puesto *m.; (part)* parte *f.;* to go from place to place corretear
plain llanura *f.*
plane *(airplane)* avión *m.,* aeroplano *m.,* aparato *m.;* plane trip viaje *(m.)* en avión
plate plato *m.*
platform *(railway)* andén *m.*
play comedia *f.; vb. (games)* jugar *(ue); (music)* tocar *(qu);* to play a game of cards echar una partida de naipes; to play hooky hacer* rabona; to play solitaire hacer* solitarios
player jugador, -ora *mf.*
pleasant *(likable)* simpático, -a
please gustar, agradar; servirse *(i),* hacer* el favor de *(+ inf.);* please (pass *or* give me)... hágame (usted) el favor de...; as you please como usted guste
pleased contento, -a
pleasure gusto *m.,* placer *m.;* it's a pleasure (to know you) tanto gusto
plot *(of a play, etc.)* argumento *m.,* fábula *f.*
point punto *m.; (tip)* punta *f.;* point of view punto de vista; to point out señalar
polish *(shoe polish)* betún *m.; vb.* dar* betún a
poor pobre
poppy amapola *f.*
pork chop chuleta *(f.)* de cerdo

position posición *f.*
possess poseer *(i, y)*
possible posible
postage franqueo *m.*
postal postal
post card tarjeta postal *f.*
post office correos *m. pl.;* (main) post office central *(f.)* de correos; at the post office en correos
potato patata *f.;* mashed potatoes puré *(m.)* de patatas
powder polvo *m.; (cosmetic)* polvos *m. pl.*
powerful poderoso, -a
practical práctico, -a
practice practicar *(qu)*
precious precioso, -a
precisely precisamente
predicament: you're really in a predicament! ¡sí que está usted divertido, -a!
predilection predilección *f.*
prefer preferir *(ie, i)*
preferable preferible
preference *(like)* gusto *m.*
prepare preparar
presence presencia *f.*
present presentar
preserved en conserva
preserves conserva *f.*
president rector, -ora *mf.*
pretty bonito, -a; lindo, -a
price precio *m.;* price reduction rebaja *(f.)* de precios
principally principalmente
probably: *often expressed by future or conditional* [7]
produce producir *(zc, -uj-);* dar*
production *(work)* obra *f.*
professor profesor, -ora *mf.;* catedrático, -a *mf.*
professorial *(doctoral)* doctoral
profit by aprovechar
program programa *m.*
project proyectar
pronunciation pronunciación *f.*

prose prosa *f.*
protest protestar
prove *(prove to be)* salir*
provided (that) con tal que
pupil alumno, -a *mf.*
puppet muñeco *m.*
purchase compra *f.*
purée puré *m.*
purse *(bag)* bolso *m.*
put poner*; to put (in) meter; to put on ponerse*; *(throw on)* echarse (encima)

Q

quality calidad *f.;* of good quality fino, -a
quarrel *or* have a quarrel reñir *(i)*
quarter cuarto *m.*
queen *(in cards)* caballo *m. (horse and rider)*
queue cola *f.*
quickly de prisa; how quickly! ¡qué de prisa!; very quickly *(on the run)* de prisa y corriendo
quiet tranquilo, -a; to quiet down *(be silent)* callar(se)
quietly con tranquilidad
quite *(very)* bien
Quixote Quijote

R

race *(run)* carrera *f.*
radio radio *f.;* radio operator radiógrafo *m.*
rage trinar
rain lluvia *f.; vb.* llover *(ue)*
raincoat impermeable *m.*
raise aumento *m.;* raise in salary aumento de sueldo
range *(mountains)* cordillera *f.,* sierra *f.*
rapidity rapidez *f.*
rascal pícaro, -a *mf.;* mala persona *f.*

rascally pícaro, -a
rather *(somewhat)* algo; *(instead)* más bien
ray rayo *m.; in the rays of the sun* a los rayos del sol
Raymond Ramón; *dim.* Ramoncete
razor: safety razor maquinilla *(f.)* de afeitar
read leer *(i, y)*
reader lector, -ora *mf.*
reading lectura *f.*
ready listo, -a; *(disposed)* dispuesto, -a
real *(true)* verdadero, -a
reality realidad *f.*
really de verdad; **really?** a ver; **really...** *(indeed)* vaya si...
reason razón *f.*
reasonable razonable
recall recordar *(ue)*
receipt recibo *m.*
receive recibir
reception recepción *f.*
recognize reconocer *(zc); (perceive)* conocer *(zc)*
record *(disc)* disco *m.*
recreation recreo *m.*
rector rector, -ora *mf.*
reddish rojizo, -a
reduction rebaja *f.*
reflection reflexión *f.*
reflective reflexivo, -a
refreshment counter ambigú *m.*
regard: with regard to en cuanto a
regional regional
register *(a letter)* certificar *(qu)*
regret sentir *(ie, i)*, lamentar
rehearse ensayar
religion religión *f.*
remain quedar(se)
remember recordar *(ue)*
remove quitar
renew renovar *(ue)*
repeat repetir *(i)*
replace reemplazar *(c)*
reply responder

represent representar
request pedir *(i)*
required *(obligatory)* obligatorio, -a
resound resonar *(ue)*
rest descanso *m.*
restaurant restaurán *m.*
return volver* *(ue); (give back)* devolver* *(ue); to return (love, etc.)* corresponder
reverse revés *m.; it is the reverse from what it is...* pasa al revés que...
revue revista *f.*
rice arroz *m.; chicken and rice* arroz con pollo
rich rico, -a
Richard Ricardo
rid of *(free from)* libre de
ride: to take a ride, to go riding pasear(se)
ridiculous ridículo, -a
right derecho, -a; *(even)* mismo; **right?** ¿no?, ¿eh?; **(to the) right** a la derecha; **right away, right now** en seguida, ahora mismo; **right over there** ahí mismo; **right straight** derechito, -a; **all right** bien, bueno; **to be right** tener* razón; **that's right** en efecto; como usted lo oye; **you're quite right** bien lo puede decir; **to seem all right** parecer *(zc)* (bien)
ring *(sound)* sonar *(ue); (call)* llamar
rise surgir *(j)*
river río *m.*
roar *(noise)* ruido *m.; to roar with laughter* reírse *(i)* a carcajadas, soltar *(ue)* la carcajada
roast meat asado *m.; roast lamb* asado de cordero
rob robar
roll lista *f.; to call the roll* pasar lista
romantic romántico, -a
room cuarto *m.; (large room)* sala *f.; (ballroom)* salón *m.;* **dining**

room comedor *m.;* **fitting room** cuartito *(m.)* de pruebas
Rosalind Rosalinda
Rosary Rosario; *dim.* Rosarito
Rose Rosa; *dim.* Rosita
round-trip de ida y vuelta
row fila *f.*
rubber goma *f.; (overshoe)* chanclo (de goma) *m.*
rugby rugby *m.;* **rugby team** equipo *(m.)* de rugby
rumba rumba *f.*
run *(race)* carrera *f.; vb.* correr; *(function)* funcionar; **to run (down)** correrse; **on the run** de prisa y corriendo; **I've got a run in my stocking** se me ha corrido un punto en la media
runway pista *f.*
rushing: what rushing around! ¡qué carreras!

S

sacrifice sacrificio *m.*
sadness tristeza *f.*
safe *(cash box)* caja *f.*
safety seguridad *f.;* **safety belt** correa (de seguridad) *f.;* **safety razor** maquinilla *(f.)* de afeitar
salad ensalada *f.*
salary sueldo *m.*
sale *(clearance sale)* saldo *m.*
salt sal *f.*
same mismo, -a; **all the same** *(still)* con todo; **it's all the same to me** me es igual; **the very same thing, exactly the same** lo mismito
Saturday sábado *m.*
save salvar
savor saborear
savory sabroso, -a
say decir*;* **we might say** *(after negative)* que digamos; **all that has been said above** todo lo dicho

arriba; **to say good-by to** despedirse *(i)* de
scandal escándalo *m.*
scandalous escandaloso, -a
scarcely apenas
scene escena *f.*
schedule horario *m.*
school *(university division)* facultad *f.;* **school year** curso *m.*
scoundrel mala persona *f.*
screen pantalla *f.*
sculpture escultura *f.*
sea mar *m. or f.*
season estación *f.*
seat asiento *m.; (theatre)* localidad *f.;* **main floor seat, orchestra seat** butaca *f.;* **have a seat** tome usted asiento
second segundo, -a
section sección *f.*
security seguridad *f.*
see ver*; (perceive)* conocer *(zc);* **see you (later)** hasta (luego); **let's see** a ver; **it's surely good to see you again** dichosos los ojos que ven a usted
seek *(try)* pretender
seem parecer *(zc);* **how does it seem to you?** ¿qué le parece?; **to seem all right, to seem best** parecer *(zc)* (bien)
seemingly al parecer
sell vender
seller: ticket seller taquillero, -a *mf.*
semester semestre *m.*
send mandar; *(by mail)* remitir
sensation sensación *f.*
September septiembre *m.*
serene sereno, -a
serious serio, -a
serve servir *(i)*
service servicio *m.;* **at your service** para servir a usted; **to be of service** servir *(i)*
set *(arrange)* concertar *(ie);* **to set fire** pegar *(gu)* fuego

setting *(scene)* escena *f.*
settle accounts ajustar cuentas
seven siete
seventeen diez y siete
seventy setenta
several *(various)* varios, -as; *(some)* algunos, -as
sh! ¡chist!
shade sombra *f.*
shadow sombra *f.*
shake *(vibrate)* trepidar
shall: *present or future tense* [7]
sharp agudo, -a
shave *(oneself)* afeitarse
she ella [3]
sheer *(thin)* fino, -a
sheet *(bed)* sábana *f.; (paper)* hoja *f.*
shine brillar
shirt camisa *f.*
shocking escandaloso, -a
shoe zapato *m.;* shoe polish betún *m.*
shoot *(a film)* impresionar; I saw a film being shot vi impresionar una película
shooting *(of a film)* impresión *f.*
shop tienda *f.;* to go shopping ir* de compras, ir* de tiendas
shore playa *f.*
short corto, -a
should *(to be obliged)* deber; *conditional* [7]
shout grito *m.; vb.* gritar, dar* gritos
shove empujón *m.*
show *(showing)* sección *f.; vb.* mostrar *(ue);* show bill cartel *m.;* show window escaparate *m.*
side lado *m.;* on the other side of al otro lado de
sidewalk acera *f.*
sierra sierra *f.*
sigh: to breathe a sigh of relief respirar
sign firmar
signature firma *f.*

signify significar *(qu)*
silent: to be silent callar(se)
silly: that silly... ese bobo de...
silver plata *f.*
simple sencillo, -a
simpleton bobo *m.*
simplicity sencillez *f.*
simply sencillamente
since *(cause)* pues, como, que
sincere sincero, -a
sincerely yours su afectísimo, -a
singer cantante *mf.*
single solo, -a; *(same)* mismo, -a
sink *(stick)* hincar *(qu);* to sink one's teeth in hincarle *(qu)* el diente a
sir señor *m.;* señorito *m. (used by servants, etc.)*
sister hermana *f.*
sit down sentarse *(ie)*
six seis
sixteen diez y seis
sixty sesenta
size *(clothes)* talla *f.;* my size is 34 mi talla es del 34
sketch dibujo *m.*
sky cielo *m.*
sleep dormir *(ue, u);* to go to sleep dormirse *(ue, u)*
sleepyhead dormilón, -ona *mf.*
sleeve manga *f.*
slide deslizarse *(c)*
slightly ligeramente
slipper *(house slipper)* chinela *f.*
slippery resbaladizo, -a
slope *(hill)* cuesta *f.*
small pequeño, -a; chico, -a; menudo, -a; very small chiquito, -a; *(tiny)* minúsculo, -a
smile sonrisa *f.;* little smile sonrisita *f.*
smirk *(little smile)* sonrisita *f.*
smoke fumar; smoking lounge saloncillo *(m.)* de fumar
smokestack chimenea *f.*
smooth *(serene)* sereno, -a
sneaky fellow pajarraco *m.*

snore ronquido *m.; vb.* dar* ronquidos

snow nieve *f.; vb.* nevar *(ie)*

snowfall nevada *f.*

so tan; *(it)* lo; **(and) so, so then** conque, de modo que; **so (that)** que, para que, de modo que

soap jabón *m.*

soccer balompié *m.,* futbol *m.*

sock calcetín *m.*

soft blando, -a

solitaire solitario *m.;* **to play solitaire** hacer* solitarios

some algún, alguno, -a; unos, -as; algunos, -as; *(any)* cualquier; **some ...or other** no sé qué...

somebody alguien

something algo, una cosa, alguna cosa; **something or other** no sé qué; **isn't that something!** ¡hay que ver!

sometimes a veces, unas veces, algunas veces

somewhat algo

son hijo *m.*

soon pronto; **quite soon** prontito

sooner *(before)* antes

sorority hermandad *f.*

sorrow pena *f.*

sorry: to be sorry *(regret)* sentir *(ie, i),* lamentar

sort *(kind)* género *m.*

soul alma *f.*

sound sonar *(ue);* **to sound loudly** *(resound)* resonar *(ue)*

soup sopa *f.*

space espacio *m.*

spade *(playing card)* espada *f. (sword)*

Spain España *f.*

Spaniard español, -ola

Spanish español, -ola; *(language)* español *m.;* **to make Spanish, to give a Spanish form to** españolizar *(c)*

specialize especializar(se) *(c)*

speedy veloz; **very speedy** velocísimo, -a

spend *(time)* pasar; estar*

spirit espíritu *m.; (mind)* ánimo *m.*

spiritual espiritual

spoil *(a party, etc.)* amargar *(gu)*

sport deporte *m.;* **(for) sports** deportivo, -a

spot *(place)* paraje *m.; (stain)* mancha *f.*

sprawl *(in a chair, etc.)* repantigarse *(gu)*

spring primavera *f.*

spur *(of a mountain range)* estribación *f.*

stain mancha *f.*

stamp sello *m.; (mark)* marca *f.;* **three-cent stamp** sello de a tres (centavos)

stand *(bear)* resistir; *(take a stand)* plantarse; **standing** de pie; plantado, -a; **to stand in line** hacer* fila; **to stand out** *(excel)* sobresalir*, destacarse *(qu)*

star estrella *f.*

stare comerse con los ojos

start moving arrancar *(qu)*

static estática *f.*

station estación *f.;* **(broadcasting) station** emisora *f.*

statue estatua *f.*

stature estatura *f.*

stay quedarse

steady firme

steel acero *m.;* **steel bird** pájaro *(m.)* de acero

stenographer mecanógrafo, -a *mf.*

step paso *m.*

steward camarero *m.*

stewardess *(hostess)* revisora *f.,* camarera *f.,* azafata *f.*

stick pegar *(gu); (sink)* hincar *(qu)*

still *(even)* aun; *(yet)* aún, todavía; *(all the same)* con todo

stitch punto *m.*

stock *(supply)* surtido *m.*

stocking media *f.*
stoop down bajarse
stop parada *f.; vb.* parar(se), hacer* parada; dejar de *(+ inf.);* **to stop by** *(remain at)* quedarse en
store tienda *f.*
story *(plot)* fábula *f.*
straight derecho, -a; **right straight** derechito, -a
strange extraño, -a
strap correa *f.*
street calle *f.*
streetcar tranvía *m.*
strict *(demanding)* exigente
strong fuerte
student estudiante *mf.;* alumno, -a *mf.*
studio estudio *m.*
study *(office)* despacho *m.; (course)* asignatura *f.; vb.* estudiar
stuff oneself with llenarse de
style estilo *m.*
subject asunto *m.; (course)* asignatura *f.*
sublime sublime
subscription abono *m.*
substitute *(replace)* reemplazar *(c)*
succulent suculento, -a
such (a) tal; tan *(+ adj.)*
suddenly de repente, de pronto
suffer sufrir, padecer *(zc)*
suffice bastar
suit traje *m.; (in cards)* palo *m.; (to be becoming)* ir* bien, sentar *(ie)* (bien); **bathing suit** traje de baño
suitcase maleta *f.*
summer verano *m.;* **summer vacationist** veraneante *mf.*
summit *(height)* altura *f.*
sun sol *m.*
Sunday domingo *m.*
sunny: to be sunny *(weather)* hacer* sol, haber* sol
sunrise salida *(f.)* del sol
sunshine sol *m.*
superior superior

supplant suplantar
supply *(stock)* surtido *m.*
suppose: *often expressed by future or conditional* [7]; **to be supposed to** haber* de *(+ inf.)*
supreme supremo, -a
sure seguro, -a
surely de seguro
surname apellido *m.*
surprise sorpresa *f.*
swallow tragar *(gu)*
sweat sudar; **"to sweat blood"** sudar tinta
sweet dulce
sweetheart novio, -a *mf.*
swift veloz
swiftness rapidez *f.*
swim baño *m.*
swimming natación *f.*
sympathy *(liking)* simpatía *f.*
syntax sintaxis

T

table mesa *f.*
tailor sastre *m.;* **tailored** estilo sastre
take tomar; *(a course)* seguir *(i; g); (to carry)* llevar; **to take (long)** tardar; **to take leave** despedirse *(i);* **to take off** *(leave the ground)* despegar *(gu);* **to take out** sacar *(qu)*
talents dotes *f. pl.*
talk hablar
tall alto, -a
tango tango *m.*
taste gusto *m.;* **for every taste** para todos los gustos
tasty sabroso, -a; rico, -a
taxi taxi *m.*
teacher maestro, -a *mf.*
team equipo *m.*
technical técnico, -a
technicolor tecnicolor *m.*
te-hee! ¡ji, ji!
telegram telegrama *m.*

telephone teléfono *m.; vb.* telefonear; **by telephone** por teléfono
tell *(say)* decir*; **to tell (about)** contar *(ue);* **tell about it** cuente usted
ten diez
tender tierno, -a
tennis tenis *m.*
test prueba *f.; vb.* probar *(ue)*
than que; de *(+ numeral)*
thank agradecer *(zc);* **thanks** *(gratitude)* agradecimiento *m.;* **thanks, thank you** gracias, se agradece
that ese, esa; aquel, aquella; *pron.* ése, ésa; aquél, aquélla; eso, aquello [4]; el, la, lo [1]; *conj. or rel. pron.* que; **that business of** eso de, aquello de
the el, la, los, las, lo; **of the** del, de la, *etc.;* **to the** al, a la, *etc.* [1]
theatre teatro *m.*
their su [4]; el, la [1, 3]
theirs suyo, -a; de ellos; *pron.* el suyo, *etc.* [4]
them los, las; les, se; ellos, -as, sí [3]
theme tema *m.*
themselves se; sí, -sigo [3]
then entonces, luego, después; *(therefore)* pues
there ahí, allí, allá [5]; **down there** allá abajo; **out there** allá; **over there** ahí, allá, por allí; **right over there** ahí mismo
Theresa Teresa
these estos, -as; *pron.* éstos, -as [4]
they ellos, -as [3]
thing cosa *f.;* **a thing of beauty** una hermosura
think pensar *(ie); (believe)* creer *(i, y);* **one might think that...!** ¡ni que...!
third tercer, tercero, -a
thirteen trece
thirty treinta
this este, esta; *pron.* éste, ésta, esto [4]; **this is...(speaking)** aquí...

those esos, -as, aquellos, -as; *pron.* ésos, -as, aquéllos, -as [4]; los, las [1]
though aunque
thought pensamiento *m.*
thoughtful *(reflective)* reflexivo, -a; *(considerate)* delicado, -a
three tres
through por (entre)
throw echar; **to throw on** *(put on)* echarse (encima)
Thursday jueves *m.*
thus así
ticket billete *m.;* **commutation ticket** billete de abono; **one-way ticket** billete sencillo; **round-trip ticket** billete de ida y vuelta; **ticket seller** taquillero, -a *mf.;* **ticket window** taquilla *f.*
time tiempo *m.; (sequence)* vez *f.; (time of day)* hora *f.;* **at times** a veces; **at the same time** al mismo tiempo, en un mismo instante; *(equally)* al par; **from time to time** de vez en cuando; **to have a good time** divertirse *(ie, i);* **I had a time of it!** ¡pasé un ratito!
tiny chiquito, -a; minúsculo, -a
tip propina *f.;* **there is no tipping here** aquí no hay propinas
tire *(fatigue)* cansar
title título *m.*
to *(direction)* a; *(purpose)* para; *(cause)* por [5]
toast *(piece of toast)* tostada *f.*
today hoy
tomorrow mañana
tone of voice voz *f.*
tonight esta noche
too *(also)* también; **too (much)** demasiado; **it's too bad** *(it's a pity)* es lástima
tooth diente *m.*
toothbrush cepillo *(m.)* de dientes
toothpaste pasta dentífrica *f.*
top: on top of encima de

tow remolque *m.;* **to tow, to have in tow** llevar a remolque
toward *(with, to)* con
towel toalla *f.*
town pueblo *m.;* **little town** pueblecillo *m.*
toy juguete *m.;* **(little) toy boat** barquito *(m.)* de juguete
track *(athletics)* atletismo *m.*
traffic circulación (de coches) *f.;* movimiento *m.*
tragic trágico, -a
train tren *m.*
tranquil tranquilo, -a
transparent transparente
traveler viajero, -a *mf.*
tray bandeja *f.*
treasure tesoro *m.*
treatment *(cure)* cura *f.; (manner)* trato *m.*
trick *(cheating)* trampa *f.*
trip viaje *m.; (excursion)* excursión *f.;* **have a pleasant trip!** ¡feliz viaje!
trolley tranvía *m.*
trousers pantalón *m.*
true verdadero, -a; **true?** ¿verdad?; **it's true** es verdad
truly de verdad
truth verdad *f.*
try querer*, pretender; tratar de *(* + *inf.);* *(rehearse)* ensayar; **to try (out)** probar *(ue);* **to try on** probarse *(ue)*
Tuesday martes *m.*
turn torcer *(ue; z);* **to turn around** volverse* *(ue);* **to turn loose of** soltar *(ue);* **to turn off (the lights)** apagar *(gu);* **to turn on** *(a radio, etc.)* poner*; **to turn out** *(prove to be)* salir*; **to turn out (the lights)** apagar *(gu);* **to turn up** *(appear)* aparecer *(zc)*
twelve doce
twenty veinte; **twenty-one** veintiún,

veintiuno, -a; **twenty-two** veintidós; *etc.*
two dos
typist mecanógrafo, -a *mf.*

U

ugh! ¡uf!
ugly feo, -a
unbelievable: it seems unbelievable parece mentira
uncle tío *m.*
under bajo
underclothes ropa interior *f.*
underneath debajo
understand entender *(ie)*
underwear ropa interior *f.*
undulation ondulación *f.*
uniform uniforme *m.*
university universidad *f.*
unpleasant: to be unpleasant *(persons)* tener* mala sombra
until hasta
untiring infatigable
unusual insólito, -a
unwillingly a remolque
up arriba; **up to** hasta; **to get up** levantarse; **get up!** ¡arriba!
upon sobre
upset *(excited)* azorado, -a
us nos; nosotros, -as [3]
use usar; *(handle)* andar* con; **to get used (to it)** acostumbrarse; **to make use of** aprovechar
usual *(as always)* de siempre
usually por lo común; soler *(ue)* *(* + *inf.)*

V

vacant vacante
vacation vacaciones *f. pl.*
vacationist *(summer)* veraneante *mf.*
valiant valiente
valley valle *m.*
value valor *m.*

variety variedad *f.*
various varios, -as
vast vasto, -a
vegetable legumbre *f.;* (Spanish) vegetable soup sopa *(f.)* de hierbas
verse verso *m.*
very muy; bien; -ísimo, -a [2]
vestibule vestíbulo *m.*
vibrate vibrar; *(shake)* trepidar
vicarage vicaría *f.*
vice-president vicerrector, -ora *mf.*
vice-rector vicerrector, -ora *mf.*
victory victoria *f.*
view vista *f.*
viewpoint punto *(m.)* de vista
violinist violinista *mf.*
visit visitar
vitamin vitamina *f.;* vitamin pill píldora *(f.)* de vitamina
vivacity viveza *f.*
vocation vocación *f.*
voice voz *f.*

W

wait (for) esperar, aguardar; waiting and waiting aguarda que te aguarda; to wait in line hacer* cola
waiter camarero *m.,* mozo *m.*
waitress camarera *f.*
walk andar*; to take a walk pasear(se)
waltz vals *m.*
want querer*; to want to *(feel like)* tener* ganas de *(+ inf.)*
war guerra *f.*
warm: to be warm (weather) hacer* calor
wash lavar; to wash (oneself) lavarse
waste *(lose)* perder *(ie)*
watch mirar; *(see)* ver*; watch out! ¡cuidado!
water agua *f.;* to make one's mouth

water hacérsele* a uno la boca agua
wave onda *f.; (undulation)* ondulación *f.*
way modo *m.;* (in) that way así; in the (Spanish) way a la (española); I'm on my way ya voy
we nosotros, -as [3]
wear llevar, vestir *(i); (put on)* ponerse*
wearing apparel ropa *(f.)* de vestir
weather tiempo *m.;* to be (good) weather hacer* (buen) tiempo; to be (beautiful) weather hacer* un tiempo (hermoso)
wedding boda *f.*
Wednesday miércoles *m.*
week semana *f.;* last week la semana pasada
weekend fin *(m.)* de semana
welcome: you're welcome de nada, no hay de que; welcome! ¡bien venido, -a!
well bien; bueno; well! ¡toma!, ¡vaya!; well... pues...; as well as *(the same as)* lo mismo que; very well (muy) bien
wet mojado, -a
wham! ¡pum!
what lo que; what? ¿qué?; what (a)! ¡qué!; what is...? *(which is...?)* ¿cuál es...?
whatsoever: not...whatsoever no ...alguno, -a
wheat trigo *m.;* wheat field campo *(m.)* de trigo
when cuando; al *(+ inf.);* when? ¿cuándo?
whenever cuando
where donde; where? ¿dónde?; *(to what place?)* ¿adónde?
whether si
which que; which? ¿cuál?; that which lo que
while mientras; a (little) while un

rato, un ratito; **quite a while ago** (hace) un rato ya largo
white blanco, -a
who que; quien; **who?** ¿quién?
whole *(entire)* entero, -a
whom que; a quien; *(obj. of prep.)* quien; **whom?** ¿a quién?; *(obj. of prep.)* ¿quién?
why *(well)* pues; **why?** ¿por qué?; **why!** ¡toma!, ¡vaya!
will: *present or future tense* [7]
willingly de buena gana
win ganar
window: **checkroom window** taquilla *(f.)* del guardarropa; **show window** escaparate *m.;* **ticket window** taquilla *f.*
winter invierno *m.*
wise sabio, -a; **wise man** sabio *m.*
wish desear, querer*; **as you wish** como usted guste; **I wish I could...!** ¡quién *(+ past subjunctive)!*
wit gracia *f.*
with con; *(manner)* a, de [5]
within dentro; *prep.* dentro de
without sin
woman mujer *f.;* **young woman** joven *f.*
wonderful magnífico, -a
wonderfully divinamente
word palabra *f.;* **words** *(speech)* palabra *f.;* **little word** palabrita *f.*
work trabajo *m.;* *(production)* obra

f.; vb. trabajar; *(function)* funcionar
worker: office worker oficinista *mf.*
world mundo *m.*
worry apurarse
worse peor
worth *(worthy)* digno, -a; **to be worth** valer*; **worth seeing** digno (-a) de verse
worthy digno, -a
would: *conditional* [7]
wrap up abrigarse *(gu)*
wrestling lucha *f.*
write escribir*; poner*

Y

year año *m.;* **school year** curso *m.*
yes sí
yesterday ayer
yet aún, todavía
you tú, te, ti; vosotros, -as, os; usted, le, lo, la, se; ustedes, los, las, les, se [3]; *(one)* se [3, 6]
young joven; **young man, young woman** joven *mf.*
youngish jovencito, -a
your tu; vuestro, -a; su [4]; el, la [1, 3]
yours tuyo, -a; vuestro, -a; suyo, -a; de usted, de ustedes; *pron.* el tuyo, *etc.* [4]
yourself, yourselves te, os, se; ti, -tigo; vosotros, -as; sí, -sigo [3]

Index

(Numbers refer to pages.)

a, 116; personal a, 99–100
adjectives, 98–101; demonstrative, 110–112; possessive, 110–111
adverbs, 115–116; used for wishes or commands, 123
articles, 92–94

commands, 123; with object pronouns, 105
comparison: adjectives, 100–101; adverbs, 116
conditional, 128

de, 117
definite article, 92–94
demonstratives, 110–112
direct object pronouns, 104–107

elliptical constructions, 121
estar, 121–122; in progressive forms, 122, 129

future indicative, 128

gender of nouns, 98–99

imperative, 123; with object pronouns, 105
imperfect indicative, 127
indefinite article, 92–94
indefinite subject, 107, 123
indicative: tenses, 127–129; contrasted with subjunctive, 133
indirect object pronouns, 104–107
infinitive: used as noun, 121; used for wishes or commands, 123; with object pronouns, 105; contrasted with subjunctive, 135

negatives, 115
neuter: definite article, 92–93; personal pronouns, 104–106; demonstrative pronouns, 110–112
nouns, 98–100; with articles 92–94; adjectives used as nouns, 100; infinitive used as noun, 121

object pronouns, 104–107

para, 117
passive voice, 122–123; reflexive for passive, 107, 123
past participle: in perfect tenses, 129; with estar, 122
past subjunctive, 135
perfect tenses, 129
personal a, 99–100
personal pronouns, 104–107
por, 117
possessive forms: nouns, 100; adjectives and pronouns, 110–111; definite article used for possessive, 92; indirect object used for possessive, 106
prepositional object pronouns, 104, 106
prepositions, 116–117; with infinitive, 121
present indicative, 127; used for wishes or commands, 123
present participle: in progressive forms, 122, 129; with object pronouns, 105; used for wishes or commands, 123
present subjunctive, 133–135; used for wishes or commands, 123

preterite indicative, 128

progressive forms, 129

pronouns: personal, 104–107; demonstrative, 110–112; possessive, 110–111; definite article used as pronoun, 93; adjectives used as pronouns, 100

reflexive forms, 104–107, 122–123

subject pronouns, 104–105; indefinite, 107, 123

subjunctive, 133–135; used for wishes or commands, 123

tenses *see* verbs

verbs: forms, 142–149; indicative, 127–129; subjunctive, 133–135; imperative, 123; passive voice, 122–123; reflexive, 106–107, 122–123

wish or command forms, 123; with object pronouns, 105